Academic Instruction for Students With
MODERATE AND SEVERE
INTELLECTUAL DISABILITIES
in Inclusive
Classrooms

Academic Instruction for Students With MODERATE AND SEVERE INTELLECTUAL DISABILITIES in Inclusive Classrooms

June E. Downing
FOREWORD BY DIANE RYNDAK

CORWIN
A SAGE Company

For information:

Corwin
A SAGE Company
2455 Teller Road
Thousand Oaks, California 91320
(800) 233-9936
Fax: (800) 417-2466
www.corwinpress.com

SAGE India Pvt. Ltd.
B 1/I 1 Mohan Cooperative
 Industrial Area
Mathura Road, New Delhi 110 044
India

SAGE Ltd.
1 Oliver's Yard
55 City Road
London EC1Y 1SP
United Kingdom

SAGE Asia-Pacific Pte. Ltd.
33 Pekin Street #02-01
Far East Square
Singapore 048763

Printed in the United States of America

Library of Congress Cataloging-in-Publication Data

Downing, June, 1950-
Academic instruction for students with moderate and severe intellectual disabilities in inclusive classrooms/June E. Downing.
        p. cm.
Includes bibliographical references and index.
ISBN 978-1-4129-7142-3 (pbk.)
    1. Students with disabilities—Education—United States. 2. Inclusive education—United States. I. Title.

LC4031.D695 2010
371.92'6—dc22   2009045334

This book is printed on acid-free paper.

10 11 12 13 14 10 9 8 7 6 5 4 3 2 1

Acquisitions Editor:	David Chao
Associate Editor:	Sarah Bartlett
Production Editor:	Amy Schroller
Copy Editor:	Jeannette K. McCoy
Typesetter:	C&M Digitals (P) Ltd.
Proofreader:	Theresa Kay
Indexer:	Sylvia Coates
Cover Designer:	Scott Van Atta
Graphic Designer:	Karine Hovsepian

Contents

Foreword

It is with a sense of honor that I write the foreword for this book! In case you are unaware of it, let me inform you that not only is June Downing one of the preeminent scholars in the field of significant disabilities, but all of her work is grounded in the reality of both the lives of students with significant disabilities and the day-to-day operational tempo of schools. Both are replete with daily frustrations and challenges that must be met with expertise, creativity, enthusiasm, and perseverance. Each of these characteristics is evident in each chapter of this book in the explanations of practices, the importance of each practice for students with significant disabilities, and strategies for educational teams to implement each practice in their own school. Just as important, this information comes at time that is crucial for the future of students with significant disabilities. Let me explain why.

The No Child Left Behind Act (NCLB, 2001) and the latest reauthorization of the Individuals with Disabilities Education Improvement Act (IDEIA, 2004), which mandates that all students have access to the general curriculum, have changed the dialogue related to services for students with significant disabilities in the education community. Specifically, school administrators, teachers, parents, researchers, and teacher educators are interpreting these mandates in different ways. On the one hand, some of these personnel are interpreting the mandates as being limited to a focus on the content of the formal general curriculum (i.e., core curriculum; state standards). This selective focus allows discussion of both group and one-to-one instruction on that curriculum content without regard for context. Personnel, therefore, do not comprehend the importance of context and do not call to question the instruction of students with significant disabilities in self-contained classes and schools. The logic used to support this interpretation is belief that the essence of these mandates relates only to the explicit content of the general curriculum at any grade level. This interpretation, however, does not consider several variables that inform us about effective instructional practices for students with significant disabilities. For instance, one such variable is the learning needs of students with significant disabilities. Research tells us to teach these students during naturally occurring activities in contexts that are meaningful and important to each student. Said another way, students with significant disabilities learn more content, and learn that content more quickly, when their instruction is embedded within activities that naturally occur in contexts that are naturally experienced by students of the same age and grade level. From preschool through 12th grade, this context is that of general education, including classes, school environments, curriculum content, instructional and noninstructional activities, and classmates; basically, all of the components that make up the general education experience for students who do not have disabilities at any given grade level. No self-contained setting (i.e., class or school) can replicate this general education context or, therefore, replicate the activities and experiences that are inherent within general education contexts.

A second variable that informs us about effective instructional practices for students with significant disabilities is the outcome data available from services previously provided for students with significant disabilities in self-contained settings. These longitudinal data tell us that teaching in self-contained classes and schools did not result in graduates having the desired type of high-quality life that reflects meaningful interdependence with individuals who are naturally present across real-life contexts. Such desired outcomes might be reflected in long-term employment in the competitive workplace, living in situations that are similar to those of most adults in the individual's home community, frequent access of the community consistent with the access of most adults in the individual's home community, and a natural support network that is consistent with networks of most individuals without disabilities. Neither such poor outcomes nor the type of services that historically have resulted in those outcomes (i.e., services in self-contained classes and schools) would be acceptable for general education students; for that reason they are not acceptable for any students, including students with significant disabilities. Consequently, efforts to provide access to the general curriculum must be grounded in meaningful participation in general education contexts.

A third variable that informs us about effective instructional practices for students with significant disabilities is the body of research related to educational services for students with significant disabilities. This body of research tells us that (a) students with significant disabilities can and do learn, including content from the general curriculum; (b) instructional strategies that are effective for students with significant disabilities have been identified and can be embedded in both instructional and noninstructional activities that naturally occur in contexts in which general education students are engaged (i.e., general education contexts); and (c) embedding instruction for students with significant disabilities in general education contexts results in more acquisition and use of content from the general curriculum of skills required to participate in general education contexts. Instruction, therefore, does not need to be provided using a one-to-one format and does not need to be provided in self-contained settings that are believed to limit distractions and focus students on an adult instead of other students. Not only is this type of instruction not provided in the least restrictive environment, but it also eliminates the motivation inherently present by the proximity of general education classmates and participation in the same activities as those classmates. It ignores the importance of peers, peer pressure, and the desire to be a "member of a group" with peers. It also eliminates the student's equal opportunity for incidental learning opportunities that are present for general education students across the school day.

In contrast, a second interpretation of the legislative mandates for access to the general curriculum uses a broader conceptualization of general curriculum, believing that the general curriculum extends beyond the explicit content (i.e., core; standards) and incorporates the contexts in which the explicit curriculum is taught. Such contexts are comprised of the expertise of a highly qualified general education teacher, the general education instructional strategies and activities implemented and evaluated by that teacher, the materials used during those instructional activities, and the instructional and noninstructional experiences of the general education students. The logic used to support this interpretation is that, when the three variables discussed above (i.e., students' learning needs, outcome data, and research findings) are considered both independently and collectively, the importance and interrelatedness of curriculum, context, and instruction for students with significant disabilities become apparent (see Jackson, Ryndak, & Wehmeyer [in press] and Ryndak, Moore, & Delano [in press] for further discussion of the importance and interrelatedness of curriculum, context, and instruction). It becomes impossible to discuss curriculum in isolation from context, or context in isolation from instruction, or instruction in isolation from curriculum. Each influences the others, and each is intertwined with practices related to the others. Thus, to meet the mandates for access to the general curriculum, educational teams must embrace the provision of effective instructional practices in general education contexts and embedded within general education instruction and experiences. Interestingly, these concepts also are consistent with the findings of a study we conducted a decade ago about the components of definitions of inclusive education submitted by experts in the field of significant disabilities (see Ryndak, Jackson, & Billingsley, 2000). The content analysis of the submitted definitions indicated that instruction for students with significant disabilities in general education contexts does not occur on the sidelines of the class or separate from the class activities. Rather, the systematic instruction needed by students with significant disabilities can occur in the center of general education instruction, allowing all students to share experiences (i.e., the positive and the negative; the successes and the struggles) and learn general education content.

The information and strategies provided in this book for developing and implementing effective instruction in general education contexts for students with significant disabilities are based in the understanding of the importance and interrelatedness of curriculum, context, and instruction for all students but especially for students with significant disabilities. In addition, the information and strategies are grounded solidly in general education practices observed in classrooms across the country. School administrators and teachers will recognize the instructional contexts and practices described and will be able to envision how the educational team strategies will complement, rather than conflict with, their current practices. June Downing offers a wealth of expertise and experience for educational teams seeking to provide true access to the entire general curriculum for all students. Enjoy reading this book, and relish the experience of implementing its strategies and seeing the difference in your students' learning and outcomes!

—*Diane Lea Ryndak, PhD*
University of Florida

Preface

Inclusion is not just putting students together of differing abilities and hoping that everyone learns. We have learned that students with disabilities, especially those with more severe disabilities, will require specific instruction to acquire the skills that they need to learn. Close physical placement with peers who are not disabled will not lead to social interactions and the development of social skills unless they are specifically taught (Carter & Hughes, 2005; C. Hughes, Carter, Hughes, Bradford, & Copeland, 2002). Likewise, these students are not likely to pick up all the possible academic skills in general education classrooms unless the material has been adapted *and* the skills taught to them.

We know that students with the most severe types of disabilities can learn a number of skills when systematically instructed in a manner that is appropriate for the task and accounts for individual learning needs. This information will be presented in Chapter 2 and so not repeated here. This acquired knowledge over many years of teaching and research should not be discarded because the placement of the students may have changed from special education environments to inclusive ones. Applying what we know about how students learn to inclusive environments makes sense, given the necessary adjustments.

This text will present evidence-based practice in the field of severe disabilities with suggestions based on personal experience of how to effectively incorporate them into general education classes. Chapter 1 provides the foundation for the text with descriptions of recommended practices that are to be assumed throughout the entire text. Such factors as family involvement, inclusion, and positive behavior support are integral to any high-quality educational program. The information hopefully will assist teachers as they include their students in general education lessons that address the core curriculum. Chapter 2 covers researched and evidence-based strategies that address the "how to" of instruction. Such strategies can be effective when students are in general education classes, although adjustments will need to be made, especially during lessons involving large group instruction. Chapter 3 targets assessment issues, both of the student and the learning environment. Identifying learning opportunities during typical classroom activities must be part of any assessment when the goal is to enhance the student's access to the core curriculum. Chapter 4 describes numerous and very specific examples of different students, ages five to twenty-one, who have severe disabilities and are learning a variety of subject matter (e.g., science, social studies, reading, Spanish). The focus is on techniques to shape desired behavior using adapted material while still keeping the student as an integral member of the overall class activity. Of course, the ideas suggested in this text will have to be adjusted to meet the individual needs of specific students.

One premise of this text is that students will have multiple teachers across any one school day who must work collaboratively to provide the most meaningful education. Chapter 5 highlights the many different potential teachers any one student may have and the need for the student to learn to work with many different individuals. Chapter 6, cowritten with Dr. Kathy Peckham-Hardin, stresses the importance of collecting data on meaningful skills to show accountability. Students cannot just be exposed to core curriculum; they must also be expected to learn and acquire new skills. Finally, the issue of next steps to take is addressed in Chapter 7. A person-centered approach is recommended, keeping the student's needs and interests in the forefront of any future steps taken to support the individual.

Too often, students with severe disabilities are denied access to general education classrooms because educational teams cannot see how they could benefit from this placement. They may not know how to adapt the core curriculum to make it meaningful for students of such different abilities. They may not know of positive behavioral support strategies to assist students with severe behavior challenges to control their unwanted and problematic behaviors. They may not know how to employ direct and systematic instruction to teach meaningful skills during typical classroom activities. While these issues are real and do pose a hindrance to inclusive learning opportunities, they should not bar the students with moderate or severe disabilities from the general education classroom. Students with disabilities have the right to obtain an appropriate education in the least restrictive environment. Those providing educational support for these students must acquire the skills needed to ensure such placement occurs. One major purpose of this text is to offer some information pertaining to this goal. My hope is that those on the educational team, both professional and family, will find the information and examples provided in this text helpful toward creating inclusive opportunities that are beneficial to all students.

Acknowledgments

Even when a book is primarily written by one person, several people offer a helping hand along the way. I owe much to these individuals and would like to acknowledge their support. First, I am very grateful to my friend and past colleague at California State University, Northridge (CSUN), Dr. Kathy Peckham-Hardin, for her contribution of Chapter 6 on assessment. Despite her hectic schedule (made worse by my departure from CSUN), she found the time to create a very practical chapter on assessment that represents a critical area of need in our field. I love writing with Kathy and admire her attention to detail and her profound belief in the need to assess what we are teaching as well as to determine what we should be teaching before jumping into the fray.

I was able to obtain a few photographs for this text with the aid of two past graduate students—one from the University of Arizona and one from CSUN. Antonia Pond, a graduate from CSUN's special education program and a high school teacher for students with severe disabilities in the Phoenix area, captured some nice photographs of students with and without disabilities learning together in typical classrooms. She has created an exemplary peer-tutor program at her high school, and these young people were very helpful in obtaining these photos. I really appreciate her contribution to this text. The photographs of elementary students were provided by Susie Speelman, one of my first graduate students from the University of Arizona. Susie has taught for many years as both a general educator and special educator and loves to see students of all ability levels learning together. She's very much a team player and so not only took pictures herself but also involved one of her paraprofessionals, Kristina Zeider, in taking pictures. I am so very grateful for these great photographs. They add so much!

Susie Speelman also shared one of many adaptations, see Figure 4.1, for inclusion in the text. She gave me lots of options, and I probably could have included nothing but her adaptations in the book—there were so many. Jean Slater of Slater Software readily agreed to permit the use of her graphics, which were part of some of these adaptations. Thanks to both of these women.

I must also acknowledge the several families who so willingly (and quickly) signed the photograph release forms and allowed their son or daughter to be pictured in this text. These pictures bring to life the concepts discussed in this text, and I'm sure they draw the attention of the reader. So a very big thank you goes out to all the students and their families who helped with this project. I'd also like to thank those parents who acted as a catalyst for me to write this text in the first place. Their questions regarding the lack of instruction occurring for their son or daughter prompted me to take on the challenge of writing another book. I'm very grateful for these family members who continue to push for the improved education of their child. I'm grateful (as I feel most professionals are) for their continued and much needed energy toward this effort.

Finally, I'd like to thank the many individuals at Corwin for their support and guidance throughout the development, editing, and publication phases. They were the ones to make this effort come to fruition. My name may be the one on the book cover, but many were involved in the process and I am very grateful to everyone for their support.

Corwin gratefully acknowledges the contributions of the following reviewers:

Nanci Lee Adkinson-Smith, Specialist in Education
Christensen Middle School
Livermore Valley Joint Unified School District
Livermore, CA

Karen Harrison, Special Education Teacher
Center Ridge Elementary School
Centerville, VA

Ronda Schelvan, Special Education Teacher
Hathaway Elementary School
Washougal, WA

Brenda Shelton, First-Grade Teacher
Lenoir City Elementary School
Lenoir City, TN

Kathy Tritz-Rhodes, Principal
Marcus-Meridian-Cleghorn Community Schools
Marcus, IA

About the Author

**June E. Downing,** PhD, is Professor Emerita of Special Education at California State University, Northridge, and prior to that was at the University of Arizona in Tucson, where she did research and prepared teachers to work in the area of moderate, severe, and multiple disabilities. She is a national leader in the field of special education that targets the needs of students with severe disabilities, especially with regard to inclusive education. She has published numerous articles, chapters, monographs, and seven books on students having severe and multiple disabilities. She served for six years on the Executive Board of TASH, an international advocacy organization for individuals with severe disabilities, and was a past president of the California Chapter of this organization—CalTASH as well as AZTASH. She has served as an associate editor of *Research and Practices for Persons With Severe Disabilities* and currently serves on this board as well as several other professional editorial boards. She is presently serving as an educational consultant, traveling extensively in the United States and abroad to do presentations on various subjects.

Teaching Students With Moderate to Severe Intellectual Disabilities in General Education Classrooms

Foundational Beliefs

KEY CONCEPTS

- 🔑 Students with moderate to severe intellectual disabilities can learn and acquire many skills.

- 🔑 Progress has been made toward the inclusion of students with severe disabilities in general education, but considerable work remains.

- 🔑 Inclusive education ensures access to the core curriculum and active participation in the general education lesson with the necessary supports and services.

- 🔑 Skilled teachers with high expectations are needed to help maximize learning potential.

- 🔑 Recommended educational practices include the presumption of competence, inclusive education, strong family involvement, positive behavior support, and self-determination training.

Education should support students' learning and ability to learn. For students with severe disabilities, this learning can occur in either special education rooms or general education rooms with peers without disabilities. While inclusive education for students with severe disabilities is strongly supported by the research (Carter & Hughes, 2006; Cole, Waldron, & Majd, 2004; Dore, Dion, Wagner, & Brunet, 2002; Downing & Peckham-Hardin, 2007; Fisher & Meyer, 2002; Idol, 2006), in actual practice, considerable inexperience and lack of knowledge hinder its effectiveness for students. Many educators in special and general education have never experienced inclusive education and may question how they would provide quality instruction.

Once all educators become comfortable in their ability to make the curriculum meaningful to all students, regardless of ability, students once considered unable to benefit from general education will have more opportunities to realize their potential. Although we have made considerable gains in the education of students with severe disabilities as described in the following section, there is much to learn and improve upon. However, the original and false presumption of students with severe disabilities being unable to learn has been replaced with the knowledge that these students can and do learn. Instead of blaming the student for lack of progress, the need to change learning environments and instructional strategies has received greater attention. Teachers can learn and grow in their instructional ability and in turn, students will reflect that increase in competence to help them learn. We need to learn from our past efforts and continue to push boundaries to discover new and more effective techniques.

■ A HISTORICAL PERSPECTIVE: WHERE WE CAME FROM

The education of students with moderate and severe intellectual disabilities has evolved substantially from initial and traditional beliefs. Originally, individuals with intellectual disabilities were considered unable to learn and were systematically assigned to institutions for care but not for learning (Blatt, 1981). Families were advised to place their children with moderate or severe disabilities into these congregate institutions shortly after birth to avoid any ill effect on the family group and society (Ferguson, 2008; Singer & Irvin, 1991). However, as early as the late 1960s and early 1970s, teachers in the field of special education began questioning the institutionalization of individuals, especially children, calling for a continuum of services offered to students from least to most restrictive in placement (Reynolds, 1962; Taylor, 1982). In addition, family members began questioning the practice of removing their children from the home to be cared for by strangers with no effort made to teach skills.

Banding together, families became a recognizable force opposing institutional placement and instigated court actions demanding educational rights for their children. Their advocacy led to the early court cases, in particular *Mills v. Board of Education* (1982) and *Pennsylvania Association for Retarded Children (PARC) v. Commonwealth of Pennsylvania* (1971, 1972), that ensured educational opportunities for children with developmental disabilities. Such federal court cases impacted the education for all students in the United States and resulted in Congress endorsing the least restrictive environment (LRE) concept in P.L. (Public Law) 94–142, The Education for All Handicapped Children Act of 1975. With the passage of this federal act, the placement of students with disabilities in general education settings was clearly the preference. However, the practice of segregating students with intellectual disabilities, especially those with more severe forms of disability, continues (McLeskey & Henry, 1999).

A Developmental Approach

When educators first were faced with the responsibility to educate students previously unknown to the public school system, initial efforts reflected a developmental approach to learning. Regardless of chronological age, students were tested on standardized tests for those who are typically developing and instruction began where students failed to perform. As a result, instruction bore little resemblance to the student's chronological age and created learning environments that looked very juvenile. Educational placement remained very specialized with students attending special education classrooms physically apart from students without disabilities. Placement either occurred in a completely separate, special school serving only students with disabilities or in a self-contained room in a public school. There was little if any interaction between students with and without disabilities and the curricula did not overlap.

The Functional Era

In the late 1970s, psychologists began to question the developmental programming for students. Educational outcomes were relatively bleak, with students leaving the school program with limited skills to enter the mainstream of adult life. Following a developmental model of education, most students with severe disabilities could not remain in school long enough to learn the skills that would most benefit them as young adults. Brown, Nietupski, and Hamre-Nietupski (1976) published a seminal work questioning the current practice of developmental teaching and proposed a new approach. This new approach adopted a top-down strategy where students' chronological age was a prime consideration in determining the most critical and functional skills for the student (Brown, Branston, Hamre-Nietupski, Pumpian, et al., 1979). This functional approach highlighted the belief that students not only could learn but also could learn meaningful skills that would improve their quality of life by providing them with critical skills to be as independent and interdependent as possible. Age-appropriate skills in the areas of self-care, safety, community access, social, recreation, and communication replaced age-inappropriate skills of stringing beads, repeating simple sounds (ba ba), coloring, and doing two-piece puzzles that were typical of the developmental approach. Students learned such life skills as doing laundry (Taylor, Collins, Schuster, & Kleinert, 2002); getting dressed (Hughes, Schuster, & Nelson, 1993); and accessing the community by riding buses, demonstrating street-crossing safely, and ordering food (Brown et al., 1983). Instruction in these areas was designed to improve students' performance in typical environments upon graduation.

The Least Restrictive Environment: A Problem With Interpretation

Despite the legal mandate to avoid infringing on the student's civil rights through placement in the LRE, schools and school districts have struggled with the principle and the imprecise definition of LRE. The continuum of placement options originally developed by Reynolds (1962) offered ten potential placements from hospitals and treatment centers (most restrictive) to regular classroom with consultation (least restrictive). Unfortunately, despite criticism of the continuum model (which preceded the mandate) for placement (see Taylor, 1988), students with severe disabilities typically were placed in special schools and special classrooms in regular schools (McLeskey & Henry, 1999). Taylor (1988) criticized the use of a continuum of placements, especially for students with severe disabilities, stating that the continuum confused services with a physical place (with more intensive services equating to more restrictive environments) and that it forced students to earn the right to move up the continuum through demonstration of readiness skills that were taught in a segregated setting. Trying to demonstrate competency to learn in a general education environment was particularly challenging when the life skills approach to these specialized settings did not address the academic curriculum typically taught in regular classrooms.

The Era of Integration

However, as students acquired more meaningful skills, attention was drawn to the positive impact that students without disabilities could have. Students without disabilities provided positive role models for communication, behavior, and social skills. Following the reauthorization of P.L. 94–142 and the renaming of the law to reflect person-first language (e.g., Individuals with Disabilities Education Act, 1990) efforts were made to physically increase the time that students with and without severe disabilities spent together during nonacademic times such as recess, lunch, music, nutrition breaks, and assemblies. The integration of students with moderate and severe disabilities gained some prominence during this time with the focus on the social benefits to the students with disabilities (Brown et al., 1983; Taylor, 1982). While students spent the majority of their school day in specialized settings working on functional skills, they also were spending a small part of the day physically close to same-age or younger students without disabilities. Through social integration, students with moderate to severe intellectual disabilities could model appropriate behavior, have access to competent communication partners, and be exposed to a much broader base for social relationships to emerge (Ford & Davern, 1989).

While functional skills were supporting their independent performance as adults, outcomes indicated that students were not making friends and not engaging in activities after school (Brown, Branston, Hamre-Nietupski, Johnson, et al., 1979). Students with disabilities, especially moderate to profound intellectual disabilities, were not gaining membership at their schools but were perceived as infrequent visitors to certain aspects of school life (e.g., assemblies, library time). Such visitation status was evident even when students with severe disabilities spent up to 50% of their school day in general education classrooms (Schnorr, 1990).

Currently, schools are in the process of opening their classrooms to all students at all times, including those with the most challenging types of disabilities. There is a growing recognition that all students should have equal access to the core academic curriculum that may not be possible when students, especially those with severe disabilities, are educated in separate classrooms (Soukup, Wehmeyer, Bashinski, & Bovaird, 2007). However, the trend to include all students, including those with the most severe disabilities, in general education classrooms is uneven at best and successful implementation rests heavily on individual teams at different schools around the country. Nationally, this is a learning phase and much work needs to be done before it can be considered universally successful for all students.

THE PRESENT SITUATION AND CHALLENGE ■

Reauthorization of the original Education of All Handicapped Children Act of 1975 led to the Individuals with Disabilities Education Act of 1990, 1997, and most currently, Individuals with Disabilities Education Improvement Act (IDEIA, 2004). With each reauthorization, greater emphasis was placed on the rights of students with disabilities to learn and to be educated with students without disabilities and by highly qualified teachers. In addition, the No Child Left Behind Act (NCLB) of 2001 has heightened awareness of the need to challenge all students and to stress the importance of all students learning core curriculum content (Browder & Spooner, 2006). Teachers are being held increasingly accountable for the learning of their students. Both of these educational acts (IDEIA and NCLB) support the inclusion of students with disabilities in general education classrooms with access to core curriculum.

While students with moderate to severe disabilities may be gaining physical placement in age-appropriate general education classrooms, questions remain as to how to teach students in these rooms, especially during large group discussion or lecture times. Such teaching arrangements pose particular challenges for students with certain intellectual disabilities due to their heavy emphasis on verbal skills, ability to recall information quickly, and the ability to focus on a teacher standing at the front of the room. Teachers who pursue inclusive education for their students with intellectual disabilities need to know strategies to use to provide the necessary individualized and systematic instruction in general education, especially when the learning arrangement is least conducive to active participation by their students. Students with moderate to severe intellectual disabilities can learn in general education environments, but they need skilled teachers to provide the adaptations and accommodations that they need to be successful.

Considerable research has been completed on effective teaching strategies for students with moderate to severe intellectual disabilities (Barudin & Hourcade, 1990; Biederman, Fairhall, Raven, & Davey, 1998; Post & Storey, 2002). Some of these practices include task analysis, constant or progressive time delay, simultaneous prompting, and least to most instructional prompting. Such practices have been shown to be effective for teaching such skills as communication (Angell, Bailey, & Larson, 2008; Light & Binger, 1998), literacy (Ault, Gast, & Wolery, 1988; Bradford, Shippen, Alberto, Houchins, & Flores, 2006), and community skills (Hughes & Agran, 1993; Zhang, Gast, Horvat, & Dattilo, 1995). What is less in evidence is the implementation of these recognized strategies within general education classes.

Most experts in the area of moderate to severe intellectual disabilities stress the need for systematic teaching procedures for these students to learn (Bradford et al., 2006; Browder, Trela, & Jimenez, 2007; Copeland, Hughes, Agran, Wehmeyer,

Fowler, 2002; Duker, Didden, & Sigafoos, 2004). Systematic instruction refers to carefully planned and direct strategies used to teach new behaviors and skills, maintain skills, and generalize skills to other environments, activities, and people. The challenge for teachers is to provide high quality systematic instruction to individual students when they are taught in general education classrooms. Instead of having control over their own special education rooms, special educators, paraprofessionals, and related service providers must share learning space with general educators and in such a way as to blend highly specialized instruction into the general education class activities. In other words, teachers have to apply what is known about the learning of students with moderate to severe disabilities within the specifications of a fully inclusive environment.

■ WHAT IS INCLUSIVE EDUCATION?

Inclusive education is full-time membership of students with disabilities in their chronologically age-appropriate classrooms with the necessary supports and services to benefit from educational activities (Lipsky & Gartner, 1992; Ryndak, Jackson, & Billingsley, 2000). Students do not need to be demonstrating grade-level performance but can gain valuable academic and nonacademic skills from participation in grade-level lessons. Supports and services include a wide variety of material adaptations and instructional accommodations, such as tactile or pictorial information, slant boards to hold materials upright, information made simpler and repeated verbally or signed, related service providers, and additional time to explore concrete items that are part of a lecture. Such supports are individualized to meet the unique learning needs of students having a wide range of moderate or severe disabilities and are embedded into the activities typically occurring in the classroom. The student is supported to learn in an environment with high expectations and is expected to be actively engaged in all learning opportunities. While the student may not be expected to learn the exact same content nor in the same manner as classmates, he or she should be challenged to learn as much as possible. Figure 1.1 highlights this expectation by showing a high school student giving a presentation to his class with the support of a peer.

Collaboration of team members is a hallmark of inclusive education. General educators, special educators, paraprofessionals, related service providers, and all critical team members share the responsibility for teaching students with moderate to severe intellectual disabilities in typical learning environments (Downing, 2008; Idol, 2002; Snell & Janney, 2005). Team members do not work in isolation or remove the student from class activities to address skills unrelated to the core curriculum. Instead, areas of need are addressed during typical class activities by various support persons who are highly qualified.

This collaborative approach entails preplanning for lessons that take into consideration the needs of the student and how the lesson will be taught. Planning so that all students of diverse needs and abilities can have access to and actively participate in class activities is termed *universal design for learning* (UDL; Rose & Meyer, 2002). Through this process of collaborative teaming to

| Figure 1.1 | A high school peer tutor supports another student giving a presentation |

Photographer: Antonia Pond

involve all students in class lessons and activities, accommodations are considered with regard to presentation of material, learning arrangements, demonstration of knowledge learned, and evaluation from the onset of the lesson and not as an add-on piece. The intent is to value and respect different ways that students learn so that all students have access to the material presented.

Inclusive education also ensures access to the core academic curriculum for the student with moderate or severe disabilities, which is a legal mandate as per IDEIA (2004) and NCLB (2001; Dymond, Renzaglia, Gilson, & Slagor, 2007). When students are educated in general education classrooms, they have immediate access to the grade-level core curriculum that the entire class receives. Such access is much harder to ensure when students are educated in specialized settings with special educators who are not as knowledgeable about different grade-level standards. Soukup et al. (2007) found that instruction in self-contained special education rooms was not linked to the general education curriculum and concluded that the best place for students with disabilities to gain access to general education curriculum was in general education classrooms. Therefore, inclusive education is the process of students learning challenging material made meaningful and appropriate for their individual needs in general education rooms alongside their classmates with no disabilities.

■ WHAT IS NOT INCLUSIVE EDUCATION

Inclusive education does not mean physically placing students in general education classrooms without the necessary supports and services. For instance, having a student with significant cognitive disabilities listen to a lecture in a high school physics class without simplifying the information, presenting it in an accessible manner, and relating it to the student's life is not what is meant by inclusive education. Unfortunately, such a practice has been associated with inclusion. As a result, it is no wonder that some educators fear its implementation in their schools (Carter & Hughes, 2006; Lohrmann & Bambara, 2006).

Inclusive education also is not hiring a paraprofessional to be with the student with moderate or severe disabilities throughout the day, getting materials for the student, telling the student what to do, assisting the student to perform tasks, and removing the student from the classroom when the student vocalizes distress. This hovering nature of paraprofessionals can lead to isolation by the student and an overdependence on an adult's assistance for all tasks (Giangreco & Broer, 2005; Giangreco & Doyle, 2007; Giangreco, Yuan, McKenzie, Cameron, & Fialka, 2005). Such a situation often occurs when the paraprofessional is not trained appropriately and is unsure of the goal of inclusive education or of the IEP goals for the student. The paraprofessional may feel the need to keep the student quiet, turn in correct work, and meet basic needs. However, when an adult is overly involved in the process and product of the student's education, learned helplessness on the part of the student can emerge (Giangreco & Broer, 2005; Giangreco et al., 2005). Once learned helplessness has been acquired, the student may not feel that he or she can perform a task without the support of an adult. Rather, the student is entitled to instruction from a highly qualified educator, which must be an important component of inclusive education.

In addition, inclusive education does not have the student sitting near the door or at the back of the room working with another adult on material that is unrelated to the class activity. Such a scenario occurs when teaming for a lesson is not occurring and the general educator has no ownership of the student with moderate or severe disabilities. The IEP for the student has been created with no attention to content standards for a particular grade and is comprised of unrelated skills that must be worked on separately from the class. In a truly inclusive classroom, the student should be an integral part of the class, actively participating in activities with peers to the maximum extent possible.

Having a student with moderate or severe intellectual disabilities visit a particular classroom for a period of time, from 30 minutes a week to several hours a day, also is not what is intended as inclusive education. Often, such visitations mean that the student comes to class when he or she can "handle" the coursework (e.g., art, music, library time) and therefore, very few if any accommodations are necessary. When a student is a visitor to a class, the manner in which the lesson is being taught may not have considered the unique adaptations and accommodations that are necessary to fully include the student. Expectations may be for the student to be physically present, quiet, and partially involved when possible. Such an arrangement does not reflect truly inclusive practices, and benefits related to inclusion are not likely to be realized. For instance, when Schnorr (1990) studied the practice of "including" a young first grader with severe disabilities for a large part of the day, she found that the other first graders did not perceive him as a member of the class but rather more of a visitor. To obtain true membership for students with moderate to severe disabilities, full-time placement in chronologically age-appropriate classrooms is recommended. For elementary students, this means full-time placement in the age-appropriate class, and for middle school and high school students, it means attending different classes with peers as determined by a combination of required courses and electives.

TARGETED STUDENTS FOR THIS TEXT ■

While all students with and without disabilities can be educated together in general education age-appropriate classrooms, the focus of this book is on those students with moderate to severe intellectual disabilities who often are denied general education access. These students, ages five to twenty-two, often have cognitive disabilities that make it quite difficult to acquire new information. They may require considerable and repeated exposure to concepts and materials so that they can recognize and make use of the information (Giangreco, 2006; Ryndak & Alper, 2003). Many of these students may not have a formal language and may be in the emergent stages of both communication and literacy. Students also may have physical disabilities (mild to severe), sensory impairments (visual and/or auditory), and/or behavior challenges. For example, Jacob is a third grader who is Jewish and lives at home with his father, mother, two brothers, and one sister. Jacob loves his pet dog and most things connected with Disney and Disneyland. He has a severe cortical visual impairment that makes it very difficult for him to recognize and interpret visual information. He uses a wheelchair and cannot stand unassisted. He has some use of his hands, but struggles with any task requiring fine motor dexterity. He is nonverbal and makes use of facial expressions, some vocalizations, body movements, and some objects and parts of objects to communicate. When he can't convey what he is trying to say, he can become very agitated, spitting at others, and biting his arm. He relies on others to help him convey his thoughts and needs. Jacob also experiences seizure activity and has other health impairments (e.g., allergies). While Jacob has numerous adults involved in his educational program (e.g., general educator, special educator, occupational therapist, vision teacher, etc.), he struggles to make friends with peers.

Students like Jacob typically fare poorly on standardized intelligence tests and may not demonstrate early cognitive skills, such as object permanence, cause-effect, or imitation. On a superficial level, it may appear that accessing age-level core curriculum, for these students, may be very challenging. However, those students have a legal right to access the core curriculum and will never be able to acquire related skills unless provided with the opportunity. For the most part, such students have been denied access based on negative perceptions of their potential for academics (Browder & Spooner, 2006). Students with such severe disabilities, however, are being educated in general education classrooms in schools all over the country, and they are benefiting from this placement (Idol, 2006; Schwarz, 2006). It is hopeful that this trend will continue to grow for the benefit of students with and without disabilities. Placement, however, is insufficient in and of itself. We must first ensure that *all* students have the necessary opportunities to learn, and then, we need to make sure that we know *how* to teach them.

■ RECOMMENDED PRACTICES AS A PREMISE OF THE TEXT

This book is written with certain foundational beliefs regarding the education of students having moderate to severe disabilities. While all of these foundational beliefs may not be in evidence at a particular school, they are recommended practices and can serve as meaningful goals to reach. The main focus of this book is on the recommended practice of individualized and systematic instruction. The chapters that follow deal with such instruction. The other obvious values apparent in this book are that of presumed competence, inclusive education for all students, family involvement, positive behavior support, and self-determination. The rationale for these fundamental beliefs is presented briefly in the following pages.

Presumed Competence

One primary premise of this text is that *all* children can and do learn. No student is considered too disabled to benefit from quality instruction. At times, the severity and complexity of some students' disabilities seem to overshadow who they are as learners. When students have limited communication skills, limited physical movement, health issues, and other disabilities, such as a severe visual impairment or hearing impairment, their ability to demonstrate what they know is severely compromised. If teachers and others on their educational team equate their challenge with self-expression with an inability to learn, then students are likely to reach this limiting expectation.

A recommended practice in the field is to assume competence and teach to that assumption (Jorgensen, 2005; Jorgensen, McSheehan, & Sonnenmeier, 2007). Since we can never be sure of what students can learn, assuming competence is the least dangerous assumption. When students are assumed to be competent, they gain access to age-level experiences and information. If assumed to not be competent, those around them can limit their access to materials, information, and experiences. The tendency may be to restrict activities to those that teachers feel students can understand and demonstrate that understanding. The danger of such an approach is that students can be denied access to a number of learning and social activities and environments, which in turn limits their ability to learn. This "catch-22" situation is best avoided by supporting all students in rich learning environments and age-appropriate activities. Furthermore, when presuming competence, the student with severe disabilities is likely to be treated with respect and not demeaned (e.g., using infantile speech patterns with an elementary, middle school–, or high school–aged student).

Concomitant with the basic principles that all students can and do learn and should be respected as competent learners is the belief that they need and deserve quality instruction to help them reach their greatest potential. In addition to curricular adaptations, they will need individualized teaching support that considers both their challenges to learning as well as their strengths. When teachers differentiate their instruction to involve all learners, students of quite different abilities will be able to demonstrate what they know (Thousand, Villa, & Nevin, 2007).

Inclusive Education

The strategies discussed in this text are specifically designed to be used in general education classes. Strategies designed to separate students based on ability are not progressive in nature nor are they recommended. Strategies that support learning in typical school, home, and community environments are more worthwhile to pursue. Students with moderate to severe intellectual disabilities need ongoing opportunities to learn from their peers without disabilities. They need regular and close contact to acquire typical interactive behaviors, typical speech patterns where possible, and appropriate behaviors in general (Carter & Hughes, 2005; Copeland et al., 2004; Hughes, Carter, Hughes, Bradford, & Copeland, 2002). They also need to learn in close proximity to their same age peers without disabilities to receive the benefit of peer modeling and tutoring (Carter, Cushing, & Kennedy, 2009; Hughes et al., 2002). Above all, they need and have a right to access grade-level content that has been made meaningful to individual needs. With no access, these learners automatically face the discrimination of low expectations and no opportunity.

The benefits of inclusive education for students with severe disabilities have been well established (Carter & Hughes, 2006; Cole et al., 2004; Fisher & Meyer, 2002; Foreman, Arthur-Kelly, Pascoe, & Smyth-King, 2004; Idol, 2006; Meyer, 2001). Communication and social skills have increased when students are educated in inclusive settings (Fisher & Meyer, 2002; Foreman et al., 2004; Harrower & Dunlap, 2001; Naraian, 2008). Enhanced academic skills also have been noted for students with moderate to severe disabilities educated in general education classrooms (Cole et al., 2004; Hedeen & Ayres, 2002; Ryndak, Morrison, & Sommerstein, 1999; Wehmeyer, Lattin, Lapp-Rincker, & Agran, 2003).

Benefits for students without disabilities include greater awareness of and appreciation for differences (Copeland et al., 2004; Downing, Spencer, & Cavallaro, 2004; Peck, Staub, Gallucci, & Schwartz, 2004). Students without disabilities have acquired skills related to teaching others, using assistive technology, and understanding different ways to learn (Downing & Peckham-Hardin, 2007; Dymond et al., 2006). Besides learning about human differences, there has been no reported negative impact on student learning (Cole et al., 2004). Hunt, Staub, Alwell, and Goetz (1994) found that the presence of a student with severe and multiple disabilities in a cooperative learning group for math resulted in no differences in academic achievement for students without disabilities compared to cooperative learning groups that had no students with such disabilities. Idol (2006) surveyed teachers, principals, and paraprofessionals at eight schools moving toward more inclusive education. At the four elementary schools, no negative impact on students without disabilities was reported, and several reported that there had been improvement. At the two middle schools and two high schools investigated, 58% stated that there was no negative impact on students without disabilities and 24% said that there was improvement across seven variables. With regard to test scores, 58% to 68% of respondents said that test scores stayed the same following inclusion and 5% to 19% said students without disabilities performed better following inclusion.

Cushing and Kennedy (1997) addressed the issue of students without disabilities falling behind academically if allowed to support a classmate with severe disabilities. What they found was just the opposite. Students who were struggling to achieve academically showed improvement of enhanced letter grades as a result of working with a classmate with severe intellectual disabilities. These researchers suggested that the additional feedback from a teacher or paraprofessional while serving in a support role may have positively influenced their performance overall. Carter and Kennedy (2006) also reported that at-risk students who supported students with severe disabilities improved their academic skill level.

In general, research findings to date support the practice of bringing students of different abilities together to learn. Benefits have been documented for all involved with minimal if any detrimental impact. Teachers have reported learning more skills and knowledge to use with an increasingly diverse student population (Downing & Peckham-Hardin, 2007; Spooner, Baker, Harris, Ahlgrim-Delzell, & Browder, 2007). Special and general education teachers working together to make core curriculum accessible for all students makes more intuitive sense than the same teachers trying to do this on their own. Ensuring access to core curriculum becomes quite challenging when special educators have students of several different grade levels in one special education room, which is typical. Making use of the skills and expertise of differently trained teachers working together in inclusive classrooms can support the learning and achievement of all students. This collaboration will be discussed in Chapter 5 of this text.

Family Involvement

A strong premise of this book is that families will be actively involved (to the degree they prefer) in their child's education. Family input is critical, as family members supply considerable information on student strengths, preference, dislikes, responses to past intervention, as well as their goals and hopes for the future. Cultural and religious values also can be shared so that these will not be compromised unknowingly by the educational staff (King, Baxter, Rosenbaum, Zwaigenbaum, & Bates, 2009; Poston & Turnbull, 2004). Without strong family input and involvement, educational teams could easily get off track with regard to critical learning needs and the most appropriate academic goals to pursue (Blue-Banning, Summers, Frankland, & Beegle, 2004; Lynch & Hanson, 2004).

Families come in a variety of configurations, sizes, linguistic backgrounds, cultural experiences, religious beliefs, and racial experiences. As a result, unique family interpretations of the educational experience for their child are essential to obtain and make appropriate use of in the planning and implementation of any educational program. Families know what and how their child has been taught in the past and can provide critical information regarding what has been most successful with their child and what strategies should be avoided. They know what motivates their child to perform and what situations create the most difficulty for their child. As a result, teachers can save considerable time developing a program for a student by talking to family members about the educational program at the outset.

Of particular importance are the goals and dreams that family members hold for their family member. The educational team needs to know what the family hopes their child will achieve. They also need to understand what the family holds little value for. For example, a teacher may feel that it is imperative that a student learn the names of colors and may spend considerable time on this one skill. However, in talking to the family, it is discovered that they place relatively little importance on this skill and would much rather that he learn how to handle money or read. The student may actually make use of colors (e.g., putting like color items together or matching an outfit to wear) but cannot name them. Family members may feel that other skills are much more important for their child and would rather that the educational team address those skills. Since teachers have limited time to teach a large number of important skills, it makes sense to listen to families to determine where the majority of instructional time should be spent. Differences in anticipated educational outcomes can be particularly impacted by cultural aspects. Expectations for certain behavioral and social outcomes can be quite different as well as the strategies used to achieve them (Rogers-Atkinson, Ochoa, & Delgado, 2003).

Family involvement and input are of particular importance during transitional times when changes in schools or graduation occur. Carter, Clark, Cushing, and Kennedy (2007) reported a strong link between parent involvement and student achievement, especially as the student transitioned from elementary to middle school. These authors stressed the need to encourage active parent involvement especially as it may wane during secondary school. As students age, their interests and skills may change. In addition, family situations may change, impacting desired educational outcomes for the student. Ensuring the involvement of family members in educational planning helps to keep the educational team on track.

Positive Behavior Support

A strong foundational belief of this text is that all interactions with students are positive and respectful and reflect the premises of positive behavior support (PBS; see Horner, Albin, Todd, & Sprague, 2006). Although detailed information on the components of positive behavior support will not be discussed in this text, some general information will be provided on schoolwide positive behavior support. PBS represents a comprehensive, systematic, and positive approach to helping all students engage in desired school behavior (Simonsen, Sugai, & Negron, 2008; Sugai, Simonsen, & Horner, 2008).

According to Horner, Sugai, Todd, and Lewis-Palmer (2005) PBS that is schoolwide is a three-tiered system. The majority of all students in a school generally respond well to a positive, supportive, and nurturing environment that praises desired behavior, teaches appropriate ways of interacting, and arranges the learning environment to prevent behavior problems (first tier). For the 15% or so of students who need more than this primary support base, a secondary level of support is provided to directly teach desired social skills and ways of dealing with frustration and anger. At the tertiary level, individualized intervention based on specific data is designed for those few students who need this level of intensive behavioral supports. With respect to the student with moderate to severe disabilities who demonstrates very challenging behavior, nondesired behavior is not perceived as negative but as efforts by the student to communicate. A functional behavioral assessment (FBA) is recommended to determine what may be initiating and maintaining the behavior for the student (Horner et al., 2006). Environments are carefully analyzed to determine potential impact on behavior. Comprehensive data are then collected on the behavior in question to determine when and where it occurs and under what conditions. The data are analyzed to determine a hypothesis regarding the intent or intents of the behavior for the student. The reason for the student to engage in the behavior (the functions it serves for the student) is then used to adjust the physical and social environment to reduce the need and/or the student is taught another way to obtain what is needed.

This assessment procedure can be lengthy and time consuming but is essential for understanding the behavior and helping the student meet specified needs in a more acceptable manner. For example, when Wyatt kept falling on the floor and screaming in his seventh-grade math class, it was not labeled as "bad" behavior. Instead, his team collected data related to the behavior, such as the time of day, activity in progress, location in the room, preceding events, consequences of the behavior, and information from home (illness, sleep patterns, etc.). The team asked what Wyatt's behavior gained for him and determined that it often followed the presentation of a math task he did not want to do. They hypothesized that the behavior was his means of commenting negatively on the task and escaping from it. To test this hypothesis, they let him choose math activities to do as well as his choice of materials to use, provided considerable support to increase his success at math, and taught him a way to say that he hated certain things (by pressing a voice output device with a pictorial symbol on it). When Wyatt's behavior improved during this class period, it was determined that the hypothesis was correct and that Wyatt needed more control over how and what he learned, as well as more support when the task was challenging.

Respect for student interest is a fundamental premise of this text. Students are not meant to be physically manipulated or forced to perform tasks, especially those for which they see no value. Rather, motivating the student to learn involves incorporating interests of the student into lessons, reinforcing positive behavior and approximations of desired behavior, and recognizing the importance of and offering the student numerous choices (Sigafoos, Arthur-Kelly, & Butterfield, 2006). For example, a student who dislikes math will be given multiple choices involving who to work with, where to work, what materials to work with, and order of activities. The student's interest in insects will be used in math for counting, recognizing amounts, comparing amounts, and ordering numbered insects sequentially. See the book by Paula Kluth and Patrick Schwarz (2008) on using the interests and passions of students to support learning.

Self-Determination

A final premise of this book relates to positive behavior support and deals with empowering the student and demonstrating respect for individual preferences. Students, despite difficulties with communication, must be listened to and must be supported in their efforts to become self-determined. Helping students experience the world to develop their interests is a critical aspect of self-determination so that students can advocate for what they desire. Instead of forcing students to learn the same material in the same way, respecting the individual student's unique interests and strengths can encourage a greater partnership in learning between teacher and student.

Self-determination skills include (but are not limited to) choice making, problem solving, self-monitoring, decision making, goal setting, and self-advocacy. The desired outcome of self-determination is that students gain and maintain as much say as possible over their lives. Some bias may exist against students with moderate to severe disabilities who have limited communication skills and who have traditionally had minimal control over their lives (Agran & Wehmeyer, 2003). To counter this bias, every effort should be made to teach these students as many self-determination skills as possible and to give them every opportunity to practice and hone these important skills.

Much has been written about the importance of self-determination for students with disabilities (Katsiyannis, Zhang, Woodruff, & Dixon, 2005; Turnbull & Turnbull, 2001; Wehmeyer, Field, Doren, Jones, & Mason, 2004). In addition, benefits of self-determination for these students, which includes improved behavior, enhanced productivity, and increased contribution in class, have been noted (Agran, Blanchard, Wehmeyer, & Hughes, 2002; Brooks, Todd, Tofflemoyer, & Horner, 2003; Wehmeyer & Palmer, 2003). While most self-determination studies have involved students with learning disabilities, emotional disorders, and mild intellectual impairments, the importance for all students is clear. Fowler, Konrad, Walker, Test, and Wood (2007) completed a literature review of the impact of the teaching of self-determination skills on academic skills of students with developmental disabilities. From the 11 studies reviewed, findings indicated that self-determination instruction strongly improved organizational skills for academic work and also provided some direct support for math and spelling skills. For students with significant cognitive disabilities, initial aspects of teaching self-determination involve respecting student interests and providing choices for students (Cannella, O'Reilly, & Lancioni, 2005; Realon, Favell, & Lowerre, 1990). Students without speech make their preferences known to others through their use of pictures, objects, or actions in general. There is no need to wait for formal communication or language to develop to teach self-determination.

Supporting students to advocate for themselves and their interests occurs when students are given choices of materials, sequence of activities, locations, and so on that do not deter from the lesson but that motivate the student to learn. Starting with simple choices that lead to immediate and positive consequences for the student (e.g., choice of where to sit or stand, rewards, food, partner to work with), the student learns the skills needed to make more complex and difficult choices regarding future events (e.g., choosing to work for a reward later in the day or week). Teachers can support the development of choice making (as an early step toward self-determination) by relinquishing some control to the student. In other words, instead of giving materials to a student to work with, the teacher can present several options to the student and then honor the one(s) chosen. The student needs to learn that choices he makes will be honored by those around him, thus empowering him to make other, more complex decisions. By starting this practice in the early years of preschool and continuing to build on these skills as the student progresses through each grade, students leaving high school should have considerable practice honing these skills to be used as adults.

■ SUMMARY

This chapter introduces the topic of the text, with an emphasis on its importance in the field. While considerable change has occurred in the field with support from judicial, legislative, and advocacy areas, many students with moderate to severe disabilities are still waiting to receive a high-quality and appropriate education in the least restrictive environment. It is insufficient for students with moderate or severe disabilities to be physically present in general education classrooms without receiving the individualized and systematic instruction that is needed to learn. Curricular adaptations are essential to allow cognitive, physical, sensory, and motivational access, but specific instruction for each student is also needed to ensure that learning occurs, and students are truly a part of the learning community.

Certain premises of the text have been highlighted in this chapter and will be assumed throughout the remainder of the text. These assumptions include presumed competence of all learners, the benefits of students learning together, the critical role that family members play in the education and assessment of their child, the use of a positive behavioral approach in all interactions with students, and the belief that students should be encouraged to advocate for themselves (self-determination). Such assumptions are considered critical to attaining a high-quality education for students with moderate to severe disabilities.

In Chapter 2, strategies that have been found to be effective in the teaching of students having moderate to severe intellectual disabilities will be described even though some of these strategies have been tested and employed in special education environments only. Considerable support exists for several different intervention strategies for students with moderate to severe disabilities that have helped these students learn. The importance of applying such strategies in inclusive classrooms will be stressed.

2

Instructional Strategies and Teaching Arrangements

KEY CONCEPTS

- Effective teachers use active learning, clear expectations, and task analysis of complicated skills to benefit all students.

- Considering student interests in learning tasks can increase student engagement.

- Many different types of prompts have been used to teach students with severe disabilities, given the need to consider individual student needs and abilities.

- A variety of prompting strategies have been used successfully to shape desired behavior.

- Students with moderate to severe disabilities can learn in a variety of teaching arrangements such as large groups, small groups, and partner learning.

Teaching students to learn means providing them with sufficient information in a clear and positive manner to which they can relate and then providing opportunities to practice and maintain skills. Given the limited amount of time and the scope of curriculum that most teachers have in any given academic year, efficiency in teaching is an important consideration. The same issues pertain to students with moderate to severe intellectual disabilities, except that learning will often require more time and more repetition, so efficiency of instruction becomes a particularly critical aspect.

Given the importance of direct and systematic instruction for students with severe disabilities, this chapter will describe known teaching strategies in the field for this population of students. Considerable information exists on what appears to be effective with students having intellectual disabilities to the point that many may be considered evidence-based according to specific criterion established by Horner et al. (2005). Skilled teachers can make use of this knowledge base for the benefit of their students' learning, adapting as needed for their particular students.

■ CHARACTERISTICS OF EFFECTIVE INSTRUCTION FOR ALL STUDENTS

When students present with several complex challenges to learning, teachers may initially feel that the instruction that is typically available for students without disabilities will be insufficient to meet their needs. Characteristics of quality instruction can be beneficial to all students, however, and so identifying and utilizing those elements whenever possible for students with severe disabilities seems the most expedient.

Active Learning

One recommended practice in education calls for active involvement of students (Greenwood, Horton, & Utley, 2002; Zemelman, Daniels, & Hyde, 2005). Instead of students being passive recipients of instruction from the teacher, participation in learning activities with opportunities to apply information is the preferred objective (Haberman, 1991; McCarthy, 2005; Scruggs, Mastropieri, & Okolo, 2008). The concept that students should be actively involved in their learning with considerable hands-on opportunities fares well for students with and without disabilities. Balancing the day's instruction between sedentary and active lessons benefits those who have a strong need to move as well as those who can demonstrate their knowledge more easily through means other than reading and writing.

Lessons that require considerable student-teacher interaction, peer interaction, and active development of a project using varied materials all require active student involvement. Exploring topics on the Internet, especially in pairs or small groups, building replicas of important monuments or artifacts, or playing a *Jeopardy*-like game on history facts as a team are all examples of active learning. Although not a requirement for inclusive education, it may be easier to achieve true academic inclusion of students with moderate to severe disabilities when teachers practice active learning. Ketterer, Schuster, Morse, and Collins (2007) found that active learning increased amount of responding for six of eight elementary students and increased time on task for all eight students.

■ CLEAR EXPECTATIONS

All students need to know what is expected both socially and academically so that they can strive to reach those expectations. Westling and Fox (2009) identify giving clear directions and other forms of input as well as having appropriately high expectations as evidence of good teaching for all students. Often, students need more than just a verbal explanation of expectations for performance. They need to see visual reminders (e.g., posters in the classroom and around the school, other students being rewarded for appropriate behavior), and they need to engage in certain behaviors and receive immediate feedback. Students with moderate and severe intellectual disabilities may have particular difficulty remembering expectations that have been given orally, and they may not have the linguistic ability to understand instructions. Therefore, with this population, it is particularly important to provide expectations for performance using a number of different modalities (e.g., pictorial and/or written reminders of expectations on their desks, gestural cues, reminders from peers). Establishing clear routines may be particularly beneficial for students who may struggle to remember behavioral expectations.

ANALYZING TASKS FOR IMPROVED LEARNING ■

When curricular material is broad and complex, analyzing it into smaller skills for students can be supportive of student learning. To ease the possibility of being overwhelmed by what might appear to be a somewhat insurmountable task, narrowing the focus and mastering smaller steps at a time clarifies what is being learned and what is causing greater difficulty. Breaking a task into its smaller steps, called task analysis, has been used to teach many skills to many students. For example, with the task of writing a letter, the teacher will typically break the task down into smaller components, such as addressing a letter, starting a letter, writing the bulk of the letter, ending the letter, and preparing the envelope for mailing. Students can work to master each individual aspect before being expected to demonstrate mastery of the entire task.

For students with intellectual disabilities, task analysis makes it easier to identify what steps are most crucial to learn and which ones can be modified, omitted, or shared with another student. The team, in its planning stages for a lesson, should identify what part or parts of the activity and/or content will be targeted for the student. Then, a careful analysis of the task for that student is undertaken. All adaptations (e.g., materials, equipment, manner in which knowledge will be demonstrated) are considered in this analysis. Then, each small step that the student must do to demonstrate mastery needs to be taught. For example, Browder, Trela, and Jimenez (2007) used task analysis and systematic instruction to engage middle school students with moderate and severe intellectual disabilities in grade-appropriate literature. Although nonreaders, the students were able to gain literacy skills, such as opening a book, pointing to text, responding to comprehension questions, learning new vocabulary, turning pages in the book, and identifying initial sounds of words. Browder, Mims, Spooner, Ahlgrim-Delzell, and Lee (2008) used task analysis to identify important skills and successfully teach three students with profound disabilities to respond to shared reading questions.

By analyzing the various steps of the task for the individual student, those teaching the student have a much clearer idea of what needs to be done. They also get a clearer idea of which aspects of a task are easier for the student and which ones are more challenging. Since each student is unique, the analysis of any learning task could be equally unique. For example, one student may be expected to make a vocalization or movement when the correct answer is verbally stated (a form of auditory scanning). Another student may be expected to pick up a marker, look at all options, and then mark the correct answer. Table 2.1 and Table 2.2 provide examples of task analyses for two different students and lessons. The smaller steps identified to complete the task are unique to the cognitive and physical needs of each student.

Table 2.1	Task Analysis of Identifying the Larger of Two Decimals for a Student With Moderate to Severe Intellectual Disabilities

Materials: Number cards and a number line
1. Look at both numbers presented.
2. Pick up one number and match to number on number line.
3. Pick up the second number and match to number on number line.
4. Touch the number that is the farthest to the right.
5. Touch the same number on the worksheet or test.
6. Pick up a marker.
7. Mark the correct answer on the worksheet or test.

Table 2.2	Task Analysis of Using Media to Obtain Information for a Student With Severe Physical and Intellectual Disabilities

Precondition: Computer is on with correct Web page selected, scanning software on, switch
1. Touch switch to start scanning software.
2. Look at options on computer screen to make decisions.
3. Touch switch to make selections of correct pictorial information.
4. Touch switch to return to scan.
5. Touch switch to select print function when all selections are made.

■ WHAT WE KNOW ABOUT TEACHING STUDENTS WITH MODERATE TO SEVERE INTELLECTUAL DISABILITIES

Most research on instructional strategies used with students having moderate to severe disabilities comes from work done in special education classrooms. In addition, much of the research has targeted nonacademic instruction, such as social skills, vocational tasks, and cause-effect learning. Several comparative studies have been done to determine the most efficient means of teaching students with moderate to severe disabilities (Colozzi, Ward, & Crotty, 2008; Gast, Ault, Wolery, Doyle, & Belanger, 1988; Schuster, Griffen, & Wolery, 1992). More recently, researchers have been examining teaching strategies that occur in inclusive general education classrooms. Such investigations are necessary if we are to transfer what we have learned as a field in specialized settings to typical educational environments. Furthermore, the field needs to target academic skills and the most effective way of teaching these skills to a wide range of students having intellectual disabilities.

Teaching involves helping others acquire skills that are new or have not been thoroughly mastered. Some students learn very quickly, only needing to hear the information one time before they are able to apply it effectively. Other students require much more time and instruction in order to understand expectations of the task and how to apply new information to various situations. When students have moderate to severe intellectual disabilities, the ability to quickly ascertain associations between concepts, recognize expectations, and then apply them can be compromised. They tend to need a fair amount of repetition to learn skills with multiple opportunities to practice on a regular basis (Westling & Fox, 2009). These students typically need a systematic and structured approach to acquire new skills, to gain some fluency with these skills, maintain them, and finally, generalize them to similar but novel situations (Browder, Spooner, Ahlgrim-Delzell, Harris, & Wakeman, 2008). Teachers need to provide information and support in such a way that it makes sense to the individual learner so that knowledge and skills can be acquired.

THE IMPORTANCE OF STUDENT INTERESTS ■

Students with moderate to severe intellectual disabilities may perform longer and with greater attention to the task if their interests are embedded into activities. Edeh (2006) investigated the impact of interest-based learning and found that the students with mental retardation in the interest-based method maintained independent problem solving skills more than the control students or those in the traditional approach. Making use of student interests could mean using what they like to solve math problems, weaving these interests into stories being read, or adding interests to social studies units being studied. Light and McNaughton (2009) suggest the use of student interests when learning literacy skills. While they recommend a sequence of literacy skills to be learned, they also advise that if a student knows certain words as a result of a strong interest, then using those words as a starting point for greater literacy learning should be respected. For example, if a student really likes vacuum cleaners, then teaching the recognition of the letter *V* and the sound it makes in the word *vacuum* might be a good starting place for the student. Interests don't replace the core curriculum but are added to what is being learned to make it more relevant for the student (e.g., We have vacuum cleaners now, but they didn't have them during the Civil War).

■ COMPONENTS OF THE TEACHING TASK

Following an operant learning model, we all learn certain behaviors in the presence of specific stimuli. We act on the environment in such a way that a consequence occurs (either positive or negative). If that consequence is positive, the action or behavior will likely reoccur. For example, when we see a book that looks interesting, we will typically read it (or some of it), and if the reading of the book makes us feel good, then we are likely to engage in this reading behavior when we again encounter a book that looks interesting to us. If the book had not been interesting or pleasing to us, then the likelihood of engaging in that same behavior is diminished. Teachers can manipulate the stimuli in the environment (e.g., make sure there are books that whet students' appetites) and can also add consequences to increase the likelihood that the desired behavior (in this case, reading) will occur again. For example, they may give out points for every book read, and those points in turn can be exchanged for a reward of a student's choosing.

Specific components of structured teaching have been identified and include (1) selecting the opportunity to teach, (2) gaining the student's attention, (3) presenting the stimulus, (4) giving directions, (5) providing time for the student to respond, (6) providing prompts, and (7) providing consequences (Wolery, Anthony, Snyder, Werts, & Katzenmeyer, 1997). Selecting the opportunity to teach, especially in general education classes, requires the teacher to recognize when specific skills fit naturally into the class activities, when it is most relevant for the student, and when it will not interfere with other class activities. For instance, teaching the student to say vocabulary out loud may not be appropriate during a lecture format. The second step in a structured teaching format is to gain the student's attention. Numerous cues can be used for this purpose depending on the student's needs, abilities, and the context of the class activity. Cues such as stating the student's name, moving materials, tapping the desk, or touching the student's shoulder could all serve as an attentional clue. Again, attention to events occurring in the class may impact the type of cue provided (e.g., loudly stating a student's name may not be appropriate during a test).

The third step, presenting the stimulus, refers directly to the task asked of the student. The stimulus, which is the antecedent to the desired response, could be verbal, visual, or tactile depending on the task and the student's access to the task. Academic tasks often involve worksheets, problems on a dry erase board, tests, or computer screen information. Typically, the general educator in the classroom provides the stimulus for the entire class prior to beginning instruction (e.g., "Class, I'm handing out various pieces of material for your project. Make sure you have one of each."). As students progress through the various grades, routine expectations can serve as the natural stimulus so that when students enter the room, they know to get out their daily logs and start writing, or they know to get out their textbook and start to read.

Once the stimulus has been presented, Step 4, giving directions, occurs. All students need to know what is expected, so this step is critical and must convey information clearly (e.g., "find all the words that start with the letter *B*").

Directions to students will depend to some degree on their ability to detect and understand prompts used (e.g., a student who is Spanish speaking only may not understand English). Following the direction(s) given, sufficient time must be provided for the student to understand what is desired and act on it (Step 5). This wait time will vary per student and is dependent on a number of variables, including physical abilities, cognitive abilities, vision and hearing, and the difficulties inherent in the task itself. One desired goal of education for students with severe disabilities is that they can respond to the natural stimulus of the task and the initial direction without additional prompts (e.g., circle specific words or write a report).

However, to teach new skills, additional prompts likely will be needed (Step 6). These prompts, discussed later in this chapter, are designed to help the student demonstrate expectations as efficiently and effectively as possible. Such prompts will vary again depending on individual student, task, and context variables. These are discussed in some detail in the sections that follow. The final step in a structured teaching format is to provide a consequence to the student's behavior. Consequences can be positive (praise or reward) or can provide corrective feedback so the student understands what is desired.

An example of the previously mentioned seven steps involved in systematic and structured teaching will be provided so that its use in general education classrooms can be better understood. In an eighth-grade life science class, the teacher has reviewed the week's lesson on reptiles and has asked the class to get into their lab groups to work on their related project. As the students move to their groups and start to discuss the project, the speech-language pathologist (SLP)—who provides support at this time—decides this is a good time to check the target student, Yelena's, understanding of the topic (Step 1— select learning opportunity). To do this, she moves picture options for Yelena in front of her to gain her attention (Step 2). Due to Yelena's visual impairment, she is most receptive to movement, and so this draws her attention to the pictorial options. For Step 3, the three pictorial options are placed in front of Yelena on an upright stand, and each option is labeled as it is pointed to. Then the direction for the task is provided (Step 4) by asking her to point to the plant (the two distracters are a wagon and a fan). The wait interval for her response (Step 5) is a slow count to four (four seconds), which has been determined as an appropriate wait time for Yelena. If Yelena does not respond, additional prompts are provided (Step 6). The verbal direction is provided again, and as each is pointed to, the SLP asks, "Is it this one?" If after another four-second wait time Yelena does not respond, she is asked to find the green one. Step 7 involves providing Yelena with a smile, an upbeat voice telling her that yes, it's the plant, and patting her arm if correct. If Yelena does not respond or picks an incorrect option, she is told and shown which one is correct. More time is spent telling her features of the picture that could help her recognize it as a plant. If needed, a real plant is used to help Yelena recognize the pictorial representation.

Typically, different prompts are provided to the student in a specified manner so as to help the student learn the desired skill and produce the behavior. Many different kinds of prompts can be used depending on the strengths, needs, and preferences of the student; the situation; and the demands of the task. The various prompts that can be used to teach a variety of skills are presented next. These prompts and prompting strategies to follow will be described later in Chapter 4 as they are used to teach academic skills within typical classrooms.

■ PROMPTS

Prompts can be visual, verbal, tactile, and olfactory. Prompts should be designed to gain a student's attention, draw that attention to the task at hand (the natural stimulus), and help the student understand what is expected and then demonstrate that expected behavior. The intent of using prompts is to assist the student to ultimately respond to the natural stimulus when it occurs in typical activities. Prompts designed to assist the student demonstrate the desired behavior are called *response prompts*, while prompts designed to draw added attention to the natural stimulus of a task are called *stimulus prompts*. For example, a highlighted area on a paper to help a student know where to put her name would be a stimulus prompt, while a nudge to a student's elbow to assist him to raise his hand to gain attention would be a response prompt.

Prompts need to fit the task as well as the student's strengths and needs. Obviously, some prompts will be ineffective for some students (e.g., visual prompts for a student who does not see or verbal prompts for someone who is unable to hear). Some students may dislike certain prompts, such as using a physical prompt with a student who dislikes being touched. Some prompts provide a lot of information as to what is expected (e.g., telling a student to line up, if the student understands the words being used), while other prompts are more vague and rely on the student to figure out what is expected (e.g., gesturing toward the line of students getting ready to go out for recess). The following prompts that are described can be used with a variety of students, but the educational team needs to discover which prompts are most effective with a given student and if they make sense given the task. Some of these prompts can be used alone, while most will be used in combination to make the instruction clearer and offer more support. Table 2.3 provides an overview of various prompts that can be supportive of a student's learning.

Verbal Prompts

Words (whether spoken or signed) are commonly used in most classrooms. Students with and without disabilities are given verbal information throughout each school day and are expected to use this information for learning, following class and school rules, and for gaining desired communication skills. Verbal prompts can be either direct or indirect. Direct verbal prompts are typically commands given to the student that state exactly what behavior is expected (e.g., "line up," "get out your science book," "do the first 10 problems on page 51," or "give your paper to the teacher"). Indirect verbal prompts refer to what is expected but require the student to figure out what is required without being directed to do so. Indirect verbal prompts could involve questions

Table 2.3 Examples of Different Types of Prompts

Type of Prompt	Example
Direct Verbal (signed or spoken)	
• Commands • Specific information	• Sign your name. • Go to the reading center. • The answer is _____.
Indirect Verbal (signed or spoken)	
• Questions • Hints • Suggestions	• What's next? • What do you need to write with? • I'm hungry, are you? • This word is ch_____ (giving initial sound).
Direct Visual	
• Clear and Specific Gesture or Model	• Point to a book. • Point to the door. • Provide a model for the student to follow.
Indirect Visual	
• Vague or Indecisive Gesture or Model	• Gesture in the direction of the desired action. • Point to the other peers doing the task. • Shrug shoulders to indicate that you don't know.
Object Manipulation	
• Employment of Items or Materials Used in Instruction	• Move worksheet closer to student. • Touch signature stamp to student's hand. • Start to turn pages in the book.
Physical Prompts	
• Touch Cues	• Touch student under elbow to prompt him to raise his hand. • Touch student on back of wrist to prompt her to activate switch.
• Wrist Cue	• Place thumb and middle finger on each side of wrist to guide hand to touch screen on computer.
• Hand-Under-Hand	• Perform desired response with student's hand over yours.
• Hand-Over-Hand	• Place hands over student's and guide student through the task.

(e.g., "What do you do now?"), hints (e.g., "I'm really hungry. I wonder what's for lunch?"), or leading (suggestive) by giving some of the desired response (e.g., giving the first letter sound to help a student spell or recognize a word or pictured item).

Verbal prompts can be provided from an adult or other student or from a previously recorded message on a cassette tape, CD, or DVD. Verbal prompts require that the student have sufficient hearing to receive the prompt, retain it, and understand the meaning of the words being used. Some students can hear but have great difficulty attending to verbal prompts. Other students may have great difficulty comprehending the words and relating them to desired actions. For some students verbal prompts are overwhelming and quickly forgotten. The temporal nature of verbal prompts means that they are quickly gone, requiring the student to recall the prompt and act on it. Many students with moderate to severe intellectual disabilities may find this temporal verbal prompt too fleeting to be effective.

Visual Prompts

Teachers typically use visual prompts with verbal prompts in a form of "show and tell" format. While giving the class information, the teacher will hold up a sample or demonstrate what is being discussed, with the class visually following along. Cues such as "look at me," "eyes up front," "watch what I'm doing," and "can you all see this?" are examples of how verbal cues are often paired with visuals. Teachers at all grade levels may rely on this combination of prompts for a considerable amount of their teaching.

Visual prompts often used with students having moderate to severe disabilities include gestural as well as pictorial information. Pictorial prompts have received considerable attention in the teaching of students with disabilities (Cihak, Alberto, Taber-Doughty, & Gama, 2006; Owens, 2006; Spriggs, Gast, & Ayres, 2007). The static nature of the pictorial prompt allows the student to study the information with as much time as is needed, whereas verbal prompts are temporal and gone as soon as they are spoken. For example, West (2008) demonstrated the effectiveness of pictorial prompts over verbal prompts to teach young children with autism to independently perform simple tasks.

Pictorial prompts can be very simple in nature and very closely represent their referent (e.g., a color photograph of a single item, such as a lunchbox to represent time to eat), or they can be more abstract and vague with regard to their intended meaning (e.g., a black-and-white line drawing of children and a teacher in a circle to represent center time). Moving the student from concrete to more abstract stimuli is typically the goal of instruction. However, beginning instruction must start with prompts that are most apparent and meaningful to the student.

Visual prompts can also be dynamic as in modeling or video prompting. Videotaped examples have been used successfully to teach a number of different tasks to students with disabilities. See Mechling (2005) for a literature review of this research. Students can watch the steps of an activity being performed by a model on a computer or more portable DVD player, or they could watch the activity unfold from a more subjective point of view. Watching a video recording from the student's perspective has been shown to be effective in teaching self-help and daily living skills to this population (Norman, Collins, & Schuster, 2001; Shipley-Benamou, Lutzker, & Taubman, 2002). Mechling and

Gustafson (2009), comparing the effects of a static picture recipe to video prompting for students with moderate intellectual disabilities, found that the video prompting of each step in the recipe was more effective than the sequence of pictures, with more steps completed and fewer errors.

Gestural cues are usually visual, although some can be discerned through touch (e.g., nodding or shaking one's head can be felt by another person). Gestural cues typically involve easily recognized body movements that have relatively clear purposes, such as pointing, waving as a greeting, or beckoning someone to come. Such prompts can be provided at a distance from the student as long as that student has sufficient vision to obtain information in this manner. Although they don't indicate exactly what is expected, as a prompt, they can provide considerable information regarding the expected behavior (e.g., to attend to the teacher, line up at the door, come to a designated center). Gestural cues are commonly used by everyone and so are easy and natural for anyone in a teaching position (paraprofessionals, peers, cafeteria workers) to use.

Object Cues

When students cannot use vision or cannot understand pictorial or other visual stimuli, representative objects and parts of objects can be used (Chen & Downing, 2006). Object cues can be used either visually if the student has sufficient vision, or tactilely if the student has minimal or no functional vision. Typically, if the student needs to examine the object tactilely, greater time will be needed. Object cues have considerable iconic value since they are often exact duplicates of the item or action they are meant to represent. For example, an empty flask can be used to show a student what is needed in science class, a book can be used to represent library time, or a backpack used to cue a transition.

When only parts of objects are used, the key strategy is to use the object part or parts that the student most often feels during the course of the activity. For example, a preschooler might be given a choice at recess to ride a tricycle (represented by the handlebars) or swing (represented by a short piece of chain that the student grips while swinging). Using parts of objects is more of an abstract cue than using the entire object and can be easier to manipulate and transport to different locations. Taking the perspective of the student when handling different items and interacting in different activities is critical when developing object and parts of object cues for a student who is blind. Otherwise, the tactile object cue can resemble a visual cue (e.g., a plastic miniature of an animal for naming) and not what that animal would feel like to the student. Such prompts can become very confusing to the student and are best avoided.

Physical Prompts

Physical prompting may be the most intrusive form of prompting and should be performed with great care so that the student does not learn to rely on being manipulated by others to perform tasks. Some students may react quite negatively to being manipulated physically by others, especially if this has been a consistent approach to teaching (Billingsley, 2003). For students who are blind, physical manipulation of the hands can be particularly intrusive, as the student uses his hands to see. Students may respond to regular manipulation of hands to touch various things by clenching fists and drawing back in an effort to protest this form of prompting. In addition, Billingsley and Kelley (1994) found that physically manipulating students can draw negative attention to students with severe disabilities who are learning in general education classrooms. Therefore, physical prompts should only be provided when needed and when they offer necessary support and information. The least amount of physical support needed by the student should be employed. For example, supporting a student's forearm so that the student can make free use of his or her hand to select a response might be very effective use of a physical prompt. Following are different types of physical prompts.

Touch Cues

A specific physical touch on the student's body is a touch cue and could signal a number of different intentions. The student's physical abilities, preferences for touch, cultural considerations, and the expectations of the activity will impact the types of touch cues for a given student. There are no universal touch cues, but rather, they are individually determined per student. For one student, a touch on the arm could indicate that the student is to reach out to find something (e.g., book, switch, or backpack), and a touch against the front of the body near the shoulder could signal for the student to stop or wait. A touch to the back of one student's hand is a greeting, while the same touch cue for another student is a signal to start to work. Touch cues are often used with students having minimal vision, if any, and limited verbal skills (Chen & Downing, 2006). The team will need to decide what cues to use, under what conditions, and for what purpose. Then consistency across team members should be assured so as not to confuse the student.

Wrist Cue

A wrist cue provides physical support to the student at the wrist (a thumb and finger on either side of the student's wrist) to guide the student's hand in the desired direction of the stimulus (e.g., pen, paper, picture, object). The prompt is designed to provide enough physical support to help the student produce the desired response without over-manipulation. With only a thumb and finger touching the student on the wrist, it may be easier to withdraw such a prompt than more intrusive physical prompts.

Hand-Under-Hand

This type of physical prompt involves the teachers guiding the student's hands from underneath (not over top) of the hands. In this manner, the student is not forced to comply but can remove his or her hands at will. This process is less intrusive than manipulating the student's hands and allows the student more control. However, it does require that the student move with the instructor, following the movement of the instructor. One benefit of this approach is that the student moves his or her own body and does not rely on someone else to do that. A hand under hand approach may be used to teach a student to reach out to examine a model in science or a tactile book in social studies. Once the student has begun to act on his or her own, the instructor would fade this prompt (perhaps moving alongside the student's hand).

Hand-Over-Hand

Perhaps the most intrusive of the physical prompting procedures, this prompt essentially takes the student's hand(s) and makes the student engage in the desired activity. In this manner, the student will engage in the desired behavior (at least to some extent), experience what is expected, and be praised and/or rewarded as a result. A problem of this approach is that the student may become dependent on the instructor, and it may become very difficult to fade the prompt. In addition, depending on the desired skills, it may be very difficult to maneuver the student's hands to the point to where the student can understand what is expected. For example, taking the student's hands and having the student touch keys on a keyboard may make it difficult for the student to see and really understand what is desired (e.g., which exact key to press). Therefore, hand-over-hand prompting may not be the most informative or helpful (Riley, 1995).

PROMPTING STRATEGIES ■

Different methods of providing systematic instruction have been compared to determine both effectiveness and efficiency for helping students with moderate to severe intellectual disabilities learn. These strategies make use of the individual prompts described earlier and are sequenced in a manner to either increase the amount of information provided or decrease the information given to the student. The ultimate goal of these strategies for instruction is to reach the greatest level of independent performance for the student.

Constant or Progressive Time Delay

One prompting strategy that has received considerable attention and analysis is providing a wait time prior to additional prompting (Gast et al., 1988; Riesen, McDonnell, Johnson, Polychronis, & Jameson, 2003). A constant and consistent pause before additional prompting is provided to allow the student the opportunity to respond is called constant time delay (CTD). This strategy may be easier to implement than progressive time delay since the amount of time provided between prompts remains the same (e.g., 5 seconds or counting slowly to a specified number; Duker, Didden, & Sigafoos, 2004). Browder and Xin (1998) completed a review of sight word recognition research and found that CTD was used most often to teach students with moderate to severe disabilities functional reading. CTD also was used by Alberto, Frederick, Hughes, McIntosh, and Chihak (2007) to effectively teach six students with moderate to severe disabilities to recognize visual logos. Jameson, McDonnell, Polychronis, and Riesen (2008) found that middle school students without disabilities could effectively learn and implement the principles of CTD to teach their peers with significant cognitive disabilities to learn skills in their art and health classes. After reviewing single-subject research to date on the use of constant time delay to teach literacy to students with severe disabilities, Browder, Ahlgrim-Delzell, Spooner, Mims, and Baker (2009) determined that this procedure of instruction can be considered an evidence-based practice for the field.

Progressive time delay occurs when increasing amounts of time are provided to the student to allow more time for the student to demonstrate what has been learned. Typically, progressive time delay is used as a student is demonstrating increasingly improved performance on a task (e.g., is beginning to perform more steps in a sequence of steps without prompts). In other words, the initial wait time between the direction given and the next prompt or a response from the student may start with one second. As the student begins to respond, the wait time can increase to four seconds, then eight seconds to give the student more time to demonstrate what is expected. Providing a wait time that increases in this manner as the student shows greater progress may be challenging for different team members to remember and, therefore, implement consistently.

Simultaneous Prompting

This technique of prompting ensures that the student will demonstrate the desired skill with the antecedent prompt without making errors (e.g., errorless learning). No corrections are needed since the student is guided to perform the skill as the controlling prompt (e.g., a verbal demand) is provided. For example, a teacher may present three numbers in front of a student and say, "find the three" and then immediately show the student the correct number. There is no delay time between the prompt and the supported behavior except when probes are done to determine if learning is occurring. These probes are done prior to any instruction when the student is given the direction without any assistance.

Morse and Schuster (2004) reviewed the literature on simultaneous prompting and found that in 18 reviewed studies, the procedure appeared to be effective for preschoolers through adults both with and without disabilities. Individuals were reported to learn both discrete tasks (one step) as well as chained tasks (multiple steps). Riesen et al. (2003) demonstrated that constant time delay and simultaneous prompting were equally effective in teaching students with moderate to severe disabilities to learn academic skills in general education classrooms.

■ CONSEQUENCES OF THE BEHAVIOR

The actions taken by the teacher following a response from the student help the student learn if the response was correct or incorrect. Correct responses should be followed immediately with something positive for the student (positive reinforcer) especially during the early stages of learning (Billingsley,

1998). Incorrect responses should be followed with a correction so that the student knows to alter the response in the presence of the natural cue. Giving immediate feedback with regard to the performance can be helpful for all learners, whether adult or child, or whether or not a disability exists.

Reinforcers

All students need to find some reason to perform a skill or activity if the activity in and of itself is not that meaningful or enjoyable, at least initially. When something positive happens to the student following a desired or correct response, the student is more likely to provide the same response the next time the natural cue or stimulus is present. Reinforcers work differently for different individuals (child and adult alike). What motivates one person to continue a task may not have the same effect at all on another. Determining what serves as a reinforcer (something that increases the desired behavior) may take some time and some investigative work. Family members often know what motivates their child and can share this information with educational staff members. Depending on the student, reinforcers can be quite unusual and unique. A common mistake made by teachers is that a designated reinforcer (e.g., music) will hold the same motivating value for all students. While some students may work quite hard for a five-minute break time to listen to favorite music, others will not find this reinforcing at all. Some will want more attention from their teacher, while some will want to be away from everyone and be allowed to sit quietly and play with dried rice. Rarely will one identified reinforcer work for one student at all times (Snell & Brown, 2006). Students become satiated with certain reinforcers at times and will require different options. For example, one student may stay at his task for a promised break and trip to the drinking fountain. However, this is not always effective, and he will need other options, such as extra time on the computer, time to sit next to a favorite peer, or time to sit at the teacher's desk to keep working throughout the day.

Types of Reinforcement

Reinforcers are either primary or unlearned, such as food for someone who is hungry or drink for someone who is thirsty. This type of reinforcer tends to meet basic needs so that the individual is more comfortable. The other type of reinforcer, secondary reinforcers, is learned. These stimuli may start out being neutral for the individual, but after being paired with a primary reinforcer, they assume their own reinforcing value. Secondary reinforcers in school can be praise, tokens, or happy faces. Students learn that tokens or stickers can be accumulated and used to obtain access to something that is desired such as music, a favorite book, or extra time on a computer to play a favorite game.

Reinforcement Schedules

The times and frequency when reinforcers are given to students are called the reinforcement schedule. Whatever is reinforcing for the student is given to the student following a specific behavior, set of behaviors, or time interval (e.g., every 10 minutes of work). Reinforcement schedules are considered fixed when they are set for a specific interval or frequency of behavior (e.g., after every other math problem). Continuous reinforcement is reinforcement on a fixed schedule that occurs after every desired behavior. Continuous reinforcement is recommended for new skills that the student is just learning (e.g., provide praise after every attempt to recognize one's name from three options; Snell & Brown, 2006). Intermittent reinforcement occurs on a more variable schedule, such as giving praise after two correct responses, then five correct responses, then eight correct responses, and then three. Although intermittent reinforcement may be somewhat harder to implement (harder to remember when to provide it), it tends to maintain and strengthen desired behaviors. Not knowing when a reinforcer will be given may make students work harder than when reinforced following every correct response. Furthermore, students learn to defer gratification so that they can work and master skills without an external reinforcer always being present. Intermittent reinforcers are recommended after students have increased new skills to a level where reinforcers can be faded without the fear of losing the newly acquired skill (Snell & Brown, 2006).

The strength of the reinforcer can change as a result of the situation, the time of day, the health of the student, the amount of time previously spent with the reinforcer, the task at hand, or a number of other variables. Such variability can become frustrating as it has a considerable impact on the student's performance during the day. The best suggestion is to maintain a number of potentially reinforcing stimuli available and give the student some choice in which one is preferred for any given task. Allowing the student to determine which of several potential reinforcers to strive for during a given work period may not only increase time on task but also may help to support the development of self-determination.

Corrective Feedback

Providing feedback to students with regard to their efforts at learning new skills is considered a characteristic of quality teaching (Westling & Fox, 2009). Errors will occur during the learning process, and the feedback for making mistakes should be prompt, nonjudgmental, and clear. The student has a right to know that an error was made and a need to know what the desired response is. Some researchers have used the correct answer as the feedback for an incorrect response (Minarovic & Bambara, 2007). For instance, if a student points to a shoe when he has been asked to find the plant during biology class, the incorrect picture will be moved farther away and the correct picture brought close to the student and labeled the plant. Schuster, Morse, Griffen, and Wolery (1996) stressed the importance of correcting mistakes and not just ignoring them when teaching grocery word reading using time delay. Ignoring a mistake and just moving on to the next trial could leave the student confused as to what occurred and whether or not it should happen again.

Providing feedback to a student should not be done in a negative or punitive manner. A very matter-of-fact approach is recommended so that the student will feel comfortable to try again. In other words, a teacher may say, "No, that's a three. This one is the five." If mistakes continue, an analysis of the learning task is necessary. Clarifying the correct and desired response for the student may be needed to help the student feel successful. Once the student is performing as desired, the task can be made more difficult (e.g., more options provided or options that are more difficult to differentiate).

Fading

To assist the student to gain independence or as much independence as possible in a given task, teaching prompts must be faded. The goal of education is to help the student perform meaningful tasks using natural cues or stimuli and without the constant support of another person. While some support may always be necessary (e.g., assisting someone to eat who cannot manipulate a utensil and bring it to her or his mouth), the intent of teaching is to help the student gain as much independence as possible. Teachers must keep in mind the need to eventually reduce the number of prompts to allow the student to engage in an activity without excessive adult support.

Fading prompts should be considered from the outset of the lesson so that it is clear to all those supporting the student when to begin fading strategies (Billingsley, 1998, 2003; Westling & Fox, 2009). Fading instructional prompts can involve reducing the number of prompts provided, increasing the wait time, using increasingly more abstract stimuli, moving from direct to indirect prompts, increasing the distance between the teacher and student, or a number of other techniques, depending on the student and the task. For example, initially a student, Mita, is asked to pick between two numbers to determine which is larger. When she can do this reliably (at whatever has been determined to be mastery for her), a third number can be added and eventually a fourth.

Care needs to be taken so that fading prompts does not occur too rapidly so that the student's performance falters, nor should it occur too slowly so that the student does not learn to perform independently. The most efficient plan may be to provide the minimal amount of prompting necessary to elicit the desired response with the intent to fade those prompts as soon as possible.

USING SEQUENCES OF DIFFERENT PROMPTS ■ TO TEACH STUDENTS: SHAPING BEHAVIOR

Getting students to respond reliably and consistently to specific stimuli (such as reading, writing, math tasks) may require shaping the desired response and providing informative prompts. Shaping is a process of gradually supporting the desired behavior by reinforcing approximations until it reaches a stage of mastery for a given task (Billingsley, 2003; Snell & Brown, 2006; Westling & Fox, 2009). For example, for the task of writing one's name, a student may be initially reinforced for grabbing the pencil. This reinforcement will be faded and only given when more steps of the skill emerge (e.g., grabbing the pencil and making a mark on the page, and then grabbing the pencil, making a fairly legible first letter).

Shaping these small behaviors can take considerable time, and so prompts are often added to increase the likelihood of the behavior emerging so it can be reinforced and, therefore, strengthened. Often, students with moderate to severe intellectual disabilities do not respond to one prompt but need more clarifying information to fully understand what is expected. How prompts are combined to shape desired behavior will depend on a number of different factors. A student facing a brand new skill will probably need more information initially to perform as desired. A skill that has not been mastered, but the student has experienced previously, may require less prompting. Some situations require that the student respond promptly or the opportunity is lost (e.g., waving in response to a peer's greeting), while other situations allow more time for the student to examine materials and figure out what response is desired (e.g., looking at a personal schedule and indicating the next activity). Some students will respond more quickly in highly motivating situations (e.g., choosing food to eat at lunch) than in less motivating situations (e.g., identifying the larger of two common objects). While every student and situation is somewhat unique, there are some general guidelines when combining prompts to help a student demonstrate the desired or expected behavior.

Least-to-Most Prompting Strategy

The key aspects of this particular approach to teaching desired behavior is that limited information is provided initially and additional information (in the form of prompts and cues) is only provided as much as the student indicates need. The student is given time to consider options and to demonstrate the skill independently. If the student does not demonstrate the desired behavior after a specified wait time, another prompt is provided that should help the student understand what is expected. Additional prompts are added following wait times if the student does not appear to understand what is expected. These prompts are designed to add information and make the desired response clearer. The progression of prompts to be used must be carefully spelled out so that all staff teaching the student know what to do and when to do it. Otherwise, inconsistencies across different "teachers" may be confusing to the student who may learn to wait to be prompted by different individuals.

Benefits of least-to-most prompting strategy involve allowing the student the opportunity to demonstrate what has been learned before being prompted as well as reducing the physical manipulation of the student. West and Billingsley (2005) compared least-to-most prompting strategies with and without verbal prompts and found the overall strategy effective in both cases, with it being most efficient without additional verbal prompts. When those engaged in teaching the student refrain from providing prompts before they are needed, students may avoid becoming dependent on adult prompts. If students learn that they should engage in the behavior prior to being prompted by an adult (or peer), they may reach independence in performance sooner than if they were prompted extensively (Giangreco, 2006). Therefore, least-to-most prompting strategy represents an effective means of guiding student learning, especially if the student has had some experience with the target skill(s). A downside to least-to-most prompting is that errors are possible during the instruction, and students can learn these mistakes as part of the process (Billingsley, 2003).

Most-to-Least Prompting Strategy

The sequence of prompts in most-to-least prompting begins with the most informative or supportive prompt to ensure accurate performance by the student. The key point of this prompting sequence is that as the student demonstrates greater efficiency in performance, the teacher would fade prompts until the student is independent. When a student is presented with a new skill that he or she has not previously encountered, giving the student as much information and assistance as possible will ensure that the student performs the skill without errors and in a timely manner. Some situations require such prompting up front because there is no time to use a least-to-most prompting strategy (e.g., responding to name being called during attendance) or the situation is dangerous (e.g., crossing the street or removing something hot from a Bunsen burner in science class).

Benefits of this approach relate to the student being supported in the desired response initially without any interference from errors that could occur. Furthermore, by engaging in the desired behavior immediately following the discriminative stimulus (e.g., name being called by the teacher), the student will likely be responded to by others in the environment in a timely way. Little opportunity exists for the student to make errors (errorless learning), and so the student can receive the reinforcer being used immediately upon engaging in the desired action (even though it is supported considerably by the teacher).

Disadvantages of this system of prompting involve the failure to fade prompts as needed so that the student can reach a more independent level of performance. Duker et al. (2004) reported on the difficulty of fading prompts using a most-to-least prompting strategy. If teachers (general educators, special educators, paraprofessionals, related service providers, etc.) become used to providing considerable prompts and supports as soon as the discriminative stimulus is provided, there may be a tendency to maintain this level of prompting well past when the student should have been learning the skill. The student, therefore, would have no opportunity to demonstrate what has been learned and in fact may learn to wait until prompted to proceed. This waiting for adults to use prompts is called *cue or prompt dependence* (Clark & Green, 2004) and can hinder a student gaining greater independence in a task. Therefore, fading the level of prompting is critically important when using a most-to-least prompting strategy.

MAINTAINING AND GENERALIZING SKILLS ■

Teaching a student a skill is the first step for teachers. However, once the student has acquired the skill, especially in the initial stages, attention must be paid to ensure that the student maintains the new skill over time (maintenance) and also generalizes it to other people, items, and environments.

Research has firmly documented our ability to teach students a vast array of meaningful skills (Browder et al., 2008; Browder, Wakeman, Spooner, Ahlgrim-Delzell, & Algozzine, 2006; Mechling, 2008). However, if students do not maintain learned skills nor use them when needed, the practicality of teaching new skills is questionable.

Maintenance

If students don't use the skills they have learned, like all of us, they are likely to forget them. Teaching new skills does little to aid students if they soon forget them and are unable to use them when needed. Teachers will need to pay careful attention to students making use of their skills across time so that reteaching of these same skills is not needed, and students can be challenged to learn other skills. The strength of the teaching procedure often determines if skills will be maintained by students or not (Miracle, Collins, Schuster, & Grisham-Brown, 2001). Furthermore, their relevance to the student is important if skills are to be maintained. Spooner, Baker, Harris, Ahlgrim-Delzell, and Browder (2007) state that general and special educators must develop lesson plans that relate to real-life problems to be most meaningful to a wide range of students. If a student cannot frequently make use of the new skill across different activities and environments, the opportunity to practice and maintain the skill is greatly reduced. If students do not use skills, they will definitely lose them.

One responsibility of teachers is to ensure that their students are maintaining skills, reinforcing their performance, and reteaching if skills fade. In other words, the maintenance of skills must be taught and not left to chance (Duker et al., 2004). Reviewing skills previously learned to criterion is essential and should be an ongoing practice in schools. Westling and Fox (2009) state that regular review and reteaching of different skills as needed are considered general good teaching practices for all students. Since many skills learned in school build on earlier learning, review of these skills occurs naturally as new skills are acquired.

Generalization

From the research on efficient and effective teaching strategies for students with moderate to severe disabilities, one finding that has emerged is the critical need to teach students to generalize these skills to the different environments and situations in which they are needed (Taylor, Collins, Schuster, & Kleinert, 2002; Westling & Fox, 2009). It is insufficient to teach skills without consideration for where those skills will be needed and whether or not the student can recognize the need to use the skill across varied environments. For instance, teaching a student to recognize the words *BOYS, GIRLS, MEN, WOMEN* is most meaningful when needing to use the restroom and not when seated at one's desk reading words on 3" X 5" cards. An overall goal of instruction is to ensure that students not only learn skills in the training environment (e.g., the general education classroom) but will also demonstrate the skills in natural environments as well. For example, a student may be deciding which of two numbers is greater in math but will need to apply this skill during lunch when he needs to decide if he has enough money to buy a food or drink item. Likewise, counting dollar bills is only helpful if the student realizes the need to do this during a purchase, such as buying something for lunch. Such generalization of skills from the learned to the natural environment may not come easily for students with moderate to severe disabilities and will need to be specifically taught (Duker et al., 2004; Westling & Fox, 2009).

Students with moderate to severe intellectual disabilities often struggle to recognize stimuli in different settings that should serve to act as catalysts for learned skills (Billingsley, 2003). Therefore, if a student learns to recognize her name on one of three signature stamps to sign her name, she also needs to be taught to recognize her name on her backpack, lunch bag, homework folder, project, and other places it is likely to occur. Likewise, learning to recognize numbers is a practical skill, but the student must learn to recognize numbers not only on cards or a dry erase board but also on one, five, 10, and 20 dollar bills, menus, the phone, and the TV remote.

TEACHING ARRANGEMENTS IN ■ GENERAL EDUCATION CLASSROOMS

Determining how students will be arranged for a given lesson will depend on the content of the lesson, the outcome that the teacher is looking for, and past experience. Students can be taught in a large group with the teacher giving information and asking questions. Such an arrangement is a staple of secondary education where a teacher often addresses a large group of students. Students can also be taught in small group arrangements, with groupings based on similar skill level (homogeneous groupings) or based on different abilities (heterogeneous groupings). The teacher may decide to have students work in pairs or buddies to help each other with the task. Finally, students may be asked to work independently. Such an arrangement often follows a large group arrangement with the intent of students demonstrating individually what they have learned. The advantages and disadvantages of such arrangements will be discussed in terms of the student with moderate to severe intellectual disabilities.

Large Group Instruction

Teachers, especially in secondary schools, frequently make use of the large group format for instruction (Wagner, Newman, Cameto, Levine, & Marder, 2003; Wallace, Anderson, Bartholomay, & Hupp, 2002). Students as a large group are to listen to the teacher, follow directions, take notes, and respond to questions asked of the group. Often, students with moderate to severe disabilities find it difficult to actively participate in large group instructional arrangements (Carter, Sisco, Brown, Brickham, & Al-Khabbaz, 2008; Wallace et al., 2002). They may find it challenging to attend to one teacher standing in front of the room at a distance and may not have the linguistic, visual, or auditory skills to benefit from this type of instruction. Given such an arrangement, students with moderate to severe intellectual disabilities may have a tendency to become distracted and bored. This in turn can lead to behavior that is not desired but that communicates the student's boredom and frustration. Considerable support may be needed during such instruction to help the student understand what the lesson is about (although at the student's level) and to help the student contribute to the overall discussion.

For example, Mrs. Trent's fifth-grade class is studying how to write persuasive letters in language arts. As a whole class, Mrs. Trent asks the class what *persuasion* means. She helps to clarify the definition from what students offer and asks students for specific examples. Mrs. Trent then talks about the parts of the letter needed to make it persuasive. The class brainstorms about potential recipients of persuasive letters. Then Mrs. Trent asks each student to work independently to create a letter focused on a cause of their choice. She walks around the room checking on individual students.

One fifth grader in this class, Maricel, is learning the letters of the alphabet and their sounds when in the initial placement of words. Maricel can write the letters, and although they are large, most are legible. During the large group discussion, Maricel has simplified notes on the topic and is asked to identify words such as *letter, write, send, want* based on their initial letter sound when compared to other words that don't start with the same letter. She is helped to understand that if you want something, you can write a letter explaining why it is important. She is given many examples on picture-word cards and uses these to respond to the teacher's questions. A special educator works with her as well as other students in the class.

Ohtake (2003) found that students with severe disabilities were more accepted as full-time members of a class if they could contribute to the learning of the entire class. Therefore, adaptations will need to be made to support such a contribution, and students must be taught how to use them. For example, a teacher might begin the discussion with a simple question to the student with moderate or severe disabilities and then use the answer to ask more in-depth and more abstract questions of the rest of the class. The teacher would keep returning to the target student with simplified questions that create opportunities for the rest of the class to build on the resulting response. For example, during the study of DNA and the role that genes play in our phenotype, a high school biology teacher might ask a student with severe intellectual disabilities the following question: "Lindsey, what color is your hair?" When she responds by choosing the correct color card in front of her and holding it up for the teacher to see, the teacher continues with the discussion by asking the class how hair color is determined and why some children may have different hair color than their parents or siblings. The teacher will return to Lindsey to ask similar questions that will lead the discussion in different directions. Table 2.4 provides more examples of different subject matter and potential questions that a teacher might ask a student that could lead to different questions with others in the class.

Table 2.4	Examples of Questions Used by a Teacher During Large Group Discussions to Include a Student With Moderate to Severe Intellectual Disabilities

Potential Questions to Ask a Student With Moderate or Severe Disabilities	Follow-Up Questions With Rest of Class
Topic: The Legend of Sleepy Hollow (Twelfth-Grade English Lit.)	
1. "What was scaring all the people in the town?"	1. "Right. The Headless Horseman. So what hypothetical events led to the creation of the Headless Horseman?"
2. "Did Ichabod Crane have a love interest or girlfriend?"	2. "Yes, he did. Was this a typical boy-meets-girl romance or were there different elements to it?"
Topic: Factoring (Sixth-Grade math)	
1. "Can you find the number 2?"	1. "That's correct. It's a 2. So, if this number 2 is written in upperscript next to a number, what does it tell us about that number?"
2. "Can you find the X?"	2. "Why not write the number as 5×5 and not 5^2?"
Topic: Hamlet (Eleventh-Grade English Lit.)	
1. "Was Hamlet happy about his mother marrying his uncle?"	1. "That's right. He wasn't happy. In what act and scene of the play are you first made aware of Hamlet's anger? What does he think of his mother at this point and why?"
2. "What happened to Hamlet's mother at the end?"	2. "Yes, she died. Was this intentional? Explain the tragedy of Hamlet."
Topic: Phonic Skills (1st Grade)	
1. "Can you find a word that starts with 'mmmmmm'?"	1. "What letter does the word *moon* end in? Can you think of other words that rhyme with *moon?*"
2. "Whose name starts with J?"	2. "That's right Jeremy! Your name starts with a J. Does anyone's name end in J? Have a J in it?"
Topic: Writing (Fifth-Grade Language Arts)	
1. "Whom will you write your interest letter to?"	1. "A fireman. OK. Good. What type of requests might you ask of a fireman? What is the best way to state your request so you get a positive response?"
2. "What will you ask the firefighter in your letter?"	2. "To go for a ride? Good! How many of you think T_____ will get his request met? Why or why not? Will how he write his letter have an impact?"

Small Group Instruction

Working with students in small groups allows the teacher the opportunity to discern exactly what each student is learning but with greater efficiency than one-to-one instruction. Carter et al. (2008) studied 23 middle and high school students with autism and cognitive disabilities and found that they were more actively involved socially and academically when instructed in small groups rather than large group instruction. Furthermore, in small group instruction, students can learn from the interaction between the teacher and a peer without actually engaging in the behavior. Several studies have investigated the effectiveness of small group instruction for students with moderate to severe disabilities (Colozzi et al., 2008; Farmer, Gast, Wolery, & Winterling, 1991; McDonnell et al., 2006). These researchers have found that students can learn skills and knowledge by observing a classmate and teacher (e.g., they can learn vicariously or observationally). For example, Falkenstine, Collins, Schuster, and Kleinert (2009) used constant time delay to teach three secondary school students with moderate-severe disabilities to learn individualized academic and nonacademic skills. A small group format was used for these three students, and results verified that not only did each student learn his or her own targeted skills but also acquired the targeted skills of the other two students. Findings suggest that each student does not need one-to-one instruction for every skill but can benefit from what others near him or her are learning. In this manner, teaching becomes much more efficient than the time involved in one-to-one instruction.

Small group instruction can be conceived of as cooperative learning with assigned roles and specific expectations for students, or it can be more loosely configured so that students are told to simply work together to complete an assignment. Cooperative learning has shown substantial benefits to various learners (Johnson & Johnson, 1987; Johnson, Johnson, & Holubec, 1993). Within a cooperative learning paradigm, all students are to contribute to shared learning by assuming different roles and responsibilities for completion of the activity. In addition to assisting each other obtain desired goals in a lesson, students are also expected to develop interpersonal skills as they work in their small groups comprised of students of varying abilities.

Paired Instruction or Buddy Learning

Pairing students to work together (either of similar or diverse abilities) is a commonly employed strategy in many classrooms (Copeland et al., 2002; Miracle et al., 2001). At times, students may be allowed to choose a partner, or they may be specifically paired depending on teacher expectations and the task to be completed. Partners can assume the roles of tutor and tutee to learn math facts, spelling words, grammar, social studies, and so on. For example, Miracle et al. (2001) found that peers were equally as effective as teachers in helping secondary aged students with moderate to severe intellectual disabilities to learn selected sight words. Paired students could also be assigned to help each other with reading, completing assignments, or doing projects. Depending on the objective for the teacher, paired arrangements may work quite well for a student with severe disabilities, or it could prove to be challenging (e.g., if each person is to have the same knowledge and skills). However, students can be paired together to learn yet have different expected outcomes. For example, pictured- and/or sight-word cards can be used by a peer to help a classmate with severe intellectual disabilities recognize pictured vocabulary. At the same time, when the student recognizes the vocabulary word, he or she can turn it over and present his or her partner with a question regarding the subject matter that is challenging for the peer. In this way, both students have appropriate expectations for learning together.

Employing the use of peer buddies or tutors in teaching arrangements has been shown to be beneficial not just for the student with moderate to severe disabilities but for all students involved (Carter, Cushing, & Kennedy, 2009; Copeland et al., 2002). Both social and academic benefits have been reported for peers working with a student having moderate to severe disabilities. Middle school students supporting students with moderate to severe disabilities in English, science, and health classes substantially increased their engagement in activities, homework completion, and classroom participation (Cushing & Kennedy, 1997). Furthermore, these students also struggled academically themselves. In fact, benefits have been particularly apparent for students who are at academic risk.

Social benefits for peers without disabilities include greater acceptance and appreciation of diversity, personal growth, and the development of advocacy skills (Carter & Kennedy, 2006; Copeland et al., 2004; Downing & Peckham-Hardin, 2007). The friendships between students with and without disabilities that may develop also represent a benefit for those involved. While friendships cannot be dictated, by increasing social circles for students with and without disabilities so that regular ongoing interactions occur, friendships can and do develop.

Independent Work

Several times during the school day, teachers may request that students work independently on the assignment, complete unfinished work, or read to themselves. At these times of the day, students may be engaged in a variety of different activities that are individually determined. Independent work may be the easiest teaching arrangement to accommodate the individual needs of students with moderate to severe disabilities. Since all students will be working on their own, applying specific and systematic instruction to support a particular student's learning should not draw undue attention. Carter et al. (2008) found that middle school and high school students with developmental disabilities were more academically engaged when working in close proximity with a special educator or general educator, but that social interactions with peers was greatly reduced. Therefore, students with moderate to severe disabilities may not benefit as much socially from teaching arrangements in classes that demand a lot of independent student work.

Soukup, Wehmeyer, Bashinski, and Bovaird (2007) found that students with disabilities had better access to the content of the class when they were in one-to-one instructional arrangements in general education classrooms.

These one-to-one arrangements, often with a special educator or paraprofessional, were typical during times when the entire class was working independently. Arrangements of this nature do not bring undue attention to the student with moderate or severe disabilities, as every student is working on something individually and may need additional support from a teacher at times.

■ SUMMARY

Chapter 2 has reviewed the types of systematic teaching that have been documented as benefiting students with moderate to severe disabilities. Several different types of prompts and combinations of prompts were described that have been used successfully with students. No one approach will be equally successful with all students, however, and characteristics of the student, the task, and the learning environment will need to be analyzed to determine an approach that may be most effective for a given student.

The various teaching arrangements encountered in most general education classrooms were described with some suggestions as to the adaptations and accommodations that are needed when a student has a moderate or severe disability. Regardless of instructional arrangement in a given general education classroom, systematic instruction can be applied as needed. The skill(s) that the target student is to learn need to guide how direct instruction is provided, where it will be taught, and by whom. Chapter 4 will provide specific examples of prompts and prompting strategies used to teach core academic curriculum to students with moderate and severe intellectual disabilities learning in a variety of instructional arrangements with their classmates.

Chapter 3 covers information regarding how to determine what skills are important to teach students as well as what skills are expected or anticipated in general education classrooms. A team approach to an authentic assessment will be stressed with the student taking the central role so that outcomes of assessment will lead to meaningful instruction. Considerations for the wishes of the student and family will be blended with those of state standards expected of all students.

3

Determining Student Needs

What to Teach

KEY CONCEPTS

- 🔑 An individualized assessment that occurs in the general education environment is recommended to identify skills and determine needs.

- 🔑 Authentic assessment that includes a student/family interview, review of past records, ecological inventories with observational recordings, and portfolios are recommended over standardized forms of assessment.

- 🔑 Identifying critical skills to teach involves observing general education lessons, interpreting content standards for a grade level, and considering family and student goals and interest.

- 🔑 Writing the Individualized Education Plan (IEP) involves clearly stating skills to be taught, the conditions under which they will be taught, and the criterion to measure progress.

A hallmark of education for students with moderate to severe disabilities is that it be individualized. Despite similarities in diagnoses, all students are unique and bring unique considerations to the learning environment. Individualizing their educational program to make it relevant and meaningful is critical. At the same time, all students are to have access to grade-level core curriculum and gain as much knowledge as possible in areas of literacy, mathematics, science, and social studies (Browder & Spooner, 2003, 2006). Determining what to teach students with moderate to severe disabilities becomes somewhat of a balancing act to ensure both individualization (as mandated by IDEA) and standardization (as mandated by NCLB).

Finding a blend or balance between the individual needs of the student and family and the national expectations of the school system will be the focus of this chapter. Arriving at such a balance will depend on an assessment that is individualized and responsive to unique familial issues as well as a clear understanding of core curriculum and performance standards at each grade level. What is taught to students should challenge them to learn as much as possible while also being tailored to their individual needs and abilities.

■ LIMITATIONS OF STANDARDIZED ASSESSMENT

Standardized formats for assessment fail to consider individual circumstances and interests and tend to assume that all students should acquire the same skills in a similar hierarchical order. Yet Tindal et al. (2003) warn that students don't necessarily progress in an orderly fashion and can demonstrate more advanced skills without exhibiting previous competence of underlying skills. Standardized assessments also fail to account for the unique culture of the student, geographic region, or impact of race and ethnicity. These assessments tend to be biased in favor of those students with solid language skills, physical abilities, vision, and hearing and as a result may fail to identify student strengths and needs.

When standardized assessments don't provide as complete or truly accurate picture of a student's abilities, interviewing those who know the student well and observing the student in natural environments are recommended practice (Li, 2009; Snell, 2002; Yell, Ryan, Rozalski, & Katsiyannis, 2009). The intent of such an assessment is not only to identify strengths and needs but also to understand how the student typically acquires new skills and under what conditions. Determining learning modalities that work for the student will support teachers in their efforts to teach.

■ FAMILY AND CHILD-BASED ASSESSMENT PROCEDURE

The merits of starting with the family and student for assessment purposes have been clearly recognized by the field (Blue-Banning, Summers, Frankland, Nelson, & Beegle, 2004; Campbell, Reilly, & Henley, 2008; Turnbull, Turnbull, Erwin, & Soodak, 2006). As stated in Chapter 1, family members are the experts of their child and bring considerable information to the assessment process. Prior to the Individualized Education Program (IEP) meeting, the family needs to be contacted to determine what strengths and limitations they see at home and what skills they'd like the school to address. The family is helped to see education as a service offered to them and their child and the need to gather information that will serve as a form of blueprint of how those services will be provided. Talking with family members can occur at the home, school, or via phone, whatever is perceived as most comfortable and convenient to the family. Instead of completing test protocols, the assessor (whether teacher, related service provider, or school psychologist) listens to the family's concerns and interests in education for their child. Listening to the family requires that educational staff be aware of and respectful of cultural, religious, and linguistic practices. These attributes of each student and family need to be acknowledged and understood to work most effectively across school and home (Bui & Turnbull, 2003; Harry & Klingner, 2006).

The focus of this part of the assessment is to concentrate on the student's strengths, not deficits. Information pertaining to how the student communicates and for what purposes, how the student moves (if a physical impairment is present), how the student handles items, and how the student socially interacts with others will need to be documented. When a physical impairment is present, formal assessments from a physical therapist and occupational therapist are essential to obtain information on proper positioning for learning, best range of motion that the student can use, and needed physical accommodations (see Downing, 2003). For students with sensory disabilities, such as a visual or auditory impairment, information needs to be obtained regarding how much vision or hearing remains if any and how the student makes use of these two sensory input modes. Information from the family can be added to information from more formal and physiological examinations from vision and hearing specialists (e.g., ophthalmologists, audiologists). Although the student may act differently at home than at school, which is quite common, obtaining this type of basic information regarding how the student interacts with the world and learns is essential (Chen & Downing, 2006). Family members know what strategies and materials have been used in the past—which ones have had a positive impact and which ones should be avoided. This information provides educators with a sound starting point for working with their child.

Besides determining how the student typically behaves in familiar routines and environments, the educational team also needs to obtain information on academic skills of reading, writing, and math. While the student may not be demonstrating academic skills at grade or age level, what the student is doing in these critical academic areas is necessary. For instance, a high school student may be reading by taking a book, orienting it, and then looking at pictures while turning pages. Although he does not have conventional reading skills of decoding or comprehension of print, these literacy skills should be documented as a starting point for further literacy instruction. A middle school student may not count or recognize numbers but can indicate which pile of two quite different amounts is the larger one. This student may also have a concept of the quantity of one. Stating what a student is doing in a given subject matter is important information that can be used during grade-level math activities in school.

Of equal importance is the need to determine what interests the student—how that student amuses himself or herself when left alone. Finding out what is inherently enjoyable for the student can become potential reinforcers at school. Furthermore, making use of a student's interests to learn core content can be an effective strategy (Kluth & Schwarz, 2008; Reis, Schader, Milne, & Stephens, 2003; Vacca, 2007). Although some students may appear to engage in a specific activity to distraction (constantly repeating its name or continually fiddling with a familiar item), embedding these interests into core content (whether math, science, social studies) can be a means of engaging the student for longer periods of time (Reis et al., 2003). For instance, a student who really likes fans can use pictures of these items to count with in math and recognize quantities or learn that fans require electricity in science and are made up of smaller parts or learn that fans were not available during times past due to lack of electricity as part of a social studies class.

Assessment that starts with the student's interests and strengths as described in the preceding paragraphs is called a *person-centered approach* to assessment (Holburn, Gordon, & Vietze, 2007; Holburn & Vietze, 2002). Instead of assessing students to determine intelligence quotient (IQ) scores, mental ages, or developmental levels, the intent of this assessment is to determine who the student is as a person, where that student would like to go as an adult, and how the educational system can work to facilitate this overall goal. Many have advocated the use of person-centered assessment and intervention over a more traditional standardized format for this population (Macy & Hoyt-Gonzales, 2007; Siegel & Allinder, 2005; Renzaglia, Karvonen, Drasgow, & Stoxen, 2003; Vacca, 2007).

■ RECORD REVIEW

To obtain a more thorough understanding of both academic and nonacademic skills of the student with moderate or severe intellectual disabilities, a review of past achievement records is recommended. Past records should reveal areas of both strengths and weaknesses for a given student. These records (informal reports, notes from observations, and progress on past IEP goals and objectives) should clarify what the student has demonstrated in educational environments and what areas are challenging for the student. This information also should provide some information as to how the student best acquires and retains skills. Instructional strategies and materials that have not been effective also should be apparent.

Portfolio assessment should be one aspect of a review of past achievement. Student portfolios contain a carefully selected body of work that highlights what the student has learned across academic subjects. When artifacts in the portfolio are aligned with grade-level content standards, student skills can be compared to expectations for students at a given grade level, helping teaching staff to determine next steps. A representative sample of work can show progress over time at a glance and represent a very authentic and individualized approach to assessment (Kearns, Burdge, Clayton, Denham, & Kleinert, 2006; Kohl, McLaughlin, & Nagle, 2006; Siegel & Allinder, 2005). Samples of work could include a spelling test using pictures, a written signature by the student, written numbers, sheet of arithmetic with information on how the student completed it, and a cloze paragraph with picture and/or word cards filled in by the student. When students are requiring special accommodations and assistance to complete work, the manner in which that assistance is provided should be noted on the student's work sample. Ideally, the student should make the decision (with help as needed) as to what best represents the student's own work and, therefore, should be included in the portfolio.

Digital video segments of the student learning in a general education classroom also may be included as part of the portfolio assessment (Kearns et al., 2006; Salend, 2009; Siegel & Allinder, 2005). Such use of technology for assessment can provide considerable information regarding how the student takes direction from the teacher and peers, length of time on a task, adaptations being used (and how used), how the student interacts with peers, handles materials, and deals with frustrations. Video recordings can also document the length of time a student can stay with a group, especially when this is difficult for the student, or work on a task. Techniques used by teachers to teach concepts, redirect when needed, and wait time needed by the student to respond all can be captured on videotape. This type of information not only shows what a student can do in general education classes but also provides valuable information to future teachers regarding how the student learns and potential strategies to use while teaching. Families also can gain information from digital video recordings to help them better understand what and how their child is learning during the course of a school day (Salend, 2009; Thompson, Meadan, Fansier, Alber, & Balogh, 2007).

OBSERVATIONAL ASSESSMENTS ■

The information obtained from the family, as well as past records, provides a starting point for assessing the student's performance at school. Observing students in natural environments and typical activities to identify what they can do can provide much more authentic results than paper and pencil assessments (Browder, Spooner, Algozzine, et al., 2003; Macy & Hoyt-Gonzales, 2007). Contextually based assessments of this nature allow the student to perform in a more natural and perhaps more meaningful way for the student. When assessment venues are more practical and contextually based for the student, assessors can identify interests, strengths, learning opportunities, and necessary supports (Losardo & Notari-Syverson, 2001; Wilson, Mott, & Batman, 2004). The focus is on the assets the student brings to the learning environment, not on deficits.

One type of observational assessment occurs in the natural environment where the demands and impact of that environment can be seen. This type of assessment, called an ecological assessment, is considered a valuable approach to assessing students with severe disabilities (Renzaglia et al., 2003; Siegel & Allinder, 2005). Unlike assessments that remove the student from a familiar context and environment, an ecological assessment occurs in context, where a student can gain informative cues from the natural environment and routine of the activity being assessed. Such an assessment is more likely than a standardized format to portray the student in the most positive and comfortable environment and as such, identify more strengths as well as opportunities to learn. Instead of expecting the student to perform specified test items that may or may not be related to anything meaningful in the student's life, the student is evaluated in familiar routines and activities with varying level of supports provided.

Ecological assessments involve observing the activities in a given context to determine what students are expected to do, what natural cues exist to prompt their behavior, and what supports or hindrances may be present. Essentially, the steps of the typical activity in class are delineated so that desired student performance that comprises the overall activity can be clearly noted. See Table 3.1 for an example of this type of analysis for an 11th-grade Spanish class.

| Table 3.1 | Ecological Assessment of an 11th-Grade Spanish Class—Identifying Expected Student Behavior |

Steps of the Activity (Desired Behavior of Students)	Natural Cues to Prompt Expected Behavior
1. Come into class and find seat	• Knowledge of schedule • See seat
2. Respond to welcome of teacher in Spanish	• Teacher welcome in Spanish • Knowledge of what to say
3. Respond to questions and comments of teacher in Spanish	• Teacher questions and comments • Knowledge of response to give
4. Get out text and turn to stated page	• Teacher direction in Spanish • Knowledge of what was said
5. Read along with teacher	• Teacher reading in Spanish with explanations in English • The text page
6. Take notes	• Needing to retain the information and wanting to refer back to it
7. Work alone or in pairs on assignment (conjugating simple verbs)	• Preference of how to work • Assignment itself • Knowledge of what to do
8. Raise hand to ask questions	• Needing help • Knowledge of how to request help
9. Write down homework assignment	• Homework assignment on board • Need to remember it
10. Pack up materials and get ready to leave for next class	• Class over • Possessions spread around

Collecting this type of information helps the assessor keep in mind what the student with moderate to severe disabilities is supposed to do, what naturally exists in the environment to support this expectation, and what may be present that prevents or hinders the desired behavior. Identifying natural cues for each expected step helps to focus on what the student with disabilities should be responding to without additional prompts (Westling & Fox, 2009). Once the expectations have been determined for typical activities during class time, a third column is added to the ecological inventory that captures the target student's performance for each step of an activity. If the student does not or cannot perform this step given the natural cues that exist for all students, teachers must determine why not and design their intervention accordingly. The fourth and fifth columns of the assessment protocol capture this information (e.g., the reason for the discrepancy in the student's performance and potential intervention options, see Table 3.2). Thus, this type of assessment ties

| Table 3.2 | Ecological Assessment of a Student With Severe Disabilities in an 11th-Grade Spanish Class |

Student: Maria Elena (loves people and music, is interested in learning, can be stubborn, has limited movement of her body, reads pictures, and has some letter recognition)

Steps of the Activity (Desired Behavior of Students)	Natural Cues to Prompt Expected Behavior	Student Performance (Maria)	Discrepancy Analysis (Why The Behavior Is Not Shown)	Initial Plans to Intervene
1. Come into class and find seat	• Knowledge of schedule • See seat	—	Cannot move her wheelchair	Let her pick (by looking) which peer she would like to push her wheelchair to her desk. Use a pictorial or written schedule to ask her what class is next (photos of teachers).
2. Respond to welcome of teacher in Spanish	• Teacher welcome in Spanish • Knowledge of what to say	—	Is nonverbal	Have a peer program her BIGmack voice output switch to greet the teacher in Spanish.
3. Respond to questions and comments of teacher in Spanish	• Teacher questions and comments • Knowledge of response to give	—	Is nonverbal and may not understand all of the Spanish	Teacher can ask her a very simple vocabulary question and she can respond by looking at one of two pictorial cards held up for her. The teacher can then use her response for further questions to the class.
4. Get out text and turn to stated page	• Teacher direction in Spanish • Knowledge of what was said	—	Cannot physically access book and does not know sequence of numbers	A peer can show her two books and she can be asked to look at the Spanish book. Peer will turn to the correct page for her.
5. Read along with teacher	• Teacher reading in Spanish with explanations in English • The text page	—	Does not read	Pictures can be used to explain the big ideas in the text. She can listen to the Spanish (which she hears at home) and the pictures can be pointed to when the teacher reads certain words.

(Continued)

Table 3.2   (Continued)

Steps of the Activity (Desired Behavior of Students)	Natural Cues to Prompt Expected Behavior	Student Performance (Maria)	Discrepancy Analysis (Why The Behavior Is Not Shown)	Initial Plans to Intervene
6. Take notes	• Needing to retain the information and wanting to refer back to it	—	Cannot write and material is somewhat abstract	The pictorial information serves as notes she will use when studying for tests.
7. Work alone or in pairs on assignment (conjugating simple verbs)	• Preference of how to work • Assignment itself • Knowledge of what to do	—	Does not read or write	When shown different pictures representing verbs and nouns, Maria will be asked to find a certain verb (by looking). After selecting it, her partner will conjugate the verb.
8. Raise hand to ask questions	• Needing help • Knowledge of how to request help	—	Cannot physically raise her hand and may not know what to ask	Ensure that she has access to her switch-activated device that she uses to gain assistance when needed across all classes. She uses a head switch to activate the recorded message on her device.
9. Write down homework assignment	• Homework assignment on board • Need to remember it	—	Does not read or write	The peer tutor or adult supporting her will show her the adapted homework and makes sure it gets in her notebook to take home.
10. Pack up materials and get ready to leave for next class	• Class over • Possessions spread around	—	Not able to physically put things away	Can be taught to look at a peer to request peer assistance packing up. She can also be shown her pictorial schedule and given two options to determine which class is next.

KEY: ___ Unable to or not performing, P = Some attempt by student, + = independent performance directly to the resulting intervention and does not have to be extrapolated from numerical scores that do not reflect who the student really is or what that student is able to do.

Typically, individuals perform better in environments in which they feel comfortable and familiar. Individuals make use of existing cues from objects and others around them to perform as expected. In addition, documenting what types of supports the student needs to perform optimally can provide useful information for future instruction. Snell (2002) described a dynamic assessment where students are observed performing typical activities with support as needed. Such information can help future teachers better understand the conditions under which the student is most likely to perform. Once needed supports have been identified for the student, those supports should be provided during both instruction time and testing (Salend, 2008). For example, if a student needs to be positioned in a particular way with support provided under the forearm to enhance the student's ability to indicate responses, those supports need to be present during instructional times as well as during testing.

Information obtained from interviews with significant others, past records, and observational assessments of the student's actual performance under authentic conditions should be compiled into a summary of results for the educational team and family members. A summary of assessment results should address all academic as well as nonacademic areas. Table 3.3 provides a sample of a summary of assessment findings in academic areas for a fourth-grade student.

Table 3.3 Sample of Observation Assessment Results for a Fourth-Grade Student

Name: China	**Special Education Label**: Severe Cognitive and Physical Impairments

Summary of Findings From Observations and Interviews With Family/Team Members
China communicates by looking at pictures and objects, slight body movement, facial expressions and vocalizations (sounds, not words)
China likes Hannah Montana, birds (she has two cockatoos), amusement park rides—especially roller coaster—and being read to

Summary of Skills in Academic Subjects

Reading and Reading Comprehension

- Recognizes where to start a book and if it is correctly oriented
- Scans words from left to right with someone providing a finger cue
- Matches pictures of simple objects
- Vocalizes to request more pages to be read
- Responds to simple comprehension questions from two pictorial options
- Recognizes some common logos (e.g., girls restroom, McDonald's arches)

(Continued)

Table 3.3   (Continued)

Writing

- Picks a topic to write on from a field of three pictorial options
- Identifies some pictured action verbs to use in sentences
- Identifies some adjectives that modify common nouns (e.g., yellow bananas)

Math

- Identifies one item from many
- Matches two shapes (circles and squares)
- Identifies the larger of two items when the difference is quite clear
- Is learning to recognize the number *1*

Social Studies

- Associates some items with certain careers and jobs (e.g., water hose with a firefighter)
- Identifies different forms of transportation
- Identifies clothes she wears versus clothes worn in another time or culture
- Is learning to identify the United States flag from other quite different colored flags

Science

- Differentiates between pictures or objects of living and nonliving things
- Understands the sun is hot and that stars appear at night time
- Identifies common mammals from birds
- Associates fur with mammals and feathers with birds and knows that birds fly while mammals walk
- Identifies common items that require electricity versus those that do not

---

■ WHAT'S THE CLASS DOING?

Identifying what students in a classroom are expected to do keeps the focus on what may be very important to teach the target student. Are students to sit and listen, take notes, write, recite, respond to questions, ask questions, and so on? Determining what the entire class is doing (how they are learning) is critical information to obtain. Otherwise, the target student with moderate to severe disabilities may be taught in a manner that sets the student aside and draws undue attention. In addition, potential learning opportunities may be overlooked. A recommended practice of team collaboration, especially between general and special educators, would alleviate this problem by ensuring that planning for instruction has been done jointly and prior to the actual lesson. Dymond et al. (2006) describe this joint process of planning prior to a science lesson so that all students with unique learning needs can be actively involved in all aspects of the lesson. Decisions are made prior to the class regarding how the student with severe disabilities will participate in lecture, large group discussion, small group cooperative learning, and other learning arrangements. Special accommodations and adaptations can be made to support this involvement.

However, when coplanning does not occur or when changes must be made at the last moment, a quick assessment of the learning environment and changing expectations for student behavior is necessary. If the teacher is lecturing on content, then the student needs to be a part of this teaching arrangement. Different teaching strategies can be used if the class is being instructed in small groups. A quick assessment of how the teacher is presenting information, how students are arranged for learning, and the demonstration of acquired knowledge is critical information to obtain so that the student with moderate to severe disabilities remains with peers and does not become isolated from the class working alone with a teacher or paraprofessional. Determining when to provide direct instruction to individual students emerges from an analysis of classroom activities and teaching arrangements. Typically, direct instruction is called for when the material is abstract and the student does not appear to be able to attend to the teacher's directions. The person providing direct instruction must continually check to see what all students are doing in the learning process so that the target student is hearing and seeing closely related information and can be most easily incorporated into the overall activity.

For example, during a lecture on weather in physical science by an eighth-grade teacher, a student teacher is working with a student with severe intellectual disabilities. At the mention of cold and warm fronts, the student teacher embeds some direct instruction on picture and/or word recognition of "cold" and "hot." She explains the difference between these concepts, talks about their meaning in relation to the student's life, highlights the initial letters, and models the act of identifying these words from a field of three words. Every time the eighth-grade science teacher or a classmate verbalizes the words *hot* or *cold fronts* or *weather*, a systematic prompting strategy is used to help the student identify these words from other nonexamples. After each instructional trial, the student teacher ascertains what the class is discussing and may signal to the teacher to ask a prearranged question of the student involving the words *hot* and *cold*, teach other vocabulary and concepts related to a new topic or direction taken, direct the student's attention to a classmate's contribution, or engage in another instructional trial to provide some repetition of the vocabulary words *hot* and *cold*. As the unit on weather progresses, the same concepts of hot and cold, related vocabulary to read and learn, and associated information relating weather conditions to the student's life will continue ensuring sufficient practice for mastery of skills related to the science standard for this area. Others supporting the student during this period (e.g., occupational therapist, special educator) will intersperse trials of directed instruction throughout the lecture or large group discussions.

Identifying Important Skills to Teach

In any lesson, many different skills can be targeted. Content standards at each grade level determine to some extent what teachers will stress. However, additional skills are also important (e.g., following directions, peer collaboration, problem solving). For students with severe intellectual disabilities as well as additional impairments, determining what to teach is of critical importance. These students typically require much longer time than their peers to master skills in general (Snell & Brown, 2006; Westling & Fox, 2009). As a result, careful selection of skills to teach each student is recommended.

Family preference for student learning must be an integral aspect of skill selection and derives from the interactions with family prior to the writing of the IEP. These family preferences are then considered with the core content standards that apply to all students of a certain age. Knight (2003) stressed the importance of the family in targeting appropriate academic curriculum and avoiding school failure. Being sensitive and responsive to different cultural influences of families when determining appropriate skills to address is critical.

Academic and Nonacademic Skills

While the focus of this particular text is on the teaching of academic skills within the core curriculum and strategies for accomplishing that within general education classrooms, nonacademic skills are equally important. The team may identify several skills that are not linked to a particular standard depending on the state and its requirements. Skills such as self-care, increased mobility, use of switches, and social and communication skills may represent critical learning objectives for a given student but may not have a direct link to a content standard. Such skills should not be ignored but should and can be taught within general education environments. The reader is referred to studies by Jameson, McDonnell, Johnson, Riesen, and Polychronis (2007) and Johnson, McDonnell, Holzwarth, and Hunter (2004) for more specific information on how these types of skills can be embedded into the general education curriculum. One example of embedding nonacademic but critically important skills into general education activities is the teaching of communication skills. Students need to learn to respond to greetings from peers and teachers (and to initiate these greetings). These skills can be taught at the beginning of each school day or class. They also need to converse with peers during passing times, cooperative learning, lunch, recess or break, and partner work. See Downing (2005) for more detailed information on how communication skills can be embedded into all activities of the general education curriculum.

Several states have expanded required standards to include subject matter such as physical education (PE), technology, vocational goals, arts, and other areas that offer opportunities to directly link compensatory skills such as self-care to these requirements for all students. For example, states that have vocational standards refer to the need for the student to demonstrate cleanliness and appropriate work behavior (see state standards for Arizona, California, Indiana, and Nevada as examples). Depending on the age of the student, self-care skills could be directly linked to such performance standards and would be targeted for instruction during natural times of the day (e.g., using the restroom, lunch break, dressing for PE).

■ INTERPRETING CONTENT STANDARDS

Content standards vary by state but are closely aligned with and resemble national standards in the same content area. For the purpose of this text, standards for different content areas and across grade levels from a variety of states will be used. Often, these standards and their performance indicators address increasingly abstract skills as the student progresses through school. They may address skills that initially may seem unrelated to the needs of the student with moderate or severe intellectual disabilities. This may be particularly true as the student enters secondary grades. The tendency may exist to ignore these content standards when planning what to teach students with severe disabilities. Research investigating the linkage between content standards and a student's IEP goals and objectives found that teachers struggled to align these two required elements of a student's program (Browder, Spooner, Ahlgrim-Delzell, et al., 2003; Browder et al., 2005; Johnson & Arnold, 2004). In general, content was vague, too broad or narrow, and age inappropriate (Browder et al., 2004).

More research is needed to determine effective ways for teachers to align age-level curriculum standards to IEP goals and objectives and ultimately to assessments for these students. Until that research is complete, teachers will need to do their best to maintain high expectations for their students and interpret standards accordingly. One way to do this is to identify the big idea underlying the content standard (see Downing, 2008). Often, this big idea can relate more easily to the critical learning needs of the target student. Table 3.4 provides some sample standards across subject matter with related skills that may be of importance to teach students with moderate to severe intellectual disabilities. How the student demonstrates understanding of the standard will of course depend on the unique characteristics of each student (e.g., age, physical ability, communication skills, cognitive skills, vision or hearing loss).

Table 3.4 Interpreting Content Standards

Examples of Content Standards Across Subjects	*Related Skills Involved in Each Standard*
Life Science: Know and understand characteristics and structures of living things, the processes of life, and how living things interact	• Distinguish between living and nonliving things with pictures or objects (e.g., sort) • Identify differences of living and nonliving things (e.g., movement, growth) with pictures and objects • Identify properties of plants • Identify properties of animals • Identify what plants and animals need to exist
Reading: Understand that text has meaning and use different strategies to recognize unfamiliar text	• Attend to literacy materials in different formats (e.g., pictures, objects, audio) • Recognize letters, words, pictures, or objects on a page • Indicate that there is something of meaning on a page • Recognize that unfamiliar words start with the same letter as a familiar word

(Continued)

Table 3.4 (Continued)	
Examples of Content Standards Across Subjects	*Related Skills Involved in Each Standard*
Writing: Use appropriate conventions, mechanics, and format to create a readable and legible written product	• Identify that a period or question mark goes at the end of a sentence • Make a period at the end of the sentence • Identify the correct first letter of words in a sentence and stamp them in the correct (underlined) place • Dictate words using a speech to text device • Follow along with finger or other tool to show left to right progression of a sentence • Use picture and word cards to complete the appropriate verb for a sentence
Math: Use data collection and analyses, statistics, and probability in problem-solving situations and communicate the reasoning and processes used in solving the problems	• Point to the tallest or smallest bar of a bar graph (or tactile graph) • Make marks associated with self-monitoring of on-task behavior • Count favorite items and mark the correct number on a Y or X axis (by matching numbers) • Listen to a problem and use different objects to represent the data sets (e.g., boys/girls in class) • Use different colored magnetic pieces to represent two different amounts on a magnetic bar graph

■ BLENDING STUDENT AND FAMILY GOALS WITH STATE STANDARDS

While all students should have meaningful access to core curriculum and be held accountable to state standards, individual needs cannot be ignored. Each student's program should be individualized to meet unique needs and interests. Therefore, creating programs that are a blend of required standards and student and family desires is recommended. This process will involve interpreting the standard to make it accessible to the student and seeing if it relates to the individual student's unique needs. The following examples are offered to highlight this approach.

Nickeshia, a 10th grader, has severe intellectual disabilities and is nonverbal. Her family would like her to improve her communication skills so she can interact with them more efficiently and be less frustrated. One content standard requires high school students to analyze a written

> passage to identify the voice and intent of the author. While Nickeshia's parents want her to experience the literature of the English class, they are more interested in supporting her communication skill development. Therefore, it was determined that a blending of these two considerations (performance standard and parent wishes) would entail teaching Nickeshia to identify the tone of the written work by pointing to one of three pictorial facial expressions for angry, happy, or sad. These words are also on her augmentative communication device, and she is being taught to use these words to explain how she is feeling throughout the day.

In another example, a third-grade team considers the science standard under scientific enterprise of demonstrating the ability to work cooperatively while respecting the ideas of others and communicating one's own conclusions about findings.

> Cooper, a student with autism, has identified needs to communicate more effectively and to interact with others in an appropriate manner. His family is concerned about his lack of friends and the frustration he expresses through physical means when he can't make his thoughts known to others. A blending of this third-grade science standard and Cooper's individual needs is fairly straightforward. He will work on sharing materials and waiting his turn during science experiments. He will also work on responding to peers to do his part of the experiment and will press the correct button on his augmentative communication device (from three options) to state what he thinks might happen. These skills directly reflect those stated in the science standard. Furthermore, Cooper will have multiple opportunities to practice these skills across the school day, not just during science.

As shown above, the same process applies to all students regardless of age. Although grade-level standards become more difficult as the student progresses through middle school and high school, the same need exists to interpret the standard in a meaningful way while also considering family and student preferences. As the student nears graduation from high school, thinking creatively about possible adult roles is important.

> For instance, LaShawn is an 11th-grade student with complex intellectual and physical challenges. A high school standard in geometry and measurement calls for the student to analyze the attributes and properties of two- and three-dimensional shapes and develop mathematic arguments about their relationships. A specific performance objective states that the student will identify the attribute of certain triangles (e.g., isosceles, equilateral, right). His family (and LaShawn) want him to be as independent as possible when he graduates from high school. LaShawn loves music and is hoping to get a job in a store selling CDs and DVDs. With some physical assistance, he could stock shelves by matching CDs. Therefore, LaShawn can work on the skill of recognizing similar versus dissimilar items using different colored geometric shapes in math to organize them by type (e.g., right triangle, isosceles). Using his augmentative communication device, LaShawn will press the correct button explaining each pile of like triangles (e.g., "The sides of this triangle are all the same."). These skills relate to the required standard yet also support LaShawn's desire to learn skills that will help with employment options (e.g., stocking shelves by matching items). IEP goals and objectives targeting these skills of discriminating and matching similar figures and using his communication device to respond to questions can be helpful to LaShawn in a number of different situations.

To help teaching teams determine the link between grade-level standards and meaningful skills for students, a series of questions to ask before developing the IEP is recommended. Table 3.5 provides some sample questions that might help guide this process.

Table 3.5	Relating Student Needs to State Standards in Core Academic Subjects: Questions for the Teaching Team

1. What is the grade-level standard in the core content to be taught? What are the specific performance indicators or objectives?
2. What are the underlying concepts of this standard and/or performance indicator?
3. What part or parts of these underlying concepts have relevance for the student?
4. What specific skills can be taught related to these concepts and performance indicators?
5. Do these skills targeted for instruction directly reflect back on the original grade-level standard?

■ IDENTIFYING LEARNING OPPORTUNITIES

Once classroom activities have been analyzed to identify their composite steps (e.g., desired student behavior), specific learning opportunities addressing a number of diverse skills can be noted for the student with moderate or severe intellectual disabilities. Each step of an activity can offer multiple opportunities to teach skills of following directions, handling materials, social interaction, and communication. While the students without disabilities may not need to work on these skills, the student with moderate to severe intellectual disabilities may benefit from direct instruction on such skills. For example, after analyzing a fifth-grade math lesson on pre-algebra, the following steps were identified.

1. Listen to the teacher explaining the lesson on variables and simple equations.

2. Respond to math questions asked by the teacher on dry erase boards.

3. Volunteer to go up to the front of the class to demonstrate a problem using a Smartboard.

4. Get into groups of four.

5. Work cooperatively on math problems—drawing illustrations of problems to explain them along with the simple algebraic equation.

6. Sign paper together and turn in to the teacher.

7. Return to seat and put math book away.

Each of these seven steps is comprised of several smaller skills that may or may not be important to teach a specific student with moderate to severe disabilities. For example, Step 3 (to volunteer) involves skills of raising one's hand to volunteer, walking to the front of the room, pointing to the numbers on the board and, of course, performing the math problem. For a student with severe intellectual disabilities, part of the math demonstration could be to identify a single-digit number or match a number shown on a card to a number in the algebraic problem.

For Step 4 of the math lesson (get into groups), smaller skills involve following directions, making a choice of fellow students, visually scanning to find other classmates, physically maneuvering to the group, and greeting or acknowledging group members. While such skills may not be necessary for most students, some students with moderate or severe disabilities could easily benefit from mastering such skills. Step 5 (work cooperatively on math problems) involves many different skills, such as handling and sharing materials, counting, making marks on paper, making choices of what to depict, recognizing single digit numbers, and so on. The skills targeted for a student to learn would depend on that student's current skills and needs.

By analyzing familiar activities across different subjects and classes, numerous skills can be identified that address both academic skills related to standards and nonacademic skills that are naturally a part of the lesson. Assessing students with moderate to severe disabilities within these activities provides practical information that can be used to determine what is most appropriate to teach these students. Analyzing common class activities also serves to identify when it makes the most sense to teach specific skills (e.g., learn vocabulary and concepts during lecture, learn use of tools during lab, or learn a social greeting or use of a conversation book during transition time). Table 3.6 provides one example of the analysis of a seventh-grade language arts class. Smaller steps for each step in the analysis are provided to assist educational teams in determining what skills would be most appropriate to teach a given student. Once those skills have been identified, IEP goals and objectives can be developed.

Table 3.6 Identifying Potential Skills for Students to Learn

Analysis of a Seventh-Grade English Activity: Discussing a Novel	Smaller Skills and Adaptations per Step of the Activity
Enter room and take seat	• Read a pictorial or tactile schedule to determine next class • Physically move into class to seat • Identify own seat • Take seat without striking other students • Socialize with other students using a conversation book

(Continued)

Table 3.6 (Continued)

Analysis of a Seventh-Grade English Activity: Discussing a Novel	*Smaller Skills and Adaptations per Step of the Activity*
Get out novel and turn to the correct page	• Match book in pack to one a peer shows • Identify color of correct book • Match first number of page number to a number shown by a peer • Find book mark and open to that page
Review what has been read to date by responding to questions asked	• Point to one of three pictures to respond to simple questions about the story • Follow teacher direction to call on a classmate to review the novel
Read aloud if called on or follow along as a classmate reads	• Activate switch when called on to "read" prerecorded section of the novel • Point to pictures of characters, settings, and so on as a classmate reads about them
Discuss plot, characters, emotions, writing style	• Point to or make a facial expression to indicate tone of section read • Point to pictures or items when asked about characters, what they did, and so on
Discuss vocabulary used in the novel	• Use pictures, items, or act out simple meaning of vocabulary words • Listen to sentences and decide which simple meanings of the vocabulary words go in the sentences
Listen to the assignment	• Look at teacher and follow directions • Read adapted pictorial assignment
Pack up materials and get ready for next class	• Follow directions to put things away • Physically put materials into backpack • Recognize own backpack from others • Read pictorial or tactile schedule to determine next class • Socialize with classmates using a conversation book

■ WRITING IEP GOALS AND OBJECTIVES

The importance of writing high quality goals and objectives that stem from comprehensive assessments has been made clear (Capizzi, 2008; Snell & Brown, 2006; Yell, 2006). In addition, linking these goals and objectives to state standards is equally important in an age of accountability (Flowers, Browder,

Ahlgrim-Delzell, & Spooner, 2006; Roach & Elliott, 2006). Spooner, DiBase, and Courtade-Little (2006) recommended the identification of performance indicators that relate to specific grade-level standards to represent skills in individualized IEP goals and objectives. Then progress toward mastering these skills or performance indicators would indicate progress toward reaching content standards for that student. For example, an objective stating that a student will sort a certain number of pictures of living creatures from nonliving things will demonstrate progress toward meeting the physical science standard of differentiating properties of substances. Such an objective might be written like this: "When given colored pictures of animals, plants, and people and objects or items, Kareem will place all pictures of living things in one pile and all pictures of nonliving items in another pile with 70% accuracy per trial for 10 trials."

Goals and objectives should state the skill (or performance indicator) to be attained, the conditions under which this skill will be attained (materials needed, preparatory prompts), and the level or criterion of mastery to be attained. These should be clearly spelled out so that all members of the team who are serving as teachers for a particular student can easily understand the objective and recognize when it has been met. More information on these elements of IEP goals and objectives follow.

State the Skill(s) to Be Learned

The skill or skills to be acquired by the student must be clearly stated to ensure appropriate documentation and measurement. The skill should be easily observable and easily identifiable by all team members. Verbs that denote what the student will do to master the objective are preferred over those that are vague or confusing (e.g., write, verbally respond, add, and *not* participate, learn, understand, experience). What the student is expected to do independently and how the student will do it provides a clearer measure of what the student has learned than when the student is prompted through tasks. For example, if a student is to spell her or his name but is nonverbal, the skill of spelling will need to be defined as per the student's skill level (e.g., by pointing at the correct letters from a field of four or typing on an adapted keyboard with enlarged letters and all extraneous keys covered).

The skills can be thought of as performance indicators that relate directly to grade-level standards across various subjects. Although this text is targeting academic skills to be taught in general education classrooms, skills can be academic or nonacademic and all should be taught within natural contexts and environments. By thinking of skills in relation to performance indicators that pertain to all students, students with moderate or severe intellectual disabilities will automatically be expected to learn academic skills in reading, math, social sciences, science, and so on. Nonacademic skills, such as communication, social skills, self-help skills, and physical skills, are all appropriate to include in the IEP and may also relate to grade-level standards in several states.

Skills can represent quite large steps in activities (e.g., completing math problems) or very small steps (e.g., printing the first letter in one's name). The complexity of the skill and the number of skills in one IEP objective will depend on the skill level of the student. Analyzing the activity to identify small, discrete skills may make it easier to document whether a student has mastered an IEP objective or not. It may be preferable to target small discrete skills that the student will master independently than larger skills that require a lot of adult intervention.

Specify the Condition

The condition(s) under which the student will demonstrate the specified skill needs to be clearly stated. Otherwise, questions may remain as to what the student is to do to reach the objective. Conditions may include a specified number and type of prompts, use of adapted materials, positioning equipment, assistive technology, or the student experiencing a series of steps in an activity before the next step is expected. Conditions set the stage for what the student will then be able to produce. There can be several different conditions for one objective. For example, in order for Jory, an 11th grader, to indicate which of three elements is lightest (a physical science performance indicator), he needs to be properly positioned and have the actual items in front of him (e.g., *helium* balloon—He, a small *lead* weight—Pb, and *copper* wire—Cu). These items need to be placed on his tray fairly close to one another so that he can use the slight physical movement of his hand and fingers to indicate his response. He also needs a minimum of five seconds following the verbal question to move his hand close enough to point to his answer. Without stating necessary conditions for the skill to be demonstrated, considerable question may arise as to whether or not the student has mastered the target skill.

The condition also can refer to the person interacting with the student to get at the desired response. This person could be a member of the teaching staff or could be individuals in the community (e.g., cashier, waitperson, coworker, employer). Critical personal support to mention in IEP objectives for many students are peers, especially for those who struggle with peer-to-peer interactions. For example, to teach Alexis, a third grader, to interact more with her peers (a family priority), the following condition is part of her IEP objective. After having a short story read to her and asked a comprehension question by a classmate, Alexis will respond to her peer by pointing to the correct answer. As a result of this particular condition, at least part of the teaching strategy must involve peers. Therefore, clearly stating the conditions under which the student will demonstrate the skill has a profound influence on how the skill will be taught.

While the number of prompts provided by an adult or peer can be perceived as a specific condition under which the student will display the desired response, it is recommended that the skills targeted for the student be performed as independently as possible. Conditions that state that a student will answer questions *when prompted by an adult* are vague and do not state how much prompting, the type of prompting, or the frequency. Prompts can be so numerous and intense that the student is simply being manipulated through the activity (see Chapters 2 and 4). To better identify what the student has mastered independently, stating skills that the student can attain on his or her own following intensive instruction is recommended.

Finally, skills targeted in the IEP goal or objective that are to occur in environments other than the classroom setting should specify those environments as a condition. For instance, if the student is to make a purchase by exchanging money for a desired item, such a skill would call for mastery in a store or restaurant. Documenting this aspect of the objective or goal makes it clear that much of the instruction must occur in typical environments where the skill is needed and not in a classroom. Exchanging money with a teacher or paraprofessional in a classroom can be quite different than making an exchange in a store. Therefore, stating this condition for those skills that should occur in specific places in the community is recommended. For example: After obtaining desired items in a grocery store and after being shown to the shortest line, Joel will put all the items from the cart onto the conveyor belt and give the cashier the adapted wallet with a note on it to remove the necessary funds and return change and receipt for 12 or 15 grocery store trips. The condition of this particular setting makes it clear where Joel will need to receive instruction as well as where this objective will be met.

Determine the Criterion for Mastery

IEP goals and objectives must be measurable. Therefore, criterion for mastery must be clearly stated, relevant to the target skill, and easy to determine by all team members. The criterion to be reached by the student should reflect a considerable amount of teaching and avoid a potential attainment of the objective by chance alone (e.g., 50% or less criterion). The team must consider the level at which the student is currently performing the skill, the amount of time that will be spent teaching the student, and opportunities to practice the skill within a year or less. The mastery criterion should be set based on how much progress is deemed possible within a maximum of one year's instructional time. The student must have sufficient time to reach the desired goal. An amendment to the IEP can occur when IEP objectives are attained prior to the allotted time.

The criterion can be stated in terms of *frequency* of the desired response, in terms of percentage of *accuracy* where appropriate, in terms of reduced response time following a question or command (*latency*), and in terms of *duration* or how long a student is to engage in a particular skill (see Downing, 2008). Often, the skill or skills targeted for the student require that the criterion for mastery include several different aspects (e.g., accuracy and frequency measures). For example: When provided with manipulatives to count and told to find how much, Keiler will count five different amounts (from 1–10) and point to the correct answer from three options with 80% accuracy per math class for 10 math classes. Sometimes just frequency is needed if the quality of the response is clear. For example: When shown a thick dark line to write her name on, Malia will print the first letter of her name legibly for 12 of 15 opportunities. For the student who is very hesitant or reluctant to act and takes a considerable amount of time to respond, adding the criterion measure of latency might be very appropriate. For example: When Michael is told to start working on a test or assignment, he will begin to work within one minute of the initial direction for 12 of 14 such directions. In this example, both a frequency measure (12 of 14 directions) and a latency measurement (within one minute) comprised the entire criterion for the objective. Duration as a criterion measure is best used when a student has difficulty attending to a specified task for any given amount of time. For example: When warming up with his PE class and when encouraged by peers, Lon will perform each different exercise for a minimum of three minutes before stopping for 10 consecutive PE classes. In this objective both frequency (10 consecutive PE classes) and duration (a minimum of three minutes) were needed to specify criterion for mastery. As an academic example using a duration measure: During sustained silent reading and when allowed to choose her book to read, Layla will hold the book appropriately, look at the pictures, and turn the pages for a minimum of two minutes before stopping for 12 of 15 reading periods. Again, this objective required both a duration measure (a minimum of two minutes) as well as the frequency measure (12 of 15 reading periods) to specify mastery of the objective and be measurable.

Although accuracy as a measurement is used in many schools and school districts, care must be taken to make sure that it makes sense given the targeted skill and the reasonableness of measuring accuracy for that skill. Accuracy measurements are recommended for those skills and activities that require several manipulations of data or material and must be done correctly. Sorting pictures into categories of mammal or insect or into categories of gases, solids, and liquids, or identifying all of the spelling words used in sentences can all be adequately measured using accuracy. However, the frequency of this accurate behavior also will need to be targeted. For example: When given five pictures each of three different shapes (e.g., circles, squares, and triangles), Maria will sort the pictures with 70% accuracy for 10 trials. Her team wants her to be consistent with this math skill, and so she must demonstrate her accuracy sorting the shapes for several occasions over time. The trials could occur on several days during the course of a unit on geometry.

Accuracy is not recommended as a criterion measure and is not measurable when applied to certain skills such as self-care skills; motoric skills of running, walking, or standing; or listening to a story while sitting quietly. Duration, latency, and frequency measures are much easier to observe and more applicable. For example, if a student is expected to raise his or her hand when his or her name is called, accuracy would not be an appropriate measure as the student is either going to perform this skill or not. Rather, stating the number of times this student is to demonstrate this skill and perhaps the allowed latency period before the skill is to be demonstrated would make more sense and thus, would be easier to document. For example: At the beginning of PE (or any other class) within five seconds of the teacher calling his name, Eric will raise his arm up past his shoulder for 15 consecutive occurrences. These 15 occurrences could conceivably occur over several different classes during a week of school or more.

Individualized Criterion

The criterion set for mastery for each individual student can be quite unique. The criterion depends on the skill(s) expected, the student's strengths and limitations, the expectations of the environment (how long is possible or desired), and the effectiveness of the instruction. Setting criterion for a student should be a team decision based on members' past experience with the student, the amount of time to be devoted to instruction, the intensity of the instruction, the importance of the skill, and the number of opportunities to practice. The criterion should be set so that it makes sense for both the student and the skill, is challenging, and yet the student is able to show progress during the course of the year.

Criterion should be set so that it is clear that the student usually performs as desired (e.g., 75% or 80% of the time). Criterion set at a 50% performance level indicates little mastery for the student. If the task is quite challenging for the student, instead of setting a low criterion for mastery (essentially at a chance level), identifying smaller skills within the task for the student to master at a much greater level would be recommended. For example, instead of setting a criterion for a student to master the following skills at 50% accuracy over 20 opportunities (e.g., recognize own name from three signature stamps, grab correct stamp, place stamp in the ink, place inked stamp on bold line on upper left hand corner of worksheet), it may be more prudent to select one or two of these skills for the student to learn (e.g., recognize name from three signature stamps) with a higher criterion to show mastery (e.g., 80% of 20 opportunities).

When the student is new to the school and/or teaching team, setting the criterion for mastery will be the team's best effort. As the educational staff gain a greater understanding of how the student learns and how quickly skills are mastered, the original criterion may need to be adjusted. Criterion that may appear very easy for one student may be very challenging for another. For example, one student may find it very challenging to recognize four different single digit numbers and match them to an enlarged calculator keypad, so the criterion may be set at 70% accuracy for 10 trials per number. Another student may have mastered the use of a calculator using double-digit numbers, and so such a criterion would under-represent this student's skills. Again, the importance of knowing the student and individualizing criterion accordingly cannot be underestimated. Identifying individualized and appropriately challenging skills for students to learn are an essential goal of meaningful assessment.

SUMMARY ■

Chapter 3 has addressed the critical role that assessment plays in determining the important skills for students to learn. Assessments that capture the student's performance in familiar activities and routines in general education classrooms are recommended over standardized tests that may not provide an accurate or reliable picture. Identifying where the student is having difficulty performing the activity helps to focus intervention on where it is most needed. The intent is not to obtain a global performance level but to determine strengths as well as where teaching and supports are needed so that the student will be most successful in accomplishing meaningful tasks. Parental or familial input is critical to the assessment process as these team members are most knowledgeable about the student's strengths, interests, and needs. Cultural differences can be addressed best when family members are actively involved in both the assessment and development of their child's program.

Assessment leads directly to the development of the IEP with a clear relationship to student need and interests, family preferences, and grade-level standards. Addressing IEP goals and objectives in general education classrooms follows accordingly. When skills identified in IEP goals and objectives are perceived as performance indicators tied directly to grade-level standards, then accountability in attaining those standards may become clearer. Chapter 4 provides multiple examples of providing direct and systematic instruction in general education classrooms to help students with moderate to severe intellectual disabilities meet individualized educational goals. The relationship of skills taught to class activities and grade-level standards will be stressed.

4

Teaching Core Curriculum to Students With Moderate to Severe Intellectual Disabilities

KEY CONCEPTS

- ☛ Response to Intervention (RTI) may require more extensive adaptations and accommodations for students with severe disabilities.

- ☛ Individualized adaptations are typically needed to make the core curriculum meaningful and accessible.

- ☛ Teachers must identify the Big Ideas in each lesson to determine what to teach students with severe intellectual disabilities.

- ☛ Individualized needs can be blended into general education lessons.

- ☛ Students with moderate to severe disabilities can and should be actively involved in the group lesson.

- ☛ Systematic instruction of individualized skills will be needed and can occur in a variety of teaching arrangements.

In this chapter, several examples will be given that demonstrate what is important to teach different-aged students and how to do that in general education classrooms. This chapter will use the information presented in previous chapters and demonstrate its applicability to the general education classroom under different teaching arrangements. First, the concept of a student's response to intervention will be described with application to students with moderate to severe intellectual disabilities. This discussion will lead naturally into the importance of meaningfully adapting core curriculum at different grade levels. Numerous suggestions for appropriate accommodations for different students will be given. Then, the focus will turn to the specific skills that the student is to learn and how those are linked to and embedded in the broader curriculum. Finally, systematic instruction procedures will be highlighted for teaching the student the targeted skills during general classroom instruction. The chapter will conclude with the importance of teaching students to generalize the skills they have learned.

■ RESPONSE TO INTERVENTION

Response to Intervention (RTI) is a process of determining how well students are responding to the instructional environment and instructional strategies used in the general education classroom (Gresham et al., 2005). Strategies are perceived along a continuum from universal measures to increasingly more intensive and extensive based on the needs of the student. Typically associated with students having learning disabilities, the RTI process involves careful observation of students receiving evidence-based practices to determine if they are performing significantly below same-age peers. More intensive intervention is applied with ongoing monitoring to determine if students who do not respond as intended should be evaluated for special education services (Fuchs, Mock, Morgan, & Young, 2003). RTI keeps the focus on the quality of instruction provided to all students and its effectiveness for individual students rather than on deficits inherent in a student. When RTI is implemented effectively, it should result in a more coordinated service delivery and improved learning for all students (Cummings, Atkins, Allison, & Cole, 2008).

Although much less researched and utilized, RTI applies to students with moderate to severe disabilities. Instead of looking at disability labels and automatically assuming instruction must occur in a specialized environment, the process of RTI looks at how the student responds to increasingly more intense instruction within the general education classroom. For some aspects of any lesson, the student with moderate or severe disabilities may respond quite appropriately to the general instruction used with the entire class (e.g., the animated reading of an interesting story with pictures shown to all students). Other aspects of the lesson may involve information that the student cannot respond to given a typical or universal approach (e.g., directions to write a brief essay on a social studies topic). When this occurs, more intensive instructional approaches will be needed to ensure adequate responding from the student. The student does not have to be removed to a specialized setting but will need a more individualized approach to be successful.

■ THE CRITICAL NEED TO ADAPT
CURRICULUM TO MAKE IT MEANINGFUL

Core curriculum becomes increasingly abstract in nature, relying on considerable verbal abilities and preceding basic skills, especially as the student enters secondary education. Students with moderate to severe intellectual disabilities should not be excluded from abstract curriculum, but will need for it to be adapted to be accessible. Considerable literature exists on adapting core curriculum for students with severe disabilities (Clayton, Burdge, Denham, Kleinert, & Kearns, 2006; Downing, 2008; Janney & Snell, 2004; Ryndak & Ward, 2003). At times this can be a very simple adaptation, such as learning to recognize pictured vocabulary words in a high school Spanish class while the rest of the class works on Spanish composition using the same vocabulary. At other times it can be more challenging, such as learning class rules while the rest of the government high school class learns about legislation. Careful thought and planning are needed to ensure that the adapted lesson clearly reflects what the class in general is learning and the link to the required standards for that class and grade level is strong. Furthermore, the curriculum must be made meaningful to the student with moderate to severe intellectual disabilities, so that the student can understand the relevance to his or her life. Adapting the curriculum, therefore, is not something that can be done haphazardly, but must have some forethought and conceptual planning. All members of the team can assist in this effort, although the primary individuals responsible for such planning are the general and special educators. Family members and paraprofessionals also can be very helpful in providing suggestions as well as material adaptations.

IDENTIFYING THE *BIG* IDEAS ■ FROM CORE CURRICULUM

Core curriculum is clearly defined by each school, school district, or state and closely follows national guidelines tied to standard forms of assessment. Schools and/or school districts use approved texts for language arts, math, science, and social studies that cover the respective curriculum and provide ideas and guidelines for teachers when presenting the material to their students. All students should have access to the material, although some will need additional interpretation of the information to make it meaningful.

Interpreting the curriculum for students with moderate or severe disabilities and identifying the big ideas for learning requires the attention of teachers prior to instruction. Knowing what to address for each student with moderate or severe disabilities requires knowledge of the student, the content, and performance standards expected of same-age students. Whatever the subject, it is important to reduce the complexity of detail and determine what main idea or ideas will be taught to a given student (Parrish & Stodden, 2009). The student will have access to all the information taught, but specific and direct instruction will focus on the big ideas identified for that student. Vocabulary related to and explaining these ideas may need to be greatly simplified and reduced in quantity as well. The goal for the student will be to master these big ideas and related vocabulary and not the breadth and depth of content expected of students without severe disabilities. Federal guidelines for students taking alternate assessments allows for a reduction in breadth and depth of the content targeted for assessment (U.S. Department of Education, 2005).

The following examples of different subject matter as well as different grade levels will be used to highlight the process used to identify the big ideas from core content. Information presented at grade level will be stated followed by the interpretation of that information for a particular student. The interpretation and resulting information to teach will vary per student. Instead of becoming bogged down in each detail provided, the intent is to paint a big picture of important general knowledge that will improve the student's ability to better understand the world and communicate that understanding to others. Doyle and Giangreco (2009) stress the importance of being actively involved in the general education classroom and learning the relevant vocabulary to improve interaction skills.

Example 1. Lesson Topic: Prohibition

Class: 11th-Grade American History

Students read a text with the following information in it:

Promoting Moral Improvement

Other reformers felt that morality, not the workplace, held the key to improving the lives of poor people. These reformers wanted immigrants and poor city dwellers to uplift themselves by improving their personal behavior. Prohibition, the banning of alcoholic beverages, was one such program.

Prohibitionist groups feared that alcohol was undermining American morals. Founded in Cleveland in 1874, the Woman's Christian Temperance Union (WCTU) spearheaded the crusade for prohibition. Members advanced this cause by entering saloons, singing, praying, and urging saloonkeepers to stop selling alcohol. As momentum grew, the union was transformed by Frances Willard from a small Midwestern religious group in 1879 to a national organization. Boasting 245,000 members by 1911, the WCTU became the largest women's group in the nation's history. (Danzer, de Alva, Krieger, Wilson, & Woloch, 2007, p. 513)

Interpretation: A long time ago, people thought it was bad to drink alcohol. Bad things happened when people drank a lot. So, a large group of women got together and tried to get people to stop drinking alcohol. Finally, it became a rule that no one could drink alcohol.

Vocabulary words to be taught: people, women, bad, a lot, work, hurt, drink, large. Pictures and actions would be used to help identify words such as *people, women, alcohol, drink, hurt, police.*

Example 2. Finding Unknown Values

Class: 10th-Grade Algebra

Students might read word problems related to determining unknown values such as determining how much more room a student will have in his bedroom if his parents are planning to increase the length of the room by four feet and the width of the room by three feet. They will need to develop the polynomial expression that will represent the area of the new bedroom: $(x+4)(x+3)$ to $(x^2+7x+12)$.

Vocabulary words to be taught: bedroom, wall, floor, bed, pictures, CD player, chair, clothes, big or bigger, more, and the numbers 3,4,7,12.

Pictures would be used to show the smaller room and the bigger room and the items that are typically found in a bedroom.

Example 3. Lesson Topic: Acids and bases

Class: Eighth-Grade Science

Students in this class read the following section of their text.

Carbonate ions contain carbon and oxygen atoms bonded together. They carry an overall negative charge (CO_3^{2-}). One product of an acidic reaction with carbonates is the gas carbon dioxide.

Geologists, scientists who study Earth, use this property of acids to identify rocks containing certain types of limestone. Limestone is a compound that contains the carbonate ion. If a geologist pours dilute hydrochloric acid on a limestone rock, bubbles of carbon dioxide appear on the rock's surface. (Frank, Little, & Miller, 2009, p. 100)

Interpretation: Things that are alive are made up of very, very small things called atoms. Like a magnet, some of these very small things are negative (–), and some are positive (+), and they can push away or pull together.

Some men and women, called scientists, study rocks. They can pour an acid, which is something you can't drink, onto a certain rock, called limestone. If bubbles appear on the rock or limestone, they know that there are small atoms called carbonate ions in it.

Vocabulary words to be taught: rock or stone, pour, small, big, drink, bubbles, men and women, push and pull (– and +). Pictures and real rocks with something to produce bubbles, as well as magnets and magnetic items, would all be used to explain the big ideas.

Example 4. Lesson: The Boston Tea Party

Class: Fourth-Grade Social Studies

In their social studies text, students read the following passage with a picture or two.

Many people think Samuel Adams planned what happened next. On the night of December 16, 1773, about 150 members of the Sons of Liberty dressed as members of the Mohawk tribe and marched down to Boston Harbor.

At the harbor, hundreds of people were gathered on the docks to watch. When members of the Sons of Liberty arrived, they boarded the ships, broke open more than 300 chests of tea, and threw it all overboard. Their angry protest became known as the Boston Tea Party. (Harcourt, 2007, p. 311)

Interpretation: A long time ago, some men didn't like what was happening to them, and they got angry. They dressed up like Indians with paint on their faces and feathers in their hair and got on some ships that didn't belong to them. The ships belonged to the British, the people wearing red, who made them angry. They opened up a lot of boxes that had tea in them, and they threw the tea into the ocean. This happened in a city called Boston, and it was called the Boston Tea Party. It really wasn't a party, but a lot of people were there.

Vocabulary words to be taught: red, tea, boxes, ship and/or boat, men, Indians, paint, feathers, watch, throw, ocean, party, angry, people. Pictures and real objects such as tea bags and feathers will be used to teach the main concepts. These concepts will also be acted out to promote greater understanding.

Those responsible for identifying big ideas from grade-level content must receive some training to be effective (Spooner, Baker, Harris, Ahlgrim-Delzell, & Browder, 2007). Practice performing such interpretation should help to ease the initial challenge experienced. Once curriculum has been adapted, it can be saved, stored on disks, shared with other teachers in the district, and used for future students. For example, Figure 4.1 shows an adapted lesson on animal adaptations for a fourth grader who does not read in a conventional manner and needs easier concepts highlighted with pictorial support. Knowing in advance what curriculum will be taught at a given age may make it possible for teachers to seek the support of other team members to assume some responsibility for adapting parts of the curriculum. These can be saved, modified, and reused over the years for any student needing such adaptations.

■ AVOIDING ISOLATION IN GENERAL EDUCATION CLASSROOMS

Although outcomes of learning may be different, instruction should not remove the student from class activities. Wehmeyer, Lattin, Lapp-Rincker, and Agran (2003) found that even when middle school students with cognitive disabilities were learning in the same classroom as peers, they often would be working with a paraprofessional on separate work. When accommodations in both instruction and instructional materials are quite extensive due to complex cognitive, sensory, physical, and behavioral challenges, a tendency may exist to separate the student from students without disabilities even though students are all in the same classroom. If the student has an adult providing individualized and systematic instruction, such separation can easily occur. For example, a general educator may be leading the class in a large group discussion, and a paraprofessional may be working with a student with severe and multiple disabilities near the back of the classroom on unrelated IEP objectives. In this case, the student may need to block out the verbal instruction from the classroom teacher as well as questions and responses from his classmates, while also attending to the visual and auditory instruction on unrelated or vaguely related work. To avoid this type of instruction from occurring (or from occurring with any regularity), the educational team must be sure that planning for lessons includes all students in the class activities and reflects Universal Design for Learning (UDL).

Figure 4.1	Adaptation for a Fourth-Grade Lesson on Animals

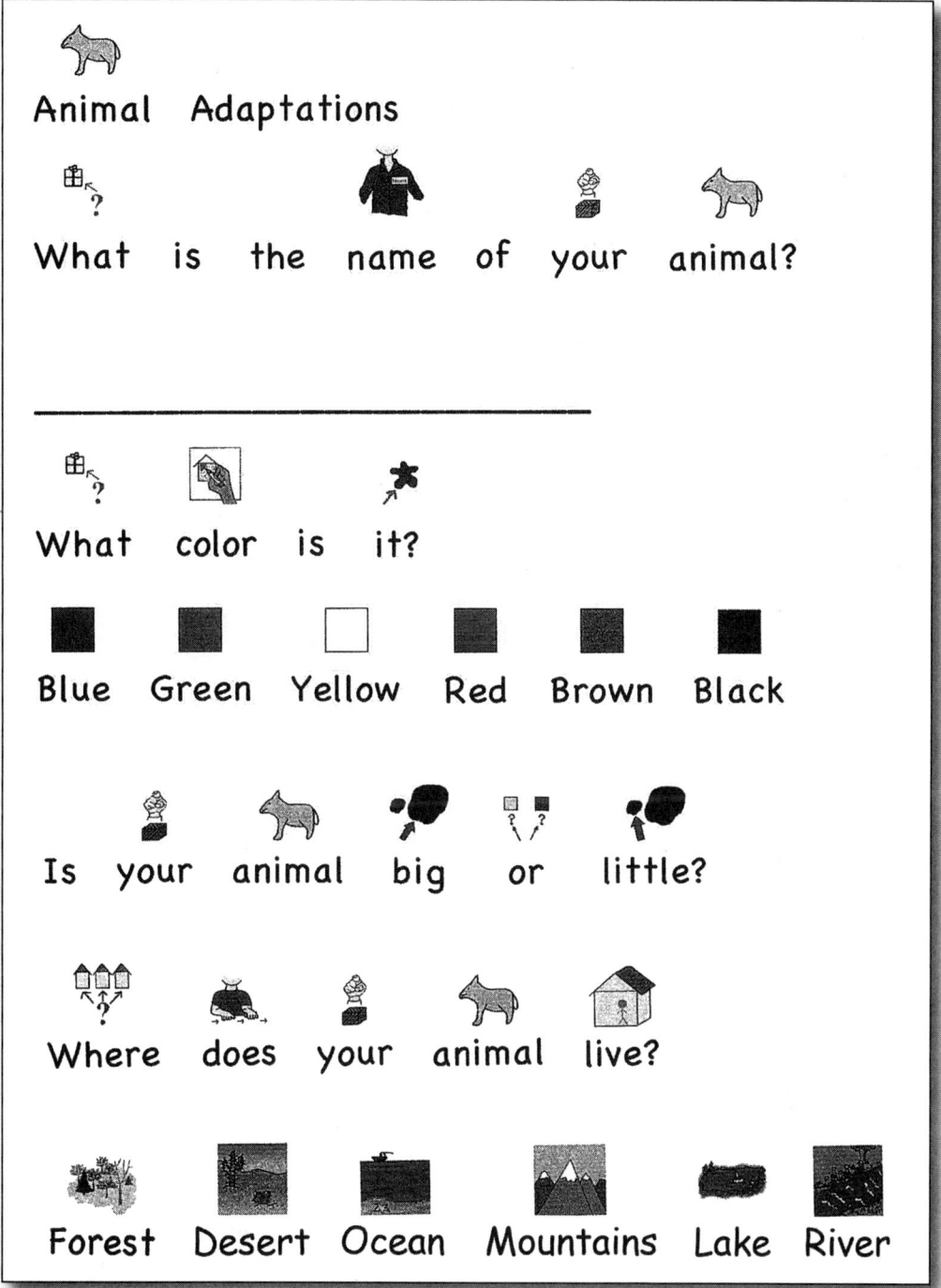

Made with PixWriter from Slater Software, Inc. Adaptation by Susie Speelman.

UDL is a process of creating learning activities and environments that are accessible to all students. General and special education teachers plan lessons from the onset (not as an afterthought) so that students of different abilities can be actively involved in the lessons (Rose & Meyer, 2002, 2006). Teachers plan to present information in different modalities (e.g., demonstration, acting out, pictorial information), plan for students to access more information through different means (e.g., reading, listening, experimenting), and plan for students to demonstrate what they have learned in different ways (e.g., writing, oral presentations, PowerPoint presentations, skits). Although universal design for learning considers all students' needs, those students with more complex disabilities will likely need additional accommodations (Dymond et al., 2006). These students are at greater risk for being isolated within general education classrooms unless more intensive support is available. For example, in a high school English literature class, students are studying the poems of T. S. Eliot. Students with learning disabilities, behavioral challenges, and mild intellectual disabilities may need a graphic organizer to help remember and better understand the use of tone, vocabulary, and analogies. They may also need prewritten notes with occasional blanks for them to fill in missing key words as the teacher discusses the material. Students with more severe intellectual (as well as other concomitant) disabilities will need pictorial material to identify what the poem is about and what it relates to as well as pictorial information of facial expressions to demonstrate understanding of the tone of a poem. As Shumaker et al. (2009) state, students may need more direct support, but they can still learn in general education classrooms given the necessary support strategies.

Ohtake (2003) presented an argument that greater class membership could be attained for the student with severe disabilities through increasing levels of class participation. She proposed four levels of contribution to the class' functioning that might help to describe a classroom and the degree to which a student with severe disabilities is an actively learning member and recognized as such by fellow classmates. These four types of contributions include *thematic*, where a student is working on related material but is not actively contributing to the lesson of the class; *social*, where a student is able to share related information to the class; *contributing*, where a student is giving direct feedback or information to assist the class in learning; and *distinctive*, where the student is adding unique and important information to the lesson of the class. Ohtake urged that classroom lessons be changed to allow for greater participation on the part of the student in the class activity to assuage the isolation that can occur even when students are physically a part of the class.

Isolation is most likely to occur when large group instruction is the teaching arrangement and the student has limited communication skills to participate. As described in Chapter 2, including the student by starting different parts of the discussion with simple questions asked of the student that lead to more abstract and in-depth questions for the rest of the class is one way of avoiding the isolation of the student with severe disabilities. The student is periodically called on to offer information to the class discussion that is used to broaden the topic and provide more comprehensive information from others in the class. For example, a biology teacher might call on a student to respond to the question of what plants need to grow. The student has three items presented in front of him (an eraser, dry erase board, water can). When the student picks up the water can, the teacher thanks him, "Yes, that's correct A. J., water," and then asks the rest of the class to explain how water impacts the plant and what happens if there is insufficient water to the plant.

This contribution from the student furthers the discussion and challenges all of the students to learn important information.

Another option for enhancing the contribution of the student to the entire class is to call on the student to assist in demonstrations or to carry a sample of the lesson to each student in the class for a closer look. Such a contribution may be particularly helpful for the student who needs to get up from the seat and move on a regular basis and for the student who is working on using a wheelchair or walker effectively or who needs to stand and weight bear and practice walking. Such participation by the student also supports efforts to teach following directions and appropriate social behavior. The teacher may also call on the student to help pass out papers, collect homework, or replace books on shelves. All such activities assist the teacher and class functioning and allow the student the opportunity to move meaningfully around the room.

Individual Student Considerations

Unique characteristics of every student need to be considered when adapting curriculum and determining the best way to help that student learn. Students come to school with different life experiences, different familial supports, different languages, cultural experiences, needs, and strengths. No one curriculum will address every student's needs and each one will require adaptations and accommodations to learn as effectively and efficiently as possible. Working with the student and the family of the student to determine the best ways of making the curriculum meaningful and relevant is essential.

Physical Considerations

Students come to school with vastly different means of using their bodies to move, manipulate items, and sit or stand. Some students may need to concentrate on using their bodies, which takes time and effort away from doing schoolwork. Typically, more time must be allotted the student who has physical limitations and needs to plan movements to carry out tasks. Efforts should be made to avoid requiring substantial physical concentration while simultaneously teaching cognitive tasks (e.g., expecting the student to maintain a sitting balance while also answering comprehension questions about a story). The balance required in independent sitting can be worked on while the student is expected to do less (e.g., listen to a story, watch a play, or cheer for a team during PE).

Students may need physical support to control their movements to respond as expected. Physical and occupational therapists on the team can provide valuable input regarding most effective positions and positioning equipment for the student, as well as which movements are most reliable and under the control of the student (Szczepanski, 2004). Movements over which the student has greatest control should be used to indicate responses. A student may use an elbow, thumb, head turn, eye gaze, knee or foot motion, or any body part to respond to a question. Teachers need to present information in such a way that students have easy access to it and can act upon it as efficiently as possible. If movements by the student require excessive effort, it may impact the willingness of the student to actively participate in lessons. Therefore, the amount of concentration and effort required of the student to perform physical skills should always be considered when planning the student's active participation in class.

Students with physical disabilities will need their prescribed positioning and other adaptive equipment in general education classrooms where they are learning. They should not need to go to a special room in order to access such essential equipment. Students may need standers for vertical positioning and weight bearing, computers with adaptive keyboards, and specialized software. Assistive technology can be very supportive of the learning of many students with a variety of disabilities, not just physical. For example, Figure 4.2 shows a fourth grader using his augmentative communication device that is interfaced with a computer to help him complete his modified work. The amount and type of assistive technology and all adaptations and accommodations are determined individually for each student as part of the IEP.

Visual Considerations

Students may have varying amounts of functional vision or no vision remaining that can compound difficulties in learning. A visual impairment may make it difficult to see things clearly at a distance (myopia) or make it difficult to see things up close (hyperopia). Some students have lost some or most of their visual field,

| Figure 4.2 | A fourth grader using his augmentative communication device to write on the computer |

Photographer: Kristina Zeider

making it difficult to detect the presence of certain information. A few students may learn better through their sense of touch and other remaining sensory input. Whenever a student has a significant visual impairment, adaptations must be made that will ensure access to the material (Downing, 2003). For some students, enlarging material will prove helpful, as well as adding color and presenting in a specific visual field. Figure 4.3 shows large alphabet stamps for writing that can be helpful for students with a visual impairment or for students who just need materials enlarged and less complex. Other students may need the information decreased in size so that they can see the entirety. Simplifying the background and highlighting the relevant information often helps students who have difficulty differentiating the foreground from background stimuli. For those students unable to presently make use of visual information tactilely relevant items that represent concepts will need to be used.

Figure 4.3 Alphabet stamps as an adaptation for writing

The vision teacher who is on the educational team for this student should be able to read visual reports and make recommendations for material accommodations, seating preferences, most appropriate lighting, and important ways to make use of other sensory input when teaching. Accommodations will need to take into account the visual impairment as well as the cognitive and physical disability, if any. The ability to make use of visual information can vary throughout the day for a student due to fatigue, medication levels, or unknown reasons, and therefore, such information is important for the teaching staff to know. How information is presented to the student will depend on a number of variables, including a student's visual skills and ability.

■ DETERMINING PROMPTS TO USE FOR A PARTICULAR STUDENT AND LESSON

Each student is unique as is each teaching situation and each skill to be learned by that student. Therefore, determining prompts to use must be planned as a team for each different skill and teaching situation. The team will need to consider what prompts work best for the student and under what conditions. Prompts that provide the most information to the student (taking into account cognitive and sensory disabilities) should be used, especially when teaching new skills. What's informative for one student (e.g., a visual cue) may not provide any information to another student (a student who does not make use of vision).

Prompts should also be selected based on their tolerance by the student and their lack of intrusiveness as the goal is to support students to learn, not to force them through activities. Physically manipulating the student to perform tasks does not necessarily relate to the student's understanding of the task or the need to do it independently (Riley, 1995). Likewise, prompts that draw undue negative attention to the student and stigmatize that student should not be used. Modeling appropriate interactions with students is critical for facilitating positive peer interactions (Carter, Cushing, & Kennedy, 2009). For example, the use of juvenile versus more adult pictures to teach basic skills would not be appropriate in a middle school or high school class (e.g., using pictures of little children and toys versus pictures of young adults or teens and cars, cell phones, etc. when discussing consumerism). The goal is to help students demonstrate their competency as much as possible. The use of juvenile material undermines such a goal.

Finally, prompts used with the student must not distract the teacher or other students or disrupt the learning process in any way. Using loud vocal prompts with a student during a teacher's lecture to the class would not be appropriate. Planning with the general educator clarifies when certain prompts can be used and when other prompts would be more appropriate. Table 4.1 lists questions to consider regarding different prompts to use with students. Table 4.2 provides an example of how specific prompts as part of a simultaneous prompting strategy are employed during large group instruction in a tenth-grade English class.

Table 4.1	Determining the Types of Prompts to Use in General Education Classrooms

What prompts work best for the student?
Which prompts provide the most information?
Are any prompts intrusive and/or disliked by the student?
Will any prompt stigmatize or draw negative attention to the student?
Will any prompt disrupt the class or distract the teacher?
Do all those supporting the student know how to provide the prompts and when?

Table 4.2	Teaching Plan for a 10th Grader on Finding the Author's Voice Using Simultaneous Prompting

Indiana 10th-Grade Reading Standard: Comprehension and Analysis of Literary Text
Performance Objective: Explain how voice, persona, and the choice of narrator affect the mood, tone, and meaning of text.
When Ms. Kleinert is lecturing about author voice and reading different pieces of literature, use the pictorial emotions to show Jadin the following:

1.	When students are doing their research on author voice, put the three emotion cards in front of him and tell him what each one is (use your own tone of voice and facial expressions to make it clear).
2.	Read a short poem or short section of a story stressing the tone of the words with inflection, facial expressions, and emphasize certain words (sorrowful, delighted).
3.	Tell the student what the tone is and touch that facial expression. (Repeat this three times with different tones, using all three emotions—happy, sad, angry.)
4.	Read one of the previously read sections or poems again and ask Jadin if it's one of the three emotions, holding them up for him as you label them.
5.	With no pause, guide his hand toward the correct answer using your hand under his forearm and tell him what the answer is.
6.	Follow this same procedure for the other two poems or sections that have different emotions of the author.
7.	Then, rearrange the three emotion cards so that they are in different places and read three different poems or sections (depending on time). Use the same prompt as described.

*Collect data on Jadin's performance before instruction—that is, read a poem or section and ask him to tell you if it's happy, sad, or angry. Do not prompt.

A Tale of Two Students

Two very different students will be used to explain more clearly how student characteristics impact teaching strategies. Kim is a fourth grader who loves books, appliances, puzzles, and silhouettes. He is nonverbal, moves very quickly, has a short attention span—especially for things he doesn't find interesting—and is labeled with severe autism and intellectual disabilities. Another fourth grader, Jeremiah, has quite different characteristics. He loves interactions with his peers, is a country music fan, and loves *Indiana Jones* movies. He has limited movement of his body and a severe visual impairment. He uses objects and some pictures to communicate and has a difficult time retaining new information. He uses a wheelchair, a stander, and adaptive seating.

Given their different strengths, interests, and needs, these two students learn somewhat differently and require different teaching strategies and supports. In general, Kim does better with limited and short verbal cues, paired with pictorial information, modeling, and visual gestures. He does not need a long wait time to respond, and in fact, can lose track of expectations if a wait time is more than about three seconds. He performs better with quick models from the teacher and clear, direct instructions. He dislikes being touched or manipulated in any way.

Jeremiah, due to his limited movement, slow processing, and severe visual loss, needs time to understand expectations, visually examine materials, make mental connections, and then act on them. A teacher working with Jeremiah needs to wait at least 10 seconds before providing more information (other prompts). Jeremiah appreciates verbal information about what he is examining as long as it is not too extensive or abstract. He often requires physical support under his forearms and elbows to stabilize the movement and allow him more accurate and controlled movement of his hands. He needs enlarged pictorial and written material with limited detail and a simple (dull) and contrasting background.

Since Kim likes to grab materials and throw them, it is better to block incorrect responses (e.g., cover the wrong options), redirect to the correct option, and quickly move on. Belaboring a particular response is not what Kim responds to. He does better using lots of different materials that address the same concept. He needs multiple opportunities to master a skill, but he likes to move through trials quickly with the focus on the materials and limited verbalizations.

The pace for Jeremiah, on the other hand, is considerably slower. Since he only sees a very small amount of information at one time, he needs time to carefully piece it together. Furthermore, once he's determined a correct answer, it takes him time to plan how to move his body to make his decision clear to others (e.g., typically by placing his whole hand on the answer). Due to these somewhat extreme differences in student learning style, teachers must be able to adapt readily and adjust their teaching strategies accordingly to be most effective.

■ EXAMPLES OF STUDENTS RECEIVING DIRECT INSTRUCTION ACROSS GRADES AND INSTRUCTIONAL ARRANGEMENTS

In general, teaching in any environment, but certainly in general education classrooms, requires certain preplanning. Teachers will need to determine how to (1) teach the target skills (share the information with the student), (2) check for acquisition (comprehension), (3) maintain acquired skills (review), and (4) generalize skills learned to other environments. The following detailed examples address the first two requirements and describe how a class and particular subject are being taught. A student with a moderate to severe intellectual disability is an active member of each class. What this student is learning as well as how the information is being taught during the whole class activity also is described. The intent of these several examples across subject matter, grade level, and teaching arrangements is to provide suggestions for addressing the needs of other students with similar disabilities in general education classrooms.

Once skills have been taught, a periodic review of the material to check for maintenance of skills also is needed. Brief reviews can occur at the start of class lessons and during lectures. Reviewing learned skills is critical to maintain a strong base from which to develop more skills. At the end of this chapter, the additional need to teach students to generalize what has been learned in one environment to other environments and situations will be discussed. For each of the lessons described, the team has considered the related content standards, the related skills that the student is to learn, adapted materials and prompts that will be needed to support student learning, and how progress will be measured. A list of questions that educational teams may wish to consider to support learning in general education classrooms can be found in Table 4.3.

Table 4.3 Steps to Consider When Teaching in General Education Classrooms

1.	What is the class learning and what standard(s) does it relate to?
2.	What skill(s) is the student to learn and how does it relate to age-level standards?
3.	What materials will be needed to highlight the critical information/skill to be learned? • Will the adapted materials be cognitively and physically accessible? • Will the adapted materials be culturally sensitive? • Will the adapted materials resemble materials/subject matter used by others in the class? • Will distracters be used (information that doesn't go with the subject)?
4.	How will the adapted materials be presented to the student? How will you get the student's attention? How will the adapted materials be used?
5.	What prompts will be used to teach the target skill(s) and in what order?
6.	How will the student's behavior be reinforced?
7.	How will mistakes be corrected?
8.	How will the student be taught during different instructional arrangements in the room (e.g., large group, small group, pairs, independent work)?
9.	What other ways will the student interact with the class that may be unrelated to the targeted skill?
10.	How will data be collected on acquisition of the targeted skill(s)?
11.	How will skills be maintained and generalized to other environments and situations?

■ SMALL GROUP INSTRUCTION

The use of small groups to teach students allows the teacher to become more acquainted with the skill level of a smaller number of students, who can serve as role models and support one another. Small group instruction also builds cooperative working relations, as students must share ideas, make decisions as a group, work toward a common goal, and compromise. Soukup, Wehmeyer, Bashinski, and Bovaird (2007) identified the small group teaching arrangement as one variable that was supportive of a student's access to the core curriculum. Researchers have identified numerous benefits (i.e., higher achievement and greater productivity, valuing of diversity, improved social skills, higher self-esteem, and greater ability to cope with adversity) as a result of small group instruction that is cooperative in nature (Salisbury, Palombaro, & Hollowood, 1993). In addition, learning vicariously, by watching other students in the group, has been documented for students with severe disabilities, making this instructional arrangement potentially more efficient than one-to-one instruction (Colozzi, Ward, & Crotty, 2008; Falkenstine, Collins, Schuster, & Kleinert, 2009). The following examples of small group instruction are provided to demonstrate how students with moderate or severe intellectual disabilities can be success-fully educated using this teaching arrangement.

Small Group Instruction—Middle School

In Mr. Edwin's sixth-grade math class, students are learning simple algebraic equations to find unknown quantities. Mr. Edwin typically presents a story problem related to something of high interest to the class (e.g., movie plots) and represents some part of it as an algebraic equation. This is done as a whole group lesson and addresses the national standard of using mathematical models to represent and understand quantitative relationships. He presents three to four different examples and then divides the class up into pairs and gives the class a page of problems to work on.

Derrick, a student in this class, is learning to recognize which of two numbers is larger (this relates to the math standard stated above). During the large group lesson, he is asked by the teacher to select a problem for the class. He does this with the use of a magnetic wand that he moves over three to four problems written on different pieces of paper with a paper clip on each one (magnetic). As the problem is being discussed, the two numbers in the problem are used to help Derrick determine which is larger. For example, in one problem Mr. Edwin writes $5x + 3x =$ ____. The numbers 5 and 3 are then used with Derrick to determine which is larger. If two-digit numbers are used, then the first digit is used to teach Derrick. Derrick sits at a table with five other students at the front of the room and in easy reach of the teacher.

The occupational therapist (OT) working with Derrick writes the two numbers on two separate cards and asks him to first point to each number as she says them. This is just to check to ensure that he still remembers the numbers and to make him feel successful. Then she asks which of the two numbers is larger. After a five-second wait to give him a chance to respond, she counts out five pictures of items related to the problem Mr. Edwin is teaching and places them over the number 5. She then counts out three pictures of items and puts them over the number 3. Then she asks Derrick again which is larger. If he points to the 5, she praises him and then listens to what problem the classroom teacher is on and does another problem with Derrick in the same way but with different pictured items (e.g., starships from the movie *Star Wars*).

If he doesn't respond after five seconds or responds incorrectly, the OT tells Derrick that he was wrong and highlights (spreads out) the five pictured items and moves the three pictured items closer together, repeats the number of each, while pointing to it. Then, she asks which number is more—which has more items. He is praised if he chooses the correct answer, and the picture items are lined up next to each other to give feedback and help him clearly see it. If after five seconds he does not choose or makes an error, he is given corrective feedback (e.g., "No, that's the three. Five is the larger number."). The OT will model and verbally explain the correct response twice (changing the location of the two numbers). Then she will change the position of the numbers and items and ask once more (waiting five seconds). If correct, he will be praised and shown why he is right. If not he will be told the correct answer and asked to find the 5.

The instruction by the OT is done quietly while Mr. Edwin is demonstrating to the class the solution of the algebraic equations. Sometimes the OT can offer several opportunities to select the larger of two numbers, using Mr. Edwin's examples and sometimes only one or two. If Derrick picks the correct number following the first request to do so, he receives credit for recognizing the larger number. The data sheet shows the two numbers being compared and the number that Derrick chose after the first question is circled (not after all of the prompts). This data is used to determine his progress toward meeting his IEP goal.

When Mr. Edwin divides the class into pairs, Derrick joins one pair of students and with the OT's support (and when she leaves, Mr. Edwin supports) continues to work on this skill using numbers in his group's assignment. He has pictured items (each on a separate small card) that go with the story problems, and his peers present different ones (three at a time) and ask him to decide which one they'll do first. Derrick enjoys this interaction, which typically results in some teasing about his choice. It also provides a brief break from the math work, which seems to help him. The procedure described above of least-to-most prompts with constant time delay is used to teach Derrick because this is not a new task for him and he is beginning to identify the correct number without several additional prompts.

Small Group Instruction—Elementary School

In a first-grade classroom, students are assigned to groups during language arts to work on different skills. One group of five is reading a story with the classroom teacher, one group of five is working with the special educator on decoding skills related to words in the story, another group is working with a parent volunteer on creating different endings to the story, and the rest of the class is working independently on reading or unfinished work. All groups are composed of students with diverse skills and ability.

In the group facilitated by the special educator, one of the five students is a curious young boy who loves pictures, especially of dinosaurs, and enjoys imitating his peers. He is nonverbal, has Down syndrome, and has a mild to moderate hearing impairment. The group is working on identifying initial, medial, and final blended sounds in words. For example, the special educator will ask the group to tell her where the *ch* sound is in words such as *witch*, *chicken*, and *kitchen*. In this group, Daniel is shown three pictures and is asked to listen to the teacher and then find the picture of the word that she has said. Once he has done this, the teacher uses the correct picture to ask the others in the group where the sound being targeted occurs. For example, Daniel is presented with pictures of a potato, a sandwich, and apple. He is asked to find the sandwich, and when he does, the rest of the group is to state that the *ch* sound occurs at the end of the word. Then they make sure everyone can spell the word correctly. Since Daniel also is working on recognizing initial letters, he is shown the three words that go with the pictures and asked to find the *s* for sandwich.

The special educator is responsible for the learning of all students in this group and must make sure that the pace of the lesson is appropriate for covering the necessary material. After showing Daniel the three pictures and naming them while pointing to each one, she waits three seconds for a response. If no response or an incorrect one, she'll quickly remove one picture and ask again while tapping each picture and stating its name. If no response in three seconds (or an incorrect one), she'll describe what each is and then asks him again. If correct, she'll praise him and go on with the rest of the group. If incorrect, she'll ask a peer to correct him and let him know which is the correct answer. She uses a least-to-most prompting strategy in this manner since Daniel recognizes the task and is beginning to become more accurate connecting the spoken word with its pictorial referent. He does not need a long wait time and typically responds immediately if he knows the answer. This procedure goes quite quickly and does not slow the group excessively. At times, the teacher will ask a classmate to describe the pictured items to Daniel to offer some practice in this skill.

Learning to recognize pictures and their meanings helps Daniel in his communication goals. Pictured items are used (either as the correct answer or distracters) that Daniel can make use of in communicating with others throughout his day at school and at home. His hearing loss interferes with his ability to clearly understand others in his environment, and so this lesson teaches him to listen and to associate what he hears with the pictured referent. Identifying letters and letter-sound associations are basic phonetic skills to aid him in creating his own messages.

Small Group Instruction—Middle School

In Mr. Benton's seventh-grade social studies class, students are learning about the Constitution and in particular, the Preamble to the Constitution. They are studying the introductory phrase of "we the people," learning what it means and comparing to other countries as well. They are also learning that federal laws supersede the power of individual states. In general, Mr. Benton uses small group instruction to explore issues in his class. After a brief introduction to the topic, he divides the class into small groups of five students and asks them to respond to questions he has selected.

Small group instruction works well for Jordan who has a harder time attending in a large group. Jordan has a very curious nature and is highly mobile. He loves to move quickly from one activity to the next. He is nonverbal and has difficulty interacting with his peers, although he often remains close to two of the boys in his group. Jordan uses picture and word symbols to communicate as well as vocalizations, a loud "no," a few gestures, and body movements (e.g., reaching, shoving, running off, kicking, and pinching). He writes by sequencing pictorial information, and he is learning to choose from different sticky labels to sign his name.

While the group explores policies in other countries, comparing and contrasting democratic societies to dictatorships, for example, a special educator provides some guidance and also provides additional support to Jordan. Pictured information is downloaded and printed from the Internet by the group and used by Jordan to identify a single leader (one man) as opposed to a large group of people. He is also learning about voting (by marking a ballot or raising one's hand) and that the greatest number of votes determines the outcome. Since Jordan often wants to ignore the group's wishes and do what he wants, this is an important lesson for him. Vocabulary words he will learn include *people, leader, vote, majority* or *most, America,* and his state, *Wisconsin.* The lesson for Jordan will involve social studies, math, reading, and writing. It relates to Wisconsin's standard in Political Science and Citizenship—specifically to identify and explain democracy's basic principles, including individual rights, responsibility for the common good, equal opportunity, equal protection of the laws, freedom of speech, justice, and majority rule with protection for minority rights.

Different members of Jordan's group assume the role of recorder, facilitator, and timer. The group decides what will be written in response to Mr. Benton's questions and decides on how many and what countries to explore and compare. All students vote, and the special educator asks the students if that is democratic or not and what would be another way to decide. When hands are in the air, Jordan is asked to count them and is given two very different numbers to identify the correct count. A peer tells him that they are voting, and he is shown a picture of people with their hands raised. The number of votes is placed on the country, and Jordan is helped to place them on a number line by matching numbers to determine which country received the majority (or most) of the votes. This occurs several times so that Jordan gets to practice the concepts of voting and determining the majority vote.

Since Jordan moves at a fairly quick pace and is easily distracted, the special educator (and anyone providing direct instruction) must keep the instruction moving with few if any delays. To ensure that Jordan is successful and does not get confused or just randomly selects any option provided to him, a simultaneous prompting procedure is used. The special educator gives Jordan four or five pictured vocabulary cards at a time and verbally labels them as Jordan looks at each one. She will repeat them for the several minutes that Jordan shows interest in manipulating the pictures. As the group formulates ideas and records them, simple sentences are written for Jordan to reflect these ideas (e.g., "A dictator is one *person* who rules."). The vocabulary word for Jordan is left blank, and Jordan is asked to find the word that completes the sentence. He is given two options placed in front of him, the sentence is read by a peer, and the special educator taps the correct vocabulary word picture as it is said. Jordan picks up the correct card (which was tapped) and is shown where it goes in the sentence. He is praised for completing the sentence. The same vocabulary and concepts are used in different ways as the lesson progresses during the week. However, before instruction begins, a quick probe is done to see if Jordan can identify any of the vocabulary words.

Small Group Instruction—10th-Grade Biology Class

Mr. Drapper's biology class has been studying DNA, the scientists who discovered DNA, and the impact on diversity. This work relates to a life science standard on the theory of biological evolution, and students must understand why genetic variation within a population is essential for evolution. The subject of study is a weeklong unit, and the class has been divided into small groups to study for the upcoming test. Mr. Drapper moves around to the different groups, checking on their progress and responding to questions.

Brad is a 10th grader in this class with severe intellectual disabilities who has a few words but typically uses alternative and augmentative forms of communication (e.g., gestures, body movement, facial expressions, and pictorial and written symbols). Brad has physical delays, which slow his movements and make his speech hard to understand. Brad is well liked by his classmates who provide a fair amount of natural support. Brad works with three of his classmates and the additional support of a peer tutor.

As Brad's group discusses the scientists responsible for the discovery of DNA and the process they undertook and ask questions of each other, Brad also works on his IEP objective of recognizing the big ideas of topics. Brad is asked to draw a number from a pile of number cards and give it to a peer of his choice in his small group. The number on the card relates to a prewritten question that the peer tutor has. The peer tutor reads the question, and the peer that Brad handed the number to must provide an answer. The peer tutor asks the others in the group if they all agree with the response or not and can refer to the answer that he has. At the same time, Brad is asked to find (from three pictorial/written options) which one is a scientist or which one is a man who is trying to find answers. The pictures are very different from one another to simplify the task.

A progressive time delay procedure is being used with Brad so that when initially asked to find the man or scientist, there is no wait provided and he is told which one is the correct picture. A zero wait of this nature is provided for the first four trials during one class, and then the wait is increased to two seconds following the direction to find the man. The three pictorial options are scrambled after every trial so that the correct response will be in a different location and Brad must carefully view each option before responding. If Brad responds within the two-second time delay by looking in the direction of the correct picture card and beginning to move his hand toward this card, then the wait time is increased to four seconds. If correct, Brad is praised and his response is reaffirmed. If incorrect, he is told what to look for in the correct response, and one of the options is removed to make the decision easier. The peer tutor assumes responsibility for ensuring the wait time increases as Brad seems to better understand the task, although the peers in his group are encouraged to give him feedback following the trials.

LARGE GROUP INSTRUCTION ■

Teachers may wish to present information to all students at once and to discuss the subject matter as a large group. Large group instruction can occur at any grade level, although it may be more prevalent and last longer in duration in secondary schools where students typically have longer attention spans. In a study observing 19 elementary students, Soukup et al. (2007) investigated ecological variables contributing to students with disabilities accessing the core curriculum. They found that students with intellectual and developmental disabilities had greater access to the core curriculum when in general education classrooms and large group instruction than when in specialized settings. The following are examples of large group instruction for different classrooms and subjects, with specific attention provided for ways to teach a student with moderate to severe intellectual disabilities during such a teaching arrangement.

Large Group Instruction—Ninth Grade

Mr. Keith's and Mr. Tybok's ninth-grade economics course is undertaking a unit on budgeting. This cotaught class by Mr. Keith (general educator) and Mr. Tybok (special educator) is very popular with a number of students. In a large group, the two teachers present different information on income, debits, and how to set up a personal budget. Mr. Keith and Mr. Tybok use lots of humor in their lectures, playing off one another, and also encouraging active student participation by having students come to the front of the room and "role play" a certain amount of income from a job and necessary as well as frivolous expensive items. The entire class can then visualize the necessity of earning enough money to obtain desired goods. Following the whole group lesson, the teachers break the students into groups of two or three students and have them work on a computer game on balancing a budget. Both teachers move around the room responding to various students' needs for assistance.

Mohammed really enjoys Mr. Keith's booming voice and his teasing nature. He also loves the attention of Mr. Tybok but doesn't care for the subject matter. His parents want him to learn some basic money concepts, and so this class offers that opportunity. Mohammed has a moderate to severe bilateral hearing impairment with a severe intellectual disability. He is nonverbal but uses his facial expressions, body language, vocalizations, objects, pictures, and a few signs to communicate. Mohammed tends to get frustrated when he isn't sure what is expected and pulls away from people and throws items when this happens. Mohammed sits at the front of the room, near the middle so he can see his teachers and they have easy access to him.

Mr. Keith always calls on Mohammed to help demonstrate concepts in the class. Mohammed will be shown pictures of certain jobs with dollar amounts attached (credit or income) or various items with price tags (debits), and he will choose which one he wants to portray. He holds the sign while standing in front of the class. The manual sign for his choice will be modeled for him several times by Mr. Tybok, the paraprofessional, or speech and language pathologist (whoever is supporting this class), and the entire class will use it along with other signs they've learned (e.g., MONEY, 1, 10, 100, 1000, FOOD, CDs, CAR).

During parts of the whole-group instruction when both teachers are teaching various aspects of budgeting, Mohammed works on sorting pictures of necessities (housing, clothing, food, transportation), jobs (with income amount attached), and desired items (computer games, CDs, TVs, movie tickets). He sits close to a classmate who is really interested in learning sign and enjoys interacting with Mohammed. On the back of each pictured item or job is a picture of the manual sign. Mohammed's classmate looks at the sign and then produces it for Mohammed and asks him which pile to put it in. This peer also uses the pictured cards to respond to teacher questions regarding income and expenses. The peer prompts Mohammed to continue working by moving a pictured item toward his hand and gesturing toward all three piles signing *WHERE? WORK, WANT, NEED?* Since this peer is also taking notes, one of the two teachers will check on Mohammed's performance, correct mistakes, and offer praise. If he has made a mistake, the correct response will be modeled, followed by a similar item that he is to sort.

Large Group Instruction—High School

In Ms. Juarez' 11th-grade Spanish class, students are expected to take notes and orally participate in the group's lesson (vocabulary, grammar, sentence structure, idioms). Typically, Ms. Juarez begins her class with a short review from the previous class, asking different students to respond to her questions. Then she'll spend some time introducing the new subject matter and will demonstrate, write on the dry erase board or Smart Board, and show pictures pertaining to new vocabulary or phrases, having the class repeat after her. She infuses a great deal of humor into her lessons, and students appear to enjoy her class. Ms. Juarez will often divide the class into pairs to work on their pronunciation, use of vocabulary, and syntax. At this time, she will either work individually with students on certain skills, or she will move around the room, helping pairs of students.

Estrella is a student in this class who comes from a Spanish-speaking family and loves hearing Spanish. She also loves the humor in the class and the interactive nature. Although Estrella does not use speech, she does have vision and enough mobility to use her fist to indicate messages through large pictorial/written cards. Her goals for this class include vocabulary development, spontaneous communication, appropriate interactions with peers, and emergent literacy skills. Estrella uses pictured/labeled cards in English to respond to questions, and her peers must provide the Spanish oral interpretation.

In this class, Estrella works with either the special educator, a paraprofessional, a high school peer tutor, or at times the classroom teacher, Ms. Juarez. Her support person depends on the schedule for that day or week. For the purpose of this example, she is working with a peer tutor. The peer tutor does not get credit for the Spanish class but does earn high school credit for serving as a student assistant to the class. This student has been trained by the general and special educators to demonstrate specific prompts that are the most effective for Estrella without over-supporting her. This student also is responsible for gathering data on Estrella's specific goals and reporting back to both teachers.

During the large group review, Estrella sits next to a student who is a high achiever and benefits from the support from this student. When the teacher asks a review question, the student will raise her hand if she knows the answer and also whispers to Estrella to identify a certain word or phrase in English. Estrella is to look at her three picture/word cards and move her hand to the correct one. When Estrella has made her choice (e.g., by putting her fist on one picture/word card), the peer tutor will gesture to the teacher who may or may not decide to call on her. If she is called on, the student next to her will state in English which one she chose and then will be expected to also respond in Spanish. If incorrect in her selection, the teacher will give her feedback and ask for another student to respond. Many students make mistakes and receive similar feedback, so Estrella is not singled out as the only one not knowing the answer.

The peer tutor and others who work directly with Estrella have learned a systematic prompting strategy of most-to-least prompts to teach her new vocabulary words when others are also learning new content. During this part of the large group instruction when the teacher is presenting new information, two quite different pictured representations are placed in front of Estrella, and the correct option is tapped and labeled or described as Estrella's arms is guided toward this option with a prompt to her elbow. When vocabulary words are reviewed at the beginning of each lesson, the support person will present two pictorial options and wait for a few seconds to see if Estrella starts to identify the correct word. If not, then those words will be used in further instruction.

During those times of the class when students are working individually or in pairs to practice their skills, much more attention and time is paid to helping Estrella understand the vocabulary and how to use it. Each new picture/word card is shown to her, and its label in English is given as well as what the word means and how it is used. Examples related to Estrella's life are provided. For example, if the word is *house* (*casa* in Spanish), then the picture is shown to her, pointing out features of a house, that it is where people live (sleep, eat, play), and that she lives in a house as well. To check for comprehension, the peer tutor will read simple sentences, omitting the last word so that Estrella has the opportunity to choose the correct vocabulary word (e.g., Estrella lives in a nice pink _____). The vocabulary Estrella is learning is used on her communication displays and in other class subjects.

Large Group Instruction—Elementary School

The first graders in Ms. Pierce's class are studying different authors and their writing styles. One author being studied is Laura Joffe Numeroff, who wrote a series of books based on amusing contingencies such as *If You Give a Mouse a Cookie*, *If You Give a Pig a Pancake*, and *If You Give a Moose a Muffin*. These popular books for young readers can be used to help children predict outcomes as well as learn a specific writing style by a given author. Ms. Pierce uses a Big Book to read to the entire class as a group, with the students sitting on a rug around her. She asks students to identify where they would find the author of the story, the illustrator, and what these terms mean. As she reads the story, she stops frequently to ask the group questions about what they are hearing, make predictions using pictorial cues, and learn new vocabulary. Standards being addressed include but are not limited to the following: identify the author and illustrator and the roles of each; identify the main idea of a story; make predictions based on evidence; and with assistance, make inferences and draw conclusions about setting and plot based on evidence. Students must be quiet and pay attention, raising their hands to ask questions or respond to questions from the teacher. Following the large group reading of the story, Ms. Pierce has the students create their own stories based on this writing style.

Bashir, a first grader in this class, enjoys stories but due to his blindness, misses out on the colorful illustrations. Although Bashir has a lot to say, he is nonverbal and uses objects and parts of objects as well as facial expressions and vocalizations to send his messages. Bashir is positioned on the floor very close to the teacher so that she can touch him at times to maintain his attention. Family members and other members of the team have gathered various objects that relate to the story as well as those that do not relate (distracters). A peer in his class has a pet mouse and that has been brought to the class for Bashir to understand what a mouse is—its size, how it feels, moves, smells, and sounds it makes. He has been told that the mouse in the story is not real and that mice really don't speak. As the story progresses, Bashir is shown various objects that go with the mouse's requests. Many of these are common objects that Bashir has encountered before. Objects are held on a simple tray in front of Bashir who feels these objects and responds to teacher questions by touching or grasping one of the options. A parent volunteer sits close to Bashir, but to the side, so that she doesn't obscure their visual access to the Big Book. This parent will repeat the question asked by the teacher to Bashir and guide his hands with a finger under his right wrist to each object while labeling them. Then she'll return his arm to midline, remind him of the question, and ask him to touch the object that is his choice. What he chooses can respond to the teacher's question regarding what is a certain vocabulary word or what the students predict will happen in the story. When a question is asked that has a correct response, the number of items placed before Bashir are reduced in number to two or three so he has less to remember and a better chance of choosing the correct item. When it is time to write their own stories, Bashir is given a prewritten form with fill in the blank options. The parent volunteer reads the story to him and offers him various object choices to make his selection. She provides the same physical cue on his wrist as previously stated. She writes in his choices as he selects them and then reads the entire story to him when they are finished. As Bashir becomes accustomed to this type of prompting, the person supporting him will repeat the teacher's question but fade the wrist prompt to his forearm and then to a nudge of his elbow. The goal is for Bashir to hear the teacher's questions and touch the correct answer without physical prompts.

Large Group Instruction—12th-Grade English Literature

In Ms. Jacobs' 12th-grade English literature class, students are studying the plays of William Shakespeare. Ms. Jacobs typically offers some preview information to the whole class, discusses Elizabethan style of English, and asks the class to compare different scenes to their current experiences. Then students get into groups of five to work on various scenes that they will enact for the class.

During the large group instruction and reading of *Romeo and Juliet*, Cody receives support from a peer tutor. (A special educator and speech-language pathologist also support on other days of the week.) As the play is discussed, the peer tutor interprets the story for Cody using small paper figures of key characters and focuses on relevant vocabulary such as *boy, girl, love, mother, father, friends, party, dance,* and so on. The peer tutor uses the paper figures to act out the action and writes out related simple sentences. The tutor also encourages Cody to use the figures of key characters to act out a scene with him since he particularly likes to manipulate items while he is learning. Cody has some letter recognition and knows some letter and sound associations, so he is asked by the peer tutor to identify some of the words in sentences he's written. At times, the teacher will direct simple questions to Cody, such as "How did one of the men get badly hurt?" and Cody will respond by acting out the swordplay. He also raises the paper figures to respond to questions related to specific characters.

When students break into groups to work on their various scenes, Cody is given an active role that involves a few lines that he says using a small voice output device. Cody's own speech is very difficult to understand, so the voice output device is used to more clearly support his efforts. Cody particularly enjoys using props (such as fake swords, masks) to engage him more in the activity.

When Cody is working on recognizing the vocabulary words that relate to the play during large group instruction, the person providing support asks him to identify a specific word (e.g., dance) from four options. He is given three seconds to find the word and then is shown the correct word (if he didn't identify it correctly). The letters in the word are pointed to as they are pronounced to help him decode the word. An effort is made to ask him to identify the same word at least three times per class as it naturally emerges during the discussion of the play (not three times in a row). Constant time delay of this nature has been effectively used with Cody in other lessons and seems to be effective during this large group lesson as well.

■ PAIRED INSTRUCTION

Considerable research has investigated the effect of students working in pairs to enhance both students' learning (see Carter et al., 2009). In this arrangement students are paired with another student as determined by the teacher to learn new skills, review skills, work cooperatively to complete projects, and study for exams. Classwide Peer Tutoring (Greenwood, Arreaga-Mayer, Utley, Gavin, & Terry, 2001) represents one type of peer buddy learning where all students in a class are engaged in a cooperative learning arrangement with another student. The teacher can decide how long specific students will be paired together during the academic year and will change the pairings based on various factors. The following serve as examples of paired instruction.

Paired Instruction—Second Grade

Mrs. Henney's second-grade class is studying plants and plant life in science. The text has many colorful pictures, which help a number of students in the class, especially those who are English language learners. Mrs. Henney makes frequent use of buddy learning—pairing students to work together—and the class has shown steady progress. Students get materials from a side table and then get with their partner to follow the directions and prepare their seeds in dirt, water, write their names on tape and add to the cup, and find a location on the windowsill for their plant. Then they complete a worksheet, which requires students to read and fill in missing words in the two paragraphs on plants.

Rika, a student with severe intellectual and physical disabilities, works with her partner, Shana, to complete the activity. Shana holds up the pictorial and written directions for Rika to see while the teacher goes over the activity with the class. Then she asks Rika if she wants her to push her wheelchair to get the materials, and Rika smiles or slightly nods her head to say yes. A list of materials with accompanying pictures is used to help Rika identify what will be needed. As the two girls collect their materials and put them on Rika's wheelchair tray, the general educator shows Rika two items and asks her which one is needed (one is offered as a distracter). Rika is to look at the item on the list of materials (e.g., dirt and not an eraser). Mrs. Henney models the first two options for Shana, who then asks Rika the same question for the last two items. If Rika looks at the irrelevant item, Shana will tell her that it's not correct and shows her the list of needed items. Mrs. Henney will point to the picture or word of the item that she needs, and Shana will repeat the question, holding up the two items. After four seconds of no response, or if Rika looks at the incorrect item, Shana will put the correct item in front of her and tell her what it is and that it is what they need. Mrs. Henney will hold up the list and point out the similarity between the picture and the item to help Rika make this association.

When the two girls follow the written and pictorial directions to plant their seeds, Shana performs the physical steps (since Rika does not possess the physical ability to assist), while Rika is asked which step to perform. She does this by looking at the appropriate item. For instance, if the step involves filling a paper cup with dirt, Shana holds up the dirt and a marker or some other distracter and asks Rika which one goes in the cup. With the pictorial directions supported vertically near Rika, she is to check the directions and then look at the correct item. If she looks at the incorrect item, Shana will wave the correct item in front of her, correct her verbally, and then perform the step. Mrs. Henney checks on all groups of students, and when she gets to Rika and Shana, she makes sure Rika is being asked each step. She'll also point out the similarity between picture and object as well as the label under the picture to draw her attention.

The same procedure is used when the girls need to complete the worksheet on the science activity. Shana will do the actual writing for both girls, but Rika will be asked questions during this aspect of the task so that her opinion is included. For instance, when the worksheet calls for the rationale for putting the plant in a certain spot in the room, Shana will show Rika a picture of a window with bright sunlight coming through and a picture of a box and ask her where they put their plant. If Rika looks at the picture of the window, Shana confirms her decision and adds that plants need light, not dark places. If Rika makes a mistake, Shana will tell her why it's wrong and show her the correct answer.

Paired Instruction—11th-Grade English Literature

This English literature class is studying poetry and the conventions used by various authors to create a very personalized tone for their poems. The class is also exploring the use of more sophisticated vocabulary words to more precisely convey mood and tone. In particular, the standard being addressed for this lesson targets the elements of literature and requires students to identify, analyze, and apply knowledge of the structures and elements of literature. Students are to demonstrate the ability to evaluate the authors' use of literary elements, such as theme (moral, lesson, view, or comment on life). Mrs. Holbrook is the English literature teacher and makes use of buddy learning or paired instruction in her class to assist students in their productivity and learn about giving peer feedback. She typically pairs students for nine to ten weeks, depending on the activities to be completed and how well students work together. For this lesson, student pairs have selected different poets to study and present their findings on their author's use of language to the class.

One eleventh grader in this class, Beth, is learning to read text at approximately a second-grade level and to express herself more effectively. She has a moderate level of intellectual impairment and is fairly shy with others. Working with one peer is much easier for her than working in a larger group given her shyness and tendency to withdraw from group involvement.

Beth is working with Janet, a classmate who does not have special needs but often struggles with her own academic achievement. The special educator, Ms. Brodsky, provides support to this pair of students, as well as other pairs.

Janet and Beth are researching Walt Whitman and how he conveyed his point of view in his poems. Ms. Brodsky helps both students interpret the poems, asking them what they think certain vocabulary means. Janet will read a poem and then ask Beth what emotion he's trying to express. Beth will express her opinion, saying that he's sad, happy, hopeful, angry, or being silly. If no response after a three-second pause, Ms. Brodsky will show her these emotion words written on cards and ask her to select the best one for the poem. Janet must decide if she agrees with Beth or not and then tell her why and make note of representative phrases that support their decisions. She explains what these phrases mean to Beth. Ms. Brodsky will write these explanations out for Beth using words at her reading level while Janet makes notes for the presentation using the poet's actual words. If Ms. Brodsky is helping other students, Janet writes the phrases for Beth to read. For example, in the poem, "O Captain! My Captain!" the line "The port is near, the bells I hear, the people all exulting" might be explained to Beth as "The boat is coming back home and everyone is happy." Rephrasing different lines and defining certain words seems to help Janet's understanding of Whitman's use of language as well.

Beth is to read the short phrase. If she doesn't read the words, Ms. Brodsky or Janet points to the first letter and ask her to think of the sound it makes. If this doesn't help her to identify the word, she is given the first sound(s). If this prompt doesn't help her, then the word is read to her. Once she has finished the phrase, she is asked to repeat it more quickly for fluency and enhanced comprehension. When her partner has written several points to make regarding the poet and his use of language, using actual phrases, she asks Beth if she agrees or wants to make changes or additions. Janet may read other poems and ask Beth if they should be added to their presentation.

When they practice their presentation, Beth will read the title with support from Janet and will state a certain tone or viewpoint held by the poet. Beth reads this information with Janet or Ms. Brodsky using least-to-most prompts as described earlier, and Janet will add to each introduction by Beth with examples from Whitman's poems. In this manner, Beth works on her verbal expressions, vocabulary development, and reading skills, while meeting class expectations.

Paired Instruction—Third Grade

Toni's third-grade class is studying Mexico for their social studies unit. They have been reading about Mexico in their textbook, and class time essentially involves working with a partner to investigate various aspects of the country. Mr. Felix, the third-grade teacher, has shared some information on geography, size, culture, language, customs, food, and music and has let various pairs of students further investigate a topic using books, travel pamphlets, and the Internet. Mr. Felix offers individual attention to the paired students to guide their learning. A culminating activity will be for all students to make short presentations to the class on their chosen topic.

Toni is working with a favorite classmate, Chloe. Toni loves bright colors and is learning to identify pictures that are enlarged to account for her visual impairment. She is very expressive and usually has a big smile that draws others to her. Toni uses a wheelchair and is learning to use an adapted keyboard to access the computer.

Since Toni loves music and often attends for longer periods of time if she can listen to music during a lesson, Toni and Chloe opted to investigate the music of Mexico. A parent of a classmate who used to live in Mexico has offered to help the girls. This mother brings in some CDs of Mexican singing artists as well as some Mexican rhythm instruments. Having the actual tactile items to relate to pictorial information helps Toni to understand what is being conveyed.

Toni's objectives for this lesson are to differentiate Mexican style of music from other forms, identify Mexican rhythm instruments from other kinds of instruments by the sound they make, recognize what instrument produces what sound, and which adjective best describes the music (e.g., happy, fast, slow, sad). Her partner's objectives involve investigative research, use of different media, comparing and contrasting Mexican music with other types of music, especially Mariachi music, and writing and oral skills involved in the final presentation.

Various sounds from CDs and instruments, the actual items, as well as verbal and physical prompts will be used to help Toni reach her objectives. The person supporting Toni will also guide Chloe in her research and will encourage interactions between the two girls as needed. Chloe has learned to seek Toni's input on a regular basis, so little external prompting is typically needed. When Chloe finds and plays Mexican music on the Internet, she tells Toni to listen and will ask her if she likes it or not. Toni will typically respond with a facial expression. Chloe will show Toni maracas and xylophone, both of which she plays and labels. She'll tell Toni that the maracas are typically what she will hear in Mexican music.

While Chloe works on the computer searching for information, the vision teacher teaches Toni the information she needs to learn. She plays a CD or shakes the rhythm instruments and tells Toni what she is doing. She describes the music (fast, upbeat, slow, etc.). She repeats this several times, asking Toni to use the instruments or use her switch to turn on the CD player. She will also ask Toni to play the rhythm instruments fast and then slow. She guides Toni's hand under the wrist while saying fast or slow. When Chloe plays some music and asks her if it's fast or slow, the vision teacher will give Toni an instrument and ask her to show Chloe if it's *fast* or *slow*. She waits five seconds, then only using her thumb and forefinger, she moves Toni's hand with the instrument either fast or slow depending on the music and states what it is. She also does this if Toni shook the instrument, but the beat was incorrect. She intersperses this instruction with instruction on whether music is Mexican or of another country and what sounds belong to what instruments. She tells Toni the correct information and then models the correct response making the selection using the actual items (CDs or instruments). For example, she plays a CD of guitar music and presents Toni with a guitar and a small drum. She asks Toni to listen and then to touch the instrument making the music. She waits five seconds for a response and then tells her that it's the guitar and points to it. She encourages Toni to strum the guitar before moving on to another question. She will use a fading procedure of first slightly moving the correct item closer to her and then waiting for five seconds before telling her. When Toni is successful at this level of prompting, the teacher will fade to asking her about a characteristic of the correct answer (e.g., which one has strings) and then wait five seconds before telling her the answer. They then practice with different types of music and instruments. A small picture of the Mexican flag is placed on the Mexican CD, and she is learning to recognize that flag as Mexican versus another country's flag. The vocabulary she is learning (e.g., flag, fast, slow, loud, soft, music, happy) are words that she will also encounter in other subjects/activities (e.g., Pledge of Allegiance, PE, music) and that she will need to use on her augmentative communication device when interacting with others.

■ GENERALIZATION OF SKILLS TAUGHT

The situations described earlier for different students, grade levels, subject matter, and teaching arrangement are specific to the lesson being taught. However, the skills learned should be applicable (or somewhat applicable) to many different lessons. The concepts, vocabulary, reading and math skills, and so on taught in one class or subject should not be restricted to this one learning environment. Skills learned in one class must also be taught across different people, different situations, and different environments. If skills identified are important to teach the student in one class, they should also be important in other classrooms or environments (e.g., lunchroom, playground, library). Identifying the big ideas or major concepts of a lesson should have broader application than the one lesson or unit currently being taught.

The transfer of knowledge and skills to different environments cannot be left to chance for students with moderate to severe intellectual disabilities but must be explicitly taught (Albin & Horner, 1988; Westling & Fox, 2009). The student needs to be taught how, when, and where the knowledge can be applied. For example, when learning about astronomy in science class, a student also needs to be taught to go outside at night (not during the day) to look for stars. A TV science program on astronomy also can support the transfer of knowledge from school to home. Such information can be incorporated into conversation books about students' interests.

Vocabulary words learned during a language arts class may be the same words studied for spelling and may be very important words to identify on an augmentative communication device. The words *boys* and *girls,* for example, may appear in a story being read in class, appear on the restroom doors, can occur in math as part of story problems, and can emerge during a social studies unit. The same can be said for the recognition or sequencing of numbers. They may be targeted in a math class but can certainly be an important aspect of stories being read in language arts, appear on doors of the school, appear on clocks, and appear in science and social studies depending on the topic. By highlighting similar information across classrooms and subjects, the student has more opportunities to practice these skills and more opportunities to respond to similar stimuli but in different environments and activities.

SUMMARY ■

Specific and systematic instruction is quite possible to provide within general education classrooms and is a necessary component of successful inclusion. Students with moderate and severe disabilities do not leave behind their unique needs when entering a typical classroom. They still need supports to learn. Carefully identifying important skills to teach a given student within core content for all students is the first step. Then systematically providing prompts, feedback, and a fading strategy to help the student master identified skills needs to occur.

Different students require different prompting strategies depending on physical, sensory, and cognitive strengths as well as the demands of the task. In addition, the teaching style and arrangements used during a given lesson have an impact on prompting strategies to use. The different scenarios described in this chapter covered a wide age range, ability level, and subject matter to show systematic instruction in general education classrooms. To ensure that the skills learned in these classrooms remain in the student's repertoire and are generalized to different environments where needed requires further instruction as well as opportunities for practice.

Learning from different instructors also is important in the education of students with moderate or severe disabilities. Students may have several different team members who will share responsibility for their learning. Therefore, Chapter 5 will discuss the potential members of the team who may be providing systematic instruction in different activities and lessons. When many different individuals are involved in instruction, collaboration and cooperation are important considerations. Teaming of this nature and the need for training will also be discussed.

5

It Takes a Village

Teaching as a Collaborative Effort

KEY CONCEPTS

- ⊙━ Each student will learn from many different "teachers" throughout each school day.

- ⊙━ Peers can provide valuable assistance in supporting their classmate.

- ⊙━ Team collaboration is a critical aspect of effective inclusive practices.

- ⊙━ Ongoing training of team members is necessary to ensure effectiveness and consistency.

Students with severe disabilities will have many different teachers in the course of a school year or even a single school day. While consistency with one teacher may support student learning, learning how to work with different people should help with generalization of important skills that result in a more flexible individual. Instead of becoming overly dependent on one person to provide instruction, students will need to learn how to adjust to different teaching styles and techniques, as well as tone of voice and other personal characteristics. Flexibility in receiving support from different individuals in school may lead to the ability to receive support from different individuals as an adult (e.g., coworker, roommates, or employers).

This chapter will identify and describe the potential teachers of a student with moderate to severe intellectual disabilities in general education classes and different ways to make the most use of each team member. Adults serving in different professional capacities as well as the use of peers will be discussed. All potential instructors will need to know systematic instructional procedures so as to ensure consistency across teachers. Furthermore, the essential goal of helping students to generalize what they have learned across different settings may be helped with the use of different individuals providing instruction.

■ THE EXPECTATION OF TEAM COLLABORATION

For students to be successfully included, team members must work in a cooperative and collaborative manner (Hunt, Soto, Maier, Muller, & Goetz, 2002; Snell & Janney, 2005; Thousand, Villa, & Nevin, 2002). Single teachers isolated in classrooms should not have to struggle alone to meet the needs of a widely diverse student population. Recognizing that everyone on the team is needed and can contribute unique expertise and experiences to the student's educational program is the recommended practice.

The complexity of teaching students with very different abilities and needs requires a collaborative approach in which different team members assume a shared responsibility for initial assessment, planning, instruction, gathering materials to create curriculum adaptations, and progress monitoring. Teams may be comprised of a few team members (e.g., general educator, special educator, family members, and paraprofessional), or they may be quite large (e.g., the individuals listed above as well as speech-language pathologist, occupational therapist, physical therapist, behavioral specialist, vision teacher, deaf and hard-of-hearing teacher, health care professional, administrator, and psychologist). Of course friends of the student will also be on the team, contributing input from a younger perspective. Coordinated input from all of these individuals (and more) is needed to develop the most cohesive and efficient program to meet the student's needs.

■ TEAM MEMBERS INVOLVED IN INSTRUCTION

Every school, whether elementary, middle, or high school, has numerous adults and peers who may serve in the capacity of teacher at some time during the school day. Some of these individuals are credentialed teachers, while others provide support with less formal training. For instance, the school cafeteria worker may ask a student to point to one of two food options as she goes through the lunch line. The librarian can read a story to a student and ask questions related to the story, with the student pointing to pictures to respond. The principal can greet a student and then wait for that student to respond to the greeting with a look or wave. Such natural learning opportunities interspersed throughout the day for any given student can support student progress in acquiring these skills.

While many different individuals can and do provide instruction to students with moderate to severe disabilities, this chapter will target credentialed teachers, paraprofessionals, related service personnel, and peers. The intent is to show how teaching support can be provided by different people within general education classrooms using a collaborative approach to instruction (Ryndak & Pullen, 2003).

■ CREDENTIALED TEACHERS

To meet the mandate that students have access to highly qualified teachers under the Individuals with Disabilities Education Act (IDEA) and No Child

Left Behind (NCLB), teachers should be credentialed by the state and for the students they are teaching. They should know about the population of students they are to serve and be well versed in recommended practices in their field. Such expectations hold for both general educators and special educators. Both are needed in the education of students with moderate to severe intellectual disabilities. Unfortunately, there exists a severe shortage in highly qualified special educators (McLeskey & Billingsley, 2008; Rosenberg, Boyer, Sindelar, & Misra, 2007). Boe and Cook (2006) found through a review of the literature that fewer individuals are entering the field of special education, forcing school districts to hire teachers who are not fully qualified. Carlson and Billingsley (2001) found that about one in every ten practicing special educators was not minimally qualified for the position.

Yet the importance of highly skilled and knowledgeable teachers is clear. Mainger, Deshler, Coleman, Kozleski, and Rodriquez-Walling (2003) write that a quality teacher is the single most important factor for a student's learning. Engaging teachers are described as warm, supportive, student-centered, intense, flexible, responsive, and are recognized for keeping students on task, providing direct and systematic instruction, supporting peer interactions, and working to enhance student autonomy (Seo, Brownell, Bishop, & Dingle, 2008). Therefore, effort must be made by every teacher, new to the field or more experienced, to continue to upgrade his or her skill level by engaging in lifelong learning. Teachers are encouraged to find the time to read the latest research in their field, attend trainings to acquire new skills, and obtain feedback on their teaching performance from administrators, mentor teachers, or peers. Considerable information also exists on the Internet, and teachers interested in gaining new ideas for lesson plans, material adaptations, classroom management, and so on can make good use of this resource. For example, see www.edhelper.com, www.enchantedlearning.com, www.starfall.com, www.brainpop.com, www.cellsalive.com, and www.cast.org for support in providing engaging and interactive instruction for students in different subject areas.

COTEACHING ■

Increased emphasis has been placed on teachers (both general and special educators) for sharing the responsibility of teaching all students in general education classrooms (Cramer, 2006; Friend & Cook, 2007; Winn & Blanton, 2005). Instead of teaching homogeneous groups of students on their own, general and special educators bring their knowledge, skills, and expertise to the classroom where students of widely diverse abilities and needs learn together. By pooling their skills and providing support for each other, teachers can address the needs of a variety of students. Instead of one teacher in a room with a certain number of students, two teachers (one general educator and one special educator) coteach in one classroom to meet the learning needs of a variety of students with and without disabilities (Friend & Cook, 2007; Keefe, Moore, & Duff, 2004). Coteaching also can occur with a general educator and a paraprofessional

(Nevin, Villa, & Thousand, 2008) or with a general educator and a related service provider (e.g., speech-language pathologist).

Many different options exist for coteaching to occur (Cramer, 2006; Friend & Cook, 2007; Keefe et al., 2004; Villa, Thousand, & Nevin, 2008). Teachers can divide the class, and each teaches the same content but to fewer students. As another option, one teacher can lead the class while the other supports. In this scenario, the general educator typically teaches the lesson to the class while the special educator supports those students with disabilities. The general educator assumes the role as the primary teacher of the class. In a more equitable framework, two teachers can alternate teaching content to all students, assuming responsibility for different aspects of the lesson. For example, one teacher can present information from the perspective of the North, and one teacher can present information from the perspective of the South during a lesson on the Civil War. Teachers can divide the class and teach sections of different but complementary information. For example, one teacher can teach about different species of animals and their characteristics while the other teacher shares information on each species' habitat. Creativity of those sharing in the coteaching situation can produce a myriad of different teaching arrangements that can be used depending on the intent of the lesson, the content to be taught, the physical arrangement of the class, and the strengths and needs of the students in the class.

Despite several different options for employing coteaching, research suggests that few teachers take advantage of the various options (Scruggs, Mastropieri, & McDuffie, 2007). The majority of teachers appear to rely on the option of the general educator assuming responsibility for the primary teaching, while the special educator supports individual students with disabilities (Scruggs et al., 2007). This situation may be particularly difficult for teachers at the high school level (Keefe & Moore, 2004). One major problem with such an arrangement is that the general educator may never get to interact directly with the student having the most intensive special education needs and may never clearly understand how that student learns or what skills are being acquired. Dividing the class into those "belonging" to the general educator and those "belonging" to the special educator does not lead to the type of learning community that is desired. Sharing the learning responsibilities for all students as well as rewards that come from student progress is preferred. The knowledge and skills of both teachers can be shared by all students to help them learn. Furthermore, both teachers can acquire valuable skills to help them improve their teaching with a much broader range of students.

While coteaching strives to share the teaching responsibility for all students, it should not interfere with qualified teachers working directly with students having the greatest need. Rather, the various arrangements possible within the coteaching paradigm should shift according to the needs of certain students who require extensive support at times. For example, it *may* be the best solution at some point in the lesson to have the general educator discussing a subject with the entire class, while the special educator provides direct instruction to the student with severe and multiple disabilities to keep that student with the group but learning related yet meaningful material (e.g., relevant vocabulary).

SUPPORTING GENERAL ■
EDUCATION OWNERSHIP

One aim of inclusive education is to support general education ownership for students with disabilities and in particular, those with moderate and severe disabilities (Broer, Doyle, & Giangreco, 2005; Ghere & York-Barr, 2007; Giangreco, Yuan, McKenzie, Cameron, & Fialka, 2005). Assuming responsibility for the learning of all students in the class helps to prevent a potential division that may occur between "my" students (those without disabilities) and "your" students (with disabilities). True membership occurs for the students with moderate to severe disabilities when the teacher of the class assumes responsibility for the education of the students and does not expect special education staff to meet the student's educational needs (Ghere & York-Barr, 2007). While the teacher may need considerable support from other team members (special educator, paraprofessional, physical therapist, speech-language pathologist, etc.), he or she should play a major role in including the student, making the content accessible and expecting the student to learn.

Students with moderate or severe disabilities should appear on the general education teacher's class list, and their unique learning needs should be considered at the onset of lesson planning. When general educators relinquish their responsibility to special education staff, they may fail to understand how the student learns and may not acquire the necessary skills to be effective working with their students who have these challenging disabilities. Time spent working directly with the student (as much as the direct instruction spent with each student in the class) helps the teacher to learn how best to interact (e.g., make use of the student's communication system, use prompts effectively, provide sufficient wait time) as well as what to expect from the student. The teacher also learns how to deal with potential behavioral challenges that may arise. For example, the teacher can learn to speak directly to the student (and not the support person), telling him or her to stop the disrupting behavior and letting him or her know what is expected. Although this may not be effective, it cues the support person to move in, redirect the student, and support the teacher's class management strategies. Furthermore, the teacher's interactions with the student help other students in the class perceive the target student as an accepted member of the class and provide them with strategies to use when they interact.

When general education teachers are familiar with their students' health care issues (e.g., seizures, tubal feedings, severe allergies, asthma), it provides one more highly qualified individual on the team who can respond quickly and effectively in a medical emergency. The safety of the student is thus further enhanced. Although general education ownership does not mean that the teacher is solely responsible for all aspects of the target student's education, it does increase the number of team members who can act knowledgeably in a variety of situations. In addition, the skills learned for one student with moderate to severe disabilities can be applied to other students with less severe disabilities. For example, when one teacher had a student who was gifted and also had seizures, she was able to apply her knowledge gained from interacting with a previous student who was blind, had severe physical and intellectual disabilities, and experienced numerous seizures. Learning about the use of wheelchairs, medical issues, and a variety of physical accommodations can assist in supporting a wide range of students in general education classrooms. Such shared knowledge makes all students with health issues safer.

■ PARAPROFESSIONALS AS TEACHERS

Paraprofessionals may not meet the same expectations for highly qualified teachers as specified by the Individuals with Disabilities Education Improvement Act (2004), but they can provide valuable assistance to the educational team, performing a number of vital activities (see Table 5.1). Paraprofessionals can receive sufficient training and guidance to gain the skills needed to be effective educators of students with moderate to severe disabilities in general education classes (Causton-Theoharis, Giangreco, Doyle, & Vadasy, 2007; Doyle, 2008). In fact, paraprofessionals often assume the role of primary instructor for students with moderate to severe intellectual disabilities in typical classrooms (Dymond & Russell, 2004; Ghere & York-Barr, 2007; Giangreco, Halvorsen, Doyle, & Broer, 2004). This situation can be problematic if paraprofessionals are not adequately trained and feel confident in their interactions with students. Giangreco et al. (2005) warn that while helpful, paraprofessionals often are the least trained member of the team. Pairing a student with the most complex learning needs with a full-time paraprofessional can lead to unintended consequences such as stigmatization, separation from teacher and peers, greater dependence, and potentially negative behavior (Giangreco et al., 2005). A legal analysis of educational issues surrounding the use of paraprofessionals revealed the pros and cons of such assistance for students (Etscheidt, 2005). Just

Table 5.1 Potential Uses of a Paraprofessional in an Inclusive Classroom

Support a small group of students with or without severe disabilities.
Direct individual student's attention to the teacher during large group instruction (those with and without disabilities).
Support the students as a paired team with one student having severe disabilities.
Coteach with the general educator by playing a particular role or asking questions of the teacher (as a model to the class).
Lead the entire class in an exercise giving the teacher time to work more closely with the student with severe disabilities.
Make materials in preparation for an upcoming activity during an activity where a peer provides support.
Help provide individual support to all students during independent work.
Monitor entire class while teacher is out of room for brief periods of time.

assigning a paraprofessional to a student does not necessarily mean quality support. Paraprofessionals need to be trained so that their support of a student when needed will be beneficial.

While paraprofessionals may assume several different tasks in a school day, the direct teaching of students is a vital responsibility. Paraprofessionals are essential supports in inclusive education where students on a teacher's designated caseload could be learning in several different classrooms concurrently (e.g., a five-year-old in kindergarten, two eight-year-olds in third grade, a nine-year-old in fourth grade, and two 10-year-olds in fifth grade, etc.). Furthermore, a paraprofessional should not be the sole support for one student but should be assigned to the classroom teacher and the students in that class for a specified period of time (Carter & Kennedy, 2006; Conroy, Asmus, Ladwig, Sellers, & Valcante, 2004). In this way, neither students nor paraprofessionals become overly dependent on just one person and learn to work effectively with a number of different individuals. Paraprofessionals must implement various lessons in different grades with different students under the direction of a qualified special educator and classroom teacher. See inset on A Day in the Life of a Paraprofessional at the middle school level. Sufficient guidance and feedback is needed to ensure that paraprofessionals know when and how to engage in systematic instruction with individual students.

A Day in the Life of a Paraprofessional

Elissa is a paraprofessional at a middle school—Grades 6 through 8. She works with a special educator and several general educators, as well as a number of related service providers. The following depicts a typical day for Elissa.

7:30 a.m. Arrival at school and brief informational meeting with special educator or general educator for the first period.

8:00 a.m. First period: Social Studies, seventh grade—Ms. Dermott's class. Support the teacher and entire class while providing extra attention as needed for Clay, who has severe autism.

8:55 a.m. Second period: Language Arts, sixth grade—Coteach with general educator, Ms. Sweeney. Support individual students during independent seatwork. Share support for Caren, who has Down syndrome, and Dayton, who has severe and multiple disabilities, with Ms. Sweeney.

9:50 a.m.—Nutrition Break. Take a 15-minute break and then assist Angelo, who has severe intellectual and physical disabilities, to PE.

10:15 a.m. Third period: PE—Mr. Kim's ninth-grade class. Help pair up students for exercise. Provide extra model for Angelo to do adapted exercises (mainly arms). Direct all students' attention to Mr. Kim when he is giving out information to the class. Make sure one student with Down syndrome has a peer buddy to follow during softball practice. Work with Angelo on standing in a stander, waving a pom-pom for cheering, keeping score with manipulatives, and practice throwing a softball on the side with a teammate.

(Continued)

(Continued)

11:05 a.m. Fourth period: Math, seventh grade. Monitor whole class doing independent work while general educator, Mr. Adams, works with one to two students at a time on specific issues. Make sure Clay has his adapted work and is getting assistance as needed.

11:55 a.m. Lunch and break. Support two students to eat and socialize with their peers. Take a 30-minute lunch break.

12:55 p.m. Fifth period: Science, seventh grade. Support Ms. Daniels by providing aid to three small groups doing lab work. Alternate between Clay's group and Manny's group giving direct instruction. (Manny has moderate intellectual disabilities.)

1:50 p.m. Sixth period: Drama, eighth and ninth grades. Work with a small group of students under the general educator's direction. One group includes Heather, who has Williams syndrome, and one group includes Angelo, who has severe and multiple disabilities. Trade off with the drama teacher.

2:40–3:10 p.m. Debrief with special educator or attend a seventh-grade team meeting.

■ RELATED SERVICE PROVIDERS

Another source of teaching expertise lies in the availability of various related service providers (e.g., speech-language pathologists, occupational therapists, vision teachers, physical therapists, behavior specialists, etc.). These highly trained and skilled professionals may serve on a given student's education team, providing both direct and indirect support. Instead of removing individual students or small groups of students with similar disabilities from class to work on specific therapy objectives, related services providers can support the student within the general education classroom to perform critical skills (Barnes, 2003; Cloninger, 2004; Cross, Traub, Hutter-Pishgaki, & Shelton, 2004). For instance, instead of taking a student from a fifth-grade classroom to a special small room to work on fine motor skills in an isolated context, the occupational therapist (OT) joins the fifth-grade lesson in progress and teaches the student to make use of fine motor skills with or without accommodations that are required to participate in the lesson (e.g., signing one's name with a signature stamp, turning pages in a book, pointing to pictures in response to comprehension questions, sharpening a pencil). In this way, more support is added to the general education classroom and the skills targeted by the therapists blend into the instruction. A therapist also can observe a student in a very natural and daily environment and determine where the student will need extra support and instruction. The concern about generalization of isolated fine motor skills to an activity where it is needed is less of an issue. In addition, the student does not miss any of the lesson, which is particularly critical for a student who may need more time to complete the work, not less. For example, general educators reported the preference for pull-in related services so that students with autism who were nonverbal would not miss any of their lessons (Finke, McNaughton, & Drager, 2009).

Although interested in a certain area of need for a student (e.g., vision or hearing loss, postural control, limited hand use, minimal communication with peers), related services providers can address these needs as part of a typical class lesson on any grade-level subject matter. Their focus is to improve a specific difficulty within a common task that all students are involved in. For example, a speech-language pathologist focusing on enhanced communication skills of a particular student can assist the student while he is responding to peers during a small group activity, learning to initiate an interaction with peers during transition times, requesting help when needed, responding to a teacher's question, or whatever else is required during the typical lesson. Furthermore, they can also support the learning of targeted academic skills, such as reading, writing, math, science, and so on.

An added benefit of pull-in therapy services is that these highly trained professionals can make suggestions to the teacher that could potentially help a number of students, whether or not they are in specific need of therapy. For example, Downing and Peckham-Hardin (2007) found that teachers appreciated the added information given them by therapists working in general education classrooms. Suggestions regarding pencil grips, seating cushions, height of seats to desks, behavioral interventions, and appropriate lighting were perceived to support students in the class who did not have disabilities. In this manner, the use of specialists for a few students benefits a much broader group of students.

PARENT VOLUNTEERS ■

While not every parent (or grandparent) has the time to volunteer in the classroom, those that do can provide quality support for a teacher. Parent volunteers are most common in the younger elementary grades (kindergarten through second grades), but such volunteers can be found in older grades as well. Most parents volunteer in their own child's class, yet some do volunteer in other classrooms as support for the entire school. While some parents are effective supporting their own child in the classroom, others may be more effective with other children. Some children with moderate to severe intellectual disabilities may find it confusing or distracting to be supported by a relative at school.

Parent volunteers may be used to monitor independent class work, providing assistance as needed, while the general educator works more closely with the student having moderate or severe disabilities. Or a parent volunteer could read a story to the entire class while the teacher works with individual students who need extra help in different areas. Additional support to the classroom should not equate with attaching that support to the student with the most severe disabilities. The teacher can decide what arrangement would be the most helpful to the class as a whole. Parent volunteers also can be very helpful gathering needed materials and helping to make adaptations for some students.

■ PEERS AS TEACHERS

Perhaps the most natural source of teaching support derives from the many same-age peers that abound in any one classroom. While not all students have the skills or the motivation to teach a classmate who has severe disabilities, several will find this to be a very positive pursuit. Since same-age peers without disabilities may see the lesson from a more student-oriented perspective, support from this teaching resource could prove quite beneficial. Hunt, Soto, Maier, Muller, and Goetz (2002) found that students with severe disabilities in general education classrooms made progress in academic responding whether taught by a general educator, special educator, paraprofessional, or another student. Likewise, Carter, Sisco, Melekoglu, and Kurkowski (2007) found that social interactions fared better with peers providing support than when paraprofessionals were involved. Therefore, the use of peers as teachers should not be perceived as a less optimal option. When peers provide support, adults can be freed up to work with other students, thus addressing the individualized needs of all students more effectively.

Figure 5.1 A Fourth Grader Reads to a Classmate

Photographer: Susie Speelman

Classmates can provide support in helping the student with moderate to severe disabilities obtain the necessary materials, open the book to a specific location, find a lunch box, or cue the student to look at the teacher. This type of assistance can be done quickly and need not interfere with the student's own need to stay on task and attend. At other times a student without disabilities may have finished the required work and may choose to volunteer to provide more systematic instruction needed for math problems, reading, writing, or any subject matter, as shown in Figure 5.1. As long as the student's own work is finished, such an arrangement provides the student without disabilities an opportunity to learn how others learn when a disability is present.

Cushing, Clark, Carter, and Kennedy (2005) suggest that two peers assigned to one student with severe disabilities may be more supportive of all three students. Two students without disabilities can troubleshoot areas of need, bounce ideas off one another, and support each other if the student with disabilities is having a difficult time learning and staying on task. Furthermore, two students without disabilities will have more friends in their friendship circles in which to include the student with severe disabilities. Enhancing a student's potential friends is an important goal of inclusive education and interacting with a same-age peer in a social manner can be highly reinforcing for certain students. Figure 5.2 shows two high school students listening to music, which is used as a positive reinforcer for the student with Down syndrome.

Figure 5.2	Two High School Students Listen to Music as a Reward

Photographer: Antonia Pond

For students at the secondary level, earning credit for assuming the role of a teaching assistant may be possible. High school or middle school students may have the opportunity to serve as a teaching assistant as an elective, supporting students in their own schools or going to an elementary school as an assistant. In this position, peers are considered peer tutors and are responsible for providing support in direct instruction, materials accommodations, simplifying concepts to be learned, and collecting data on progress. In this capacity, peers offer an alternative to the heavy reliance on paraprofessionals and other adults to provide instruction (Carter, Cushing, & Kennedy, 2009; Carter, Sisco, et al., 2007; Downing, 2006).

Considerable research has focused on the impact of peers and peer tutors on the learning of their classmates who have moderate to severe disabilities

(Carter & Hughes, 2005; Carter, Cushing, Clark, & Kennedy, 2005; Ohtake, 2003). Benefits have been confirmed for both students involved in this relationship (Carter & Kennedy, 2006; Carter, Sisco, Brown, Brickham, & Al-Khabbaz, 2008; McDonnell, Mathot-Buckner, Thorson, & Fister, 2001). For example, Logan et al. (1998) found that five students with profound levels of disability showed more alert and happy behavioral states when interacting with their peers without disabilities than when educated with students having similar disabilities. Junior high students with moderate to severe disabilities and those without disabilities had higher rates of academic responding (e.g., writing, reading, talking about subject matter) in pre-algebra and history class and less off-task behavior as a result of a classwide peer-tutoring program (McDonnell et al., 2001). Carter and Kennedy (2006) found that when students at risk for academic failure work with a student with severe disabilities, they perform better than if they had done the work alone. See Carter et al. (2009) for an in-depth coverage of the use of peer support strategies.

■ A FEW CAUTIONS WHEN USING PEERS

Using peer support can be quite helpful to students as well as teaching staff, yet some precautions are in order. Supporting a student with moderate to severe disabilities should never take away from students without disabilities completing their own work. A few students may gain such self-esteem from being perceived as a helper that they avoid performing their work, which may be more challenging. They may find it more interesting to work with their classmate who has disabilities than to listen to a teacher, take notes, and respond to questions. Some students develop a pattern of volunteering as a peer tutor to avoid engaging in required class work. Being alert to such possibilities and making sure that one student does not assume the role of sole peer tutor to a classmate is necessary. Under no circumstance should serving as a peer tutor interfere with the tutor's opportunities to learn. Research in this area has demonstrated that involvement with a student with moderate to severe disabilities does not interfere with learning (Carter, Cushing, Clark, & Kennedy, 2005; Idol, 2006; McDonnell et al., 2001). However, recognizing the role of peer tutor as a potential bid to escape challenging curriculum content and instruction is warranted for some students.

Not all students make good peer tutors. Some are not interested in teaching, and some do not have the creativity or initiative to provide the needed adaptations and support. Students must be trained to perform this role and then monitored to ensure that they are performing as desired and the student they are supporting is making the desired and expected progress. Although students should never be forced to serve as peer tutors, care must also be taken in recruitment efforts. Talking to teachers and counselors may help to identify those peers who might best benefit from participating in such a program. See Carter et al. (2009) for specific information on effective means of peer recruitment.

As with adults, unhealthy dependencies can develop between the two students who are often chosen to work together. The goal is not to teach the student with moderate or severe disabilities to work only with one chosen peer but rather to respond to direction and assistance from a number of peers serving in that role. Students are likely to form friendships and special bonds with certain peers, but that should not interfere with the student's ability to work with different classmates or peer tutors. Carter et al. (2009) suggest rotating students so that students with moderate to severe disabilities can get to know many different classmates. Furthermore, if a certain pair of students does not appear to be working well together, regular and customary rotation can handle this issue without drawing negative attention to a student or pair of students.

THE NEED FOR INFORMATION AND TRAINING ■

All members of the educational team and prospective teachers (whether credentialed, nonprofessional, or peer) need to know the goals of inclusive education so that they can support the goals and not hinder them. In other words, they need to know that students are in general education classrooms to be exposed to all aspects of the curriculum, to learn as much as possible within that curriculum, and to engage in peer interactions. Although we want all students to be safe, the primary goal of education is not to shelter and protect students with disabilities and keep them isolated from peers. Team members need to know the importance of accessing the core curriculum and the critical need to adapt the curriculum and teach this to students. Those offering instruction need to know how to task analyze the various steps within lessons, identify potential learning opportunities for those who learn quite differently, identify the big ideas of lessons, and determine what additional materials will be needed to ensure meaningful access. Effective teaching will require that team members know the components of systematic instruction and how to implement it. Each member needs to clearly recognize the skills that are to be taught and the goal for attainment of these skills (i.e., criteria for mastery). The entire team needs to know the specific teaching prompts to be used, the order in which they are to be used, and what to do following a student response (e.g., give corrective feedback, praise, and adjust the learning materials). Furthermore, they need to be consistent in implementing these prompts. It takes considerable skill to know when to move in to work closely with a student and when to back off to allow the student to be more independent. As McLeskey and Billingsley (2008) stress, an inadequately trained or lack of a highly qualified teaching force results in a negative impact on student learning. To avoid this consequence, all members of the team need to receive information and guidance to be optimally effective.

Learning how to adapt the curriculum and teach the use of the adaptation to students is imperative if students are to truly access the core curriculum (Soukup, Wehmeyer, Bashinski, & Bovaird, 2007). All team members need to be familiar with principles of Universal Design for Learning and know how to actively include the student in all aspects of the lesson so as to enhance that student's contribution to the class. Although the goal may not be complete independence in all areas, those providing instructional support should be striving for the acquisition of meaningful skills (both academic and nonacademic), less adult intervention, and greater interactions with peers.

Team members must find time to discuss how they plan to implement the teaching strategy and what they intend to do if the student does not respond as anticipated. Numerous researchers have determined that finding time to provide trainings is imperative and yet those to receive training want it done in the most time efficient manner (Bolton & Mayer, 2008; Leblanc, Ricciardi, & Luiselli, 2005; Sarokoff & Sturmey, 2004). Teachers, paraprofessionals, and others working with a student appear to want the information to make them more effective but want it to be done as quickly as possible to fit into their somewhat harried schedule.

Finding Time to Collaborate

Perhaps one of the greatest challenges to effective collaboration is finding the time to bring team members together. Ideally, short face-to-face meetings for all critical team members (those working daily with the student) that occur on a regular basis would be preferred. However, most educational staff have heavy caseloads and extremely limited time to meet, and therefore, information on lesson plans, curricular adaptations, and instructional strategies often must be shared "on the run" (Snell & Janney, 2005). Team members use different strategies depending on their unique situation (e.g., grade levels, number of team members, individual preferences, and administrative support). Sharing information quickly can occur as teachers transition to different classes, during playground supervision, and at lunch. Team members also may use texting, e-mail, notes in mailboxes, and phone calls before and after school. Scheduling specific meeting times can occur with the support of the administration by allowing teachers to meet when another teacher is in charge of the class (e.g., substitute or floating aide), during specials (PE, music, art), when an educational movie is being shown and a parent volunteer is in charge, or when the principal or assistant principal assumes responsibility for the class. See Snell and Janney (2005) for different innovative ways to find time for team members to share information on students' programs during the school day.

Training Paraprofessionals

Paraprofessionals have complained of inadequate training and lack of knowledge, which made their experiences in the classroom challenging (Downing, Ryndak, & Clark, 2000; Ghere & York-Barr, 2007). All students have a right to learn from highly trained teachers. Therefore, a critical need exists to ensure that paraprofessionals on the team receive the necessary guidance and instruction from qualified educators and not be left on their own to determine what or how to teach. They certainly should not be left to their own strategies in the case of students exhibiting behavioral challenges during class time. In these cases in particular, considerable support and direction from credentialed and experienced special education teachers are needed.

Much has been written about paraprofessional training, especially for those supporting students with disabilities in general education classrooms (Carnahan, Williamson, Clarke, & Sorenson, 2009; Doyle, 2008; Giangreco, Backus, Cichoskikelly, Sherman, & Mavropoulous, 2003). Carnahan et al. (2009) recommend a very systematic instructional approach to train paraprofessionals using a series of prompts, reinforcement, and fading, and charting behavior to demonstrate a change in performance. Doyle (2008) offers a very detailed account of ways for paraprofessionals to be trained to support individual students, perform effectively as team members, adapt curriculum to meet student needs, and maintain confidentiality. Training is not a one-time event that occurs at hiring but must take place on a regular basis over time as the paraprofessional learns about student ability and needs and understands more clearly the challenges of providing effective support. Paraprofessionals will need monitoring and feedback on a consistent basis to improve skills and better meet the needs of individual students.

Training Peer Support

When students without disabilities are serving in a teaching support role, they also must receive critical information to be most effective (Carter et al., 2009). Teachers must take the time to provide training to these students so that they can assist with the desired support without doing too much for the student (or not enough). Modeling the desired strategy with feedback is recommended along with reminders not to do too much for the learner to avoid over prompting. Peers may support their classmate excessively to help him or be successful. For example, a young peer might give the student the answer prior to any instruction. At the other extreme, a high school peer tutor may just keep repeating prompts that are not effective for the student. In each case, feedback and redirection are needed to correct the situation. Peers can be effective teachers, but they do need training and support. They cannot be considered equal to highly qualified teachers and need guidance to be most beneficial.

While such training takes time, the initial training and subsequent follow-up are necessary to ensure that peers are in fact teaching and not just sitting next to a student with quite challenging disabilities. When they are unsure of what to do, these peer tutors are expected to report back to the special or general educator so that additional training can be provided or additional accommodations can be developed for the student with moderate to severe disabilities. Peers can help with this feedback when they present challenges to the teachers regarding appropriate adaptations and accommodations, strategies that were employed but that appeared to be ineffective, and challenging behaviors. Bond and Castagnera (2003) describe a peer-tutoring training program for students at a San Diego high school that occurred five times during an 18-week term. Training involved lectures, activities, homework, and group discussion. The goal of the program was for tutors to learn not only how to support their peer with disabilities but also about the value of diversity.

■ EFFECTIVE USE OF TEAM MEMBERS

How team members provide support should be thoughtfully considered. While a tendency may exist to pair a particular support person (i.e., special educator, related services provider, paraprofessional) with the student having complex needs, alternatives to such assignments may be more advisable. Always assigning one support person to a particular student may serve to isolate that student from the general education teacher as well as from classmates (Giangreco & Broer, 2005; Giangreco et al., 2005). From interviewing high school students with intellectual disabilities, Broer et al. (2005) found that despite a very close relationship with the paraprofessional, the majority of students felt disenfranchised and embarrassed by having a paraprofessional assigned solely to them. They reported wanting more time with the teachers and more friends. A careful balance is needed throughout the day to ensure sufficient support but not to the point of creating an artificial separation within the classroom.

A different way to conceptualize the use of support personnel is to consider these team members as support to the classroom teacher and entire class and not to just one student. Tables 5.2 through 5.4 offer suggestions for different ways various team members can be supportive of the learning in a classroom at the elementary, middle, and high school levels. Instead of "attaching" a paraprofessional or specialist to one student, that support person can be more effectively used to facilitate peer interactions and address the needs of a variety of students to ensure the smooth operation of the class, providing support as needed. For example, a speech-language pathologist may work with a small group during a high school science lab to support a particular student's use of conventional gestures as well as an augmentative communication device in interactions with other students in the group. However, this professional also responds to questions asked by others concerning the science lab and the science involved. In this manner, all students receive the support from all available adults in the room (lowering the student-to-teacher ratio). In addition, the general educator has more time during the day to work with a student having severe disabilities while the paraprofessional, special educator, or parent volunteer monitors the class. As a result, adults teaching in a classroom acquire more skills and knowledge to be used with a variety of different students and teaching situations.

Support But Not Hovering

To avoid creating an artificial and special education look and feel to a room, those providing support to a student with moderate to severe disabilities should refrain from sitting next to the student for an entire lesson. Rather, some direct teaching can be given, then when possible (even if just for a few minutes), the adult can stand, move around the room, check on others' work, and then return to the student needing more support. Moving away from the student provides opportunities for the student to request or signal the need for help and for classmates sitting close by to respond to that request. Whenever possible, the adult should encourage these natural offers to help. Causton-Theoharis and

| Table 5.2 | Diverse Support Provided to a Second-Grade Student With Severe Autism Who Is Fully Included in His Neighborhood School | | | | | | |

| Time | Subject/Activity | Targeted Skills for Student | Persons Providing Support | | | | |
			M	T	W	TH	F
8:25–9:00	**Attendance, Lunch count, News, Journal**	Responding to teacher, counting, use of communication device, writing by filling in blanks of prewritten sentences	Para	PV	PV	PV	Para
9:00–10:00	**Language Arts** Read a story and discuss, discuss new vocabulary, write an alternative ending	Vocabulary, reading pictorial and/or written material, sitting near peers and attending, sequencing pictures to write, responding to teacher questions with pictures	Para	Para	Para	OT	Para
10:00–10:20	**Recess**	Social skills, communication, coping strategies	PV	PV	PV	Para	Para
10:20–11:00	**Math** Subtraction and understanding word problems of subtraction	Recognizing numbers 6 through 10, recognizing smaller and larger amounts stamping numbers	SE	SE	SE	SE	SE
11:00–11:40	**Math** Drawing math problems; creating math problems as a small group	Numerical amounts of numbers 1 through 10, sequencing numbers 1 through 10, communication, social skills, fine motor skill of drawing, copying peers	SE	SE	SE	SE	SE
11:40–12:10	**Science** Activity related to the story read in language arts—an experiment talked about in the story, group report to complete	Sequencing pictorial and/or written information, responding to questions via use of pictures, making decisions, responding to peers, signing name	SLP	Para	Para	SLP	PV

(Continued)

Table 5.2   (Continued)

Time	Subject/Activity	Targeted Skills for Student	Persons Providing Support				
			M	T	W	TH	F
12:10–12:55	**Lunch and Recess**	Following directions, sitting with peers, social skills, communication, clean up self and area	PV	Para	OT	APE	Para
1:00–1:30	**Language Arts** Spelling activity with words from story and science activity	Vocabulary, counting, writing numbers with number stamps, completing sentences with fill in the blank picture and word cards	Para	SE	Para	SE	PV
1:30–2:20	**Social Studies** Learn about careers and a social skills lesson	Vocabulary, associations, social skills, self-determination skills	Para	SE	Para	SE	GE
2:20–2:30	**Debrief, go over homework, dismissal**	Organization skills, following directions, social skills, communication skills	GE and peers (all week)				

APE = adapted physical educator, PV = parent volunteer, OT = occupational therapist, SLP = speech-language pathologist, GE = general educator, SE = special educator, Para = paraprofessional

Table 5.3   Diverse Support Provided to Seventh-Grade Student With Down Syndrome Who Is Fully Included in a Local Middle School

Period/Time	Subject/Activity	Targeted Skills for Student	Persons Providing Support				
			M	T	W	TH	F
1 8:00–8:50	**Social Studies** China—its people, customs, contributions, geography	Reading CVC words, vocabulary, articulation, writing	Para	Para	Para	Para	Para
2 9:00–9:50	**Math** Conversion of compound	Writing numbers, determining	SE	SE	SE	SE	SE

Period/Time	Subject/Activity	Targeted Skills for Student	Persons Providing Support				
			M	T	W	TH	F
	fractions to decimals	largest of three amounts (using fractions)					
9:50–10:10	**Nutrition Break**	Making purchases, conversing with peers, articulation	8th-grade peers	Para	8th-grade peers	8th-grade peers	Sister
3 10:15–11:05	**Language Arts** *Treasure Island—*reading aloud and silently, discussing the plot and characters	Reading comprehension, articulation, reading CVC words, asking questions	SE	Para	SE	Para	OT
4 11:15–12:05	**PE** Basketball drills, practice, short game	Following directions, balance, eye-hand coordination, counting, strength building	Coach	APE	Coach	APE	Coach and peers
12:05–12:50	**Lunch/Break**	Conversing with peers, making purchases, articulation, fine motor strength to open pkgs.	Peers	Peers	SLP	Peers	Peers
5 1:00–1:50	**Drama T TH Music MWF** Practice for the musical, *Annie*	Reading, articulation, speaking loudly, following directions	Peers and GE	Peers and GE	Peers and GE	Peers and GE	Peers and GE
6 2:00–2:50	**Science** Electromagnetic fields—force fields, attraction, repulsion (lecture and lab)	Vocabulary, general knowledge, articulation, reading and writing, social skills	SLP	Para	OT	Para	GE

APE = adapted physical educator, PV = parent volunteer, OT = occupational therapist, SLP = speech-language pathologist, GE = general educator, SE = special educator, Para = paraprofessional

| Table 5.4 | Diverse Support Provided to a 10th-Grade Student With Severe Disabilities Who Is Fully Included in High School |

Time/Period	Class/Activity	Targeted Skills for Student	Person Providing Support				
			M	T	W	TH	F
1 8–8:55	**English** Reading and discussing *The Hunchback of Notre Dame*	Vocabulary development, writing with picture and word cards, communication, enjoyment of age-level literature	SE	SE	SE	SLP	SE
2 9:05–10:00	**Biology** Lecture and lab work on animal species	General knowledge, counting, number amounts, matching, vocabulary, communication, socialization	Para	Para	OT	Para	Para
10–10:25	**Nutrition Break**	Communication, social skills, self-feeding, use of vending machines	12th-grade peer tutor (Monday through Friday)				
3 10:30–11:25	**PE—swimming** Warm up, laps	Controlled movement, relaxation, strength building, water safety skills, communication	APE	PT	APE	PT	APE
4 11:35–12:25	**Spanish 1** Working on skits to demonstrate conversational Spanish	Vocabulary, social skills, communication, counting, writing	Para	Para	Para	Class-mates	Class-mates
12:25–1:10	**Lunch**	Feeding self, communication, social skills, use of money	VI	OT	Peer tutor	Peer tutor	Para
5 1:15-2:10	**World History** Studying World War I by viewing movie clips, discussing readings, anticipating alternative results to the war with different scenarios	Vocabulary (men, fight, hurt, bad), making decisions, operating the DVD player, following directions from the teacher	SE	SE	SLP	Para	Para

Time/Period	Class/Activity	Targeted Skills for Student	Person Providing Support				
			M	T	W	TH	F
6 2:20–3:15	**Student Council** Work in small groups to address the issue of bullying on campus	Self-determination, communication, general knowledge, social skills, vocabulary	Peer tutor	Peer tutor	Peer SE	Peer SE	Peer SE

APE = adapted physical educator, PV = parent volunteer, OT = occupational therapist, SLP = speech-language pathologist, GE = general educator, SE = special educator, Para = paraprofessional

Malmgren (2005) studied the impact of a four-hour inservice to paraprofessionals on increasing peer interactions for elementary-aged students with severe disabilities. As a result of the training, student interactions increased and less isolation of the student occurred. Devlin (2005) also studied the effects of training the team on student interactions and found that when paraprofessionals were trained to step back from students with the most severe disabilities, student-teacher interactions increased.

Moving around the room to help other students does not eliminate direct instruction for the student with moderate or severe intellectual disabilities. However, whenever possible, the adults should step away and encourage the student to work alone (if even for a few minutes) or with the support of a peer. Otherwise, students may become so used to having an adult next to them that they may falsely learn that they need such a presence to learn. Team members should keep track of the length of time that students are able to work alone with the intent of increasing this independence throughout the student's school years.

THE IMPORTANCE OF CONSISTENCY ■

When a variety of individuals are assuming responsibility for providing direct instruction to a particular student with moderate to severe disabilities, ensuring consistency in instructional approaches across potential teachers is imperative. Team members who use different prompts and prompt sequences to teach similar skills may confuse the students and produce undesired responses. Such a concern emphasizes the necessity of sharing information among team members quickly and efficiently so that techniques used with each student are understood and capable of being replicated.

To make instructional plans easily readable and understood, it is recommended that clear, simple, and familiar words be used. Table 5.5 highlights the difference between technical language versus lay language in a written instructional plan for the purpose of teaching a student to sign his name. Plans should be easy for all team members to read, understand, and implement successfully to support consistency in instruction.

Table 5.5	Comparison of an Instructional Plan in Technical and Lay Language to Teach a Student to Sign His Name Using a Signature Stamp With a Least-to-Most Prompting Strategy

Student: Daniel	Task: Signing his name
Technical Language	Conversational or Lay Language
1. Provide an indirect verbal cue to student to perform skill.	1. Ask the student what he needs to do now.
2. Provide an indirect visual cue to the paper.	2. Point to the area on the paper where he is to put his name.
3. Provide a model prompt using your own materials. Add verbal instruction.	3. Sign your name on a piece of paper in front of the student and describe what you're doing.
4. Visually cue to the signature stamp and paper.	4. Point to the signature stamp and then to the paper.
5. Give direct verbal and visual prompts to elicit desired behavior.	5. Tell the student to sign his name while tapping on the bold line on his paper.
*Prior to each succeeding prompt or cue, provide a five-second constant time delay.	*Before each prompt, count to five slowly.

■ GENERALIZATION OF SKILLS ACROSS TEAM MEMBERS

Despite the effort to be consistent, differences across a variety of instructional personnel are inevitable. When the student experiences instruction from different individuals, he or she must be able to deal with different personal characteristics. While the type and sequence of prompts should be the same and provided consistently, variance is to be expected. Different individuals will teach from different positions, use different tones of voice, move at different rates of speed, handle materials somewhat differently, wear different clothing, and in general, have a personal style of interaction that is quite unique. Dealing with such differences can help students become accustomed to working with different individuals throughout their school and post-school environments.

■ SUMMARY

The importance of a highly qualified and skilled teaching force for all students, but especially those with moderate or severe disabilities, is clear. This chapter has provided information on the varied potential members of the teaching force. These individuals can work directly with the student with moderate or severe disabilities and/or can provide more generalized support to the classroom teacher for the benefit of the entire class. Working collaboratively as a team and sharing skills and knowledge to support the learning of each student was presented as a recommended practice.

Although not credentialed teaching staff, the use of peers to provide educational support can produce very positive results. Benefits for both students with and without severe disabilities have been documented (Carter et al., 2009; Carter & Kennedy, 2006; Conroy et al., 2004). The learning of students without disabilities has not been negatively impacted but in fact, in some instances, has shown gain. Therefore, encouraging peer-to-peer interactions and support may serve to extend limited resources in inclusive classrooms while also preparing students with and without disabilities for an adult life that is naturally integrated.

In addition to teaching responsibilities, those supporting the student must also assume responsibility for collecting data to measure progress. Chapter 6 takes a practical look at this documentation by reviewing the different types of data that can be collected and relating them to different types of skills that the student may be learning. Recommendations are made for developing data collection forms as well as for making data collection an accepted and natural part of good instructional practice. Ease and efficiency of data collection is recommended.

6

Keeping Track of Student Progress

Kathryn D. Peckham-Hardin and June E. Downing

<table>
<tr><td colspan="2" align="center">**KEY CONCEPTS**</td></tr>
<tr><td>🔑</td><td>Collecting objective data is critical to measure student performance.</td></tr>
<tr><td>🔑</td><td>Targeted skills on Individualized Education Plan (IEP) objectives determine the type and amount of data that need to be collected.</td></tr>
<tr><td>🔑</td><td>Data collection sheets need to connect to IEP objectives to capture relevant student performance.</td></tr>
<tr><td>🔑</td><td>Information on data collection sheets can also be used to modify instruction and plan next steps.</td></tr>
<tr><td>🔑</td><td>Data collection should be quick, easy, and fit into a regular routine.</td></tr>
<tr><td>🔑</td><td>All members on the team can collect data, sharing this responsibility.</td></tr>
</table>

As discussed in Chapter 3, all students eligible to receive special education services must have an IEP that identifies specific skills the student needs to learn as manifested through written goals and objectives. These goals are unique to each student, as determined through assessment. Keeping track of students' progress in meeting these goals enables teachers to better plan for instruction (Roach & Elliott, 2006; Stecker, Lembke, & Foegen, 2008). Specifically, if the child is making steady progress, then the teacher will continue to provide instruction but perhaps increase the difficulty of the task to promote more advanced skills. The teacher may also increase the teaching opportunities across different environments to promote generalization of skills. In contrast, if the student is not making progress toward one or more goals, then the teacher must make changes to the instruction. This may entail revising instructional strategies (e.g., infusing errorless learning, creating additional teaching opportunities), scaling back the expected behavior and shaping the response (e.g., reinforce if the student stamps his name somewhere on the top of the page—slowly requiring the stamp to be placed directly on the name line), and/or further modifying the instructional materials (e.g., using photos versus line drawings to depict content, infusing student interests into instructional materials).

Ensuring access to challenging curricula is insufficient as students must also be expected to demonstrate progress as well (Wehmeyer, 2006). Keeping track of student progress is a practice required of teachers as mandated through the Individuals with Disabilities Education Improvement Act (IDEIA) 2004. Whenever progress reports are submitted for general education students and at the annual IEP meeting, teachers are required to report to parents the progress students are making toward meeting IEP goals and objectives, as well as describe how this progress is being measured (IDEIA, 2004). These regular reports should be based on actual data gathered versus "guesstimates" of performance. Unfortunately, Etscheidt (2006) reports that there is less compliance with monitoring student progress than with any other component of the IDEIA.

Finally, this requirement of accountability has assumed even greater significance now that *all* students—including students with the most significant needs—participate in statewide testing. The 1997 amendments to the IDEA and the No Child Left Behind Act (NCLB) of 2001 require that states use standardized methods to measure student performance at the end of the school year (Browder & Spooner, 2006). States must demonstrate that all students are making adequate progress in three key content areas: language arts, math, and science. Students with severe disabilities take an "alternate" version of the test required of students without disabilities and those with mild disabilities. The alternate assessment also tests student performance in key content areas; however, these assessments can be based on modified achievement standards (US Department of Education, 2005). While the bulk of this chapter will address assessment for the purpose of evaluating student progress in meeting IEP goals and objectives, issues related to alternate assessment will be addressed briefly at the end of the chapter.

■ TYPES OF DATA COLLECTION STRATEGIES

Information on student performance can be gathered using a number of different methods from simple frequency count (the number of times) to more complex data such as noting the level of prompt the student needed to perform the response. This next section discusses some of the most common types of data gathered in classroom and school settings.

Frequency Data

Frequency data refers to how often the student performed a given skill or response. This type of data lends itself well to skills that are discrete in nature—meaning they have a clear beginning and ending. Examples include how many spelling words were spelled correctly, how many times a student correctly identified his name stamp from a field of three, and how often the student asked for help. For more complex responses, the skill can be broken into smaller steps (task analysis) and information can be gathered on each step. Table 6.1 displays a simple data sheet that notes the number of times (tally marks) Jack requested assistance.

Table 6.1   Frequency Data

Jack's objective: Throughout the school date when Jack needs help with a task or activity, he will use his communication device to ask for help, 10 times per day for 10 days.				
Instructions: Note (tally mark) how many times Jack asks for help.				
Monday 5/4/09	Tuesday 5/5/09	Wednesday 5/6/09	Thursday 5/7/09	Friday 5/8/09
𝓣𝓗𝓛 // (7)	𝓣𝓗𝓛 (9)	/// (3)	/// (3)	// (2)

While frequency data is a fairly common form of data collection, a word of caution is in order. Frequency data by itself can be incomplete and therefore misleading. Continuing with Jack, let's take a closer look at the data. Note that on Day 1, Jack asked for help seven times; on Day 2, nine times; Day 3, three times; Day 4, three times; and Day 5, twice (see Table 6.1). At first glance, Jack's performance appears to be variable at best; and if the goal is to increase the skill of asking for assistance, these data suggest his performance is actually decreasing or getting worse over time. However, this may not be the case at all. Specifically, what is missing is information on how often Jack *needed* help. It may be that for days one and two, Jack needed greater assistance for a variety of reasons—e.g., introduction of new material or more physical demands than usual; yet on days three through five, less assistance was needed, thus explaining the lower number of requests. It could also be that data were collected at different times of the day. For example, for days one and two data were collected during ceramics and science lab—both classes that are hands-on in nature. Jack may have needed more assistance due to physical limitations or because he is unfamiliar with the objects used in these classes (e.g., fettling knife or beveled edge cutter in ceramics; a Bunsen burner or beaker in science lab); this may account for the higher number of requests on these days. In contrast, for the other days, data were collected during times in which Jack typically needs less support, thus explaining the lower frequencies (e.g., computers and PE). Thus, while the data sheet is simple and easy to use, the information gained may not be meaningful or particularly informative. Teachers are encouraged to take this into consideration when using frequency data as the sole measure.

Success Out of Opportunity Data

Success out of opportunity (S/O) data are frequency data that include information on how often a student displayed a given skill but also include the number of opportunities that were present to perform the skill. Continuing with Jack, by adjusting the data sheet to include the number of times Jack asked for help (successes) as well as the number of times he needed help (opportunities), the information gathered is more meaningful and informative (see Table 6.2). With the addition of this information, we can see that Jack's performance is less variable than Table 6.1 would suggest. Furthermore, the addition of noting the class in which the data were collected helps us to better understand the conditions in which assistance is requested and/or needed.

Table 6.2 Success out of Opportunity (S/O) Data

Jack's Objective: Throughout the school date when Jack needs help with a task or activity, he will use his communication device to ask for help, 80% of all opportunities for two weeks.

Instructions: Note the number of successes (asked for help) out of the number opportunities (needed help).

	Monday 5/4/09	Tuesday 5/5/09	Wednesday 5/6/09	Thursday 5/7/09	Friday 5/8/09
Date →					
Class →	Ceramics	Science Lab	Computers	Computers	PE
# times asked for help	ⅧⅡ (7)	Ⅷ ⅢⅠ (9)	ⅢⅠ (3)	ⅢⅠ (3)	ⅠⅠ (2)
# of times needed help	Ⅷ ⅢⅠ (8)	Ⅷ ⅢⅠ (9)	ⅢⅠⅠ (4)	ⅢⅠⅠ (4)	ⅠⅠ (2)
S/O	7/8 (88% of opportunities)	9/9 (100% of opportunities)	3/4 (75% of opportunities)	3/4 (75% of opportunities)	2/2 (100% of opportunities)

As noted earlier, a primary purpose of collecting data is to inform instruction. In this case after reviewing these data, the teacher may decide to infuse additional supports in ceramics and science lab (e.g., pictured list of needed items). This simple change serves not only to decrease the need for assistance but also promotes greater independence, as well as teaching other important academic skills (e.g., reading picture and written vocabulary and teaching the concept of "same-different" through match to sample). Furthermore, based on this information, the teacher may decide to collect data consistently in one setting in order to get a better understanding of the student's performance. Later, the teacher may add additional settings to gauge generalization of the skill.

Using Task Analysis

Data collection also can occur using task analyses to identify small skills within a larger activity and documenting a student's progress according to these smaller skills. Breaking tasks into smaller, discrete skills can be an effective teaching strategy as discussed in Chapter 2 as well as a means of assessment (see Chapters 3 and 7). Task analysis can be highly individualized for different students to take into account characteristics such as special visual needs, physical needs, or communication needs. For example, a fourth grader, Susan, has physical, visual, and intellectual challenges that she must deal with during a math lesson on multiplication. One step in the math lesson is for the class to complete approximately 20 multiplication problems in their text. This one step in the math lesson can be analyzed into smaller skills specifically designed to document Susan's progress in identifying and matching numbers. She uses an adaptive keyboard (IntelliKeys©) with a calculator and/or math overlay to do her work on a computer. This adaptation helps her both visually and physically as the keys are large and bright with a contrasting background, spaced further apart with a keyguard to prevent accidently hitting other numbers, and a large and bright computer display for easier viewing. See Table 6.3 for data collection using task analysis for Susan in math.

Table 6.3 Task Analysis Used for Data Collection

Susan's Objective: When using an enlarged calculator, Susan will find the numbers and symbols to be inputted and tap the correct numbers and symbols in the correct order on the calculator with 80% accuracy for a total of 20 math problems.

Instructions: Note Susan's performance for each step (see key below).

Key:

+ = independent

p = problem or keyboard tapped to draw attention (prompt)

− = incorrect response or no response

	Skills	Trial 1	Trial 2	Trial 3	Trial 4	Trial 5	Trial 6
a.	Look at enlarged math problem and find the first number.	+	+	+	p	+	p
b.	Press same number on keyboard.	+	+	p	+	+	p
c.	Look back at problem to find x sign.	p	p	p	p	p	p
d.	Press same symbol on keyboard.	+	+	+	+	p	+
e.	Look back at problem to find next number.	p	p	+	p	p	p

(Continued)

Table 6.3 (Continued)

	Skills	Trial 1	Trial 2	Trial 3	Trial 4	Trial 5	Trial 6
f.	Press same number on keyboard.	+	+	p	p	+	+
g.	Look back at problem to find = sign.	–	–	p	p	–	p
h.	Press same symbol on keyboard.	–	–	–	p	p	–
i.	Look at answer and confirm or deny the answer written on her problem by a support person.	–	–	–	–	–	–

Note: One trial is equal to one attempt to input an entire problem. Although the last step in this analysis is not required in the IEP objective, it involves the same skill of matching numbers, which gives her more practice and also completes the problem.

Duration Data

Duration data note how long the student is engaged in a given activity. This type of data can be particularly helpful if the goal is to increase the time a student performs a target response. Examples include increasing time spent in close proximity to the large group, conversing with a peer, or working with a peer before requesting a break. Duration data can also be used to gather information on behaviors you are trying to decrease, such as challenging behaviors such as screaming and/or yelling, crying, or self-injurious behavior (e.g., frequent self-hitting).

Gathering duration data does require access to some form of time measurement, which could be as simple as noting the time on a clock or watch (start and stop time), or, if more exact information is needed, use of a stop watch. There are different ways to gather this information; how the data sheet is designed ultimately depends on what information is most helpful. For example, if the objective is to increase time on task while engaged in various activities with a partner, then simply noting the total time engaged (e.g., in minutes) during these activities is probably sufficient.

It may also be helpful to note the name of the peer the student worked with and/or the activity (see Table 6.4). Gathering this additional information can prove valuable in helping to understand what peers the focus student is most or least likely to interact with for extended periods of time. Similarly, the activity the student is engaged in may influence his or her participation. For example, Kari is more likely to disengage fairly quickly when the activity is math work, an activity she dislikes, but will stay engaged for longer periods of time when reading a favorite book with a peer (see Table 6.4). This additional information can help teachers better understand a student's likes and dislikes—information that can be used later during instruction (e.g., count favorite stories she's read to solve math problems).

Table 6.4 Duration Data for Time on Task

Kari's Objective: During partnered activities, Kari will work with a peer for five minutes before requesting a break, for 10 consecutive activities.			
Instructions: Note date, activity, the peer Kari worked with, and the time engaged (approximation) in the activity.			
Key: ~ = approximation to the nearest minute			
Date	*Activity*	*Peer*	*Duration*
3/7/09	Math Game	Sarah	~ 1 minute
3/8/09	Reading a story she selected	Sarah	~ 3 minutes
3/10/09	Reading a story she selected	Mark	~ 4 minutes

It is important to note that these additional data (peer and specific activity) are not always relevant and therefore should not be added to the data sheet. For example in Table 6.4, based on the data provided, it appears that *who* (peer) Kari works with is of minimal consequence; instead, the activity she is engaged in seems to be the more important variable. In this situation, the suggestion would be to drop the information on peers from the data sheet since it adds very little information. Note also that the "approximation" of the total time engaged in an activity may, in many cases, be sufficient; this strategy is easier while still being informative.

When designing data sheets for challenging behaviors, it may be helpful to note the time the behavior occurs as well as the total duration. This information can help to better understand the antecedents associated with the challenging behavior (Horner, Albin, Sprague, & Todd, 2000). For example, in Table 6.5 we can see from the data gathered thus far that tantrum-like behaviors occur approximately once a day; however, longer tantrums occur in the afternoon and approximately at the same time (e.g., time for math). Knowing this information, the teacher can then look more closely at math to better understand why the student displays challenging behaviors.

Table 6.5 Duration Data for Challenging Behavior

Corey's Objective: During the school day, Corey will reduce duration of tantrum-like behavior defined as screaming, yelling, and/or crying to 2 minutes or less for 8 consecutive episodes.				
Instructions: Note start and stop time (approximate to closest minute) for each episode; calculate total duration.				
Date: 3/9/09	Date: 3/10/09	Date: 3/11/09	Date: 3/12/09	Date: 3/13/09
Start: 1:45 p.m.	Start: 1:30 p.m.	Start: 9:00 a.m.	Start: 1:35 p.m.	Start: 11:15 a.m.

(Continued)

Table 6.5 (Continued)

Stop: 1:53 p.m.	Stop: 1:40 p.m.	Stop: 9:02 a.m.	Stop: 1:45 p.m.	Stop: 11:16 a.m.
Total: 8 min.	Total: 10 min.	Total: 2 min.	Total: 10 min.	Total: 1 min.
Date: 3/16/09	Date: _____	Date: _____	Date: _____	Date: _____
Start: 1:25pm	Start: _____	Start: _____	Start: _____	Start: _____
Stop: 1:40pm	Stop: _____	Stop: _____	Stop: _____	Stop: _____
Total: 15 min.	Total: _____	Total: _____	Total: _____	Total: _____

Latency Data

Latency data are also a measure of time; however, what is being calculated is the time it takes the student to complete the desired response. The goal is often two-fold—teach a skill *and* teach the student to display the skill within a reasonable period of time. For example, when a teacher asks a question of a student during a lesson, a typical response is the expected answer or to say, "I don't know." Furthermore, this response usually appears within a few seconds following the question. For students with more significant disabilities, the typical latency period may take considerably longer to allow for additional time to process the information and/or to provide for allowances due to physical limitations (to use augmentative communication). Since most teachers cannot afford to wait for any length of time for a response, a controlling prompt (as described in Chapters 2 and 4) may be needed to help the student display the expected behavior immediately (e.g., a lift up at the elbow to raise a picture or word card as a response). Again, how this information is recorded can vary and ultimately depends on what information is most valuable to help the student learn.

In Table 6.6, instead of denoting the time period (latency) in seconds, recording "yes" or "no" is probably sufficient. In this case, a "yes" notation

Table 6.6 Latency Data When Responding to Questions

Vic's Objective: In science lab when asked a question (by teacher or peer), Vic will respond using gestures (pointing and nodding) or use his communication device, three of three questions per day for two weeks.
Instructions: Note the question asked, who (teacher or name of peer) asked the question, and whether Vic responded within four seconds or not.

Key: Y = yes; responded within four seconds
        N = no; took longer than four seconds or didn't respond at all
        T = teacher
        P = note peer's name

Date	Question	Question asked by . . .	Responded within 4 seconds
3/11/09	Which beaker is bigger?	T	Y
	What do I put in next, water or salt?	P = Letica	Y
	Which beaker has more water in it?	P = Allison	N
3/11/09	How many test tubes do we have?	P = Letica	Y
	Which tube is longer?	T	Y
	Which number matches the weight on the scale (presented with two options)?	P = Yuki	N
3/12/09	Did the water turn blue or green?	P = Allison	N
	Can we turn the water back to the color it was?	P = Yuki	N
	Which water should we drink (presented with two options)?	P = Ben	N

indicates that Vic responded to the teacher's or peer's question within four seconds, and a recording of "no" means it took longer than four seconds for Vic to respond *or* he didn't respond at all. This is easier data to collect than using a stop watch to note the exact number of seconds. The ease of the data collection system must be taken into consideration when designing data sheets. Note also in Table 6.6 that the name of the person who asked the question (whether teacher or peer) is recorded. This information can provide insight into the individuals Vic is more likely to respond to. For example, if Vic consistently responds to the teacher and one peer (e.g., Letica) but no others, this tells us that Vic may not be generalizing the response and thus additional instruction is needed. Again, this type of added information is not always needed or relevant; teachers are encouraged to create data sheets that capture the most essential information while keeping the form easy to use.

Latency data may also be used when the focus is increasing the fluency of a response. In this situation, the student may already know how to do the response, but it takes him or her longer than usual to complete the task. In science, Kareem is learning to categorize pictures of living things (e.g., plants, animals, etc.) by sorting pictures of living and nonliving things into different piles. Over time, he mastered this task, correctly identifying 9 of 10 pictures for 10 opportunities. However, he is easily distracted and often stops in the middle of the task, requiring that he be redirected numerous times. It can take him up to 20 minutes to complete a task that he could complete in 10 minutes or less if he were more focused. So, a second objective has been identified to increase fluency of response—in this case, to complete the sorting task within 10 minutes. In this situation, noting the actual time in minutes (rounded to the nearest one half minute) will be more informative than simple "yes or no" data (see Table 6.7). This form of data will enable the teacher to note progress over time.

Table 6.7	Latency Data for Completing Tasks

Kareem's Objective: During his science class, Kareem will sort pictures of living and nonliving things within 10 minutes, correctly sorting 8 of 10 pictures for 10 opportunities.

Directions: Note how long it takes Kareem (rounded to the nearest 1/2 minute) to complete the task.

Date	Time needed to complete task	Date	Time needed to complete task
3/9/09	18 1/2 minutes		_____ minutes
3/10/09	17 minutes		_____ minutes
3/11/09	18 minutes		_____ minutes

Prompt Level Data

A final type of data collection is noting the type of prompt(s) the student needed in order to display the desired response. Students with severe disabilities often learn new skills at a much slower rate (Westling & Fox, 2009). The advantage of prompt-level data is that it can show increments of progress over time. For example, Geri takes her spelling test using a computer and an adapted keyboard (e.g., IntelliKeys© keyboard). She listens to the word being said and then selects the appropriate picture on the adapted keyboard. Initially, she needed partial physical (PP) assistance to select the correct response (e.g., a touch at the elbow to guide her arm toward the correct picture and letting go half way). As time went on, the teacher was able to slowly fade the prompt to a gesture cue (e.g., scanning the options with her finger to cue Geri to look at the different options) and finally to an indirect verbal cue (e.g., what do you need to do?). This fading process took several weeks (see Table 6.8—data presented for Weeks 1, 5, 10, and 15 only). Simple frequency data noting the number of correct pictures she identified independently would not show this subtle but very important growth in performance.

Table 6.8	Prompt Level Data

Geri's Objective: During spelling tests, Geri will use an adapted keyboard to select the picture of the spelling word, correctly identifying four of five spelling words per test for 10 spelling tests.

Instructions: Note spelling word, if she selected the correct or incorrect picture, and highest prompt level needed.

Key:

+ = independence	G = gesture cue	C = correct
IV = indirect verbal cue	PP = partial physical prompt	I = incorrect

Week 1 3/6/09 Spelling Word	Correct/ Incorrect	Prompt Level	Week 5 4/3/09 Spelling Word	Correct/ Incorrect	Prompt Level
1. candle	C	PP	1. couch	C	G
2. basket	C	PP	2. bed	C	PP
3. tree	C	PP	3. lamp	C	G
4. apple	C	PP	4. rug	I	G
5. squirrel	C	PP	5. desk	C	IV
Week 10 5/8/09 Spelling Word	Correct/ Incorrect	Prompt Level	Week 15 6/12/09 Spelling Word	Correct/ Incorrect	Prompt Level
1. car	C	PP	1. circle	C	IV
2. house	I	G	2. triangle	C	+
3. garden	C	PP	3. square	C	IV
4. bottle	I	G	4. solid	C	IV
5. river	C	G	5. round	C	+

Due to a slower learning pace, taking prompt-level data on a daily basis may not be necessary. Instead, "probes" can be taken once a week (e.g., every Friday) to get a sense of what, if any, changes are notable in the student's performance. For example, with Geri, it may be that prompt level data are taken once a week for 15 weeks; once she begins to require less assistance, data can be taken more frequently.

Combination of Measures

In some cases, two or more types of measures will be used, for example, prompt-level and duration data, frequency data in the form of "yes or no," plus latency data, and so on. Ultimately, the data sheet that is created must link with the IEP objective. If the IEP objective notes more than one type of measure, then all forms of measurement must be captured in the corresponding data sheet.

LINKING DATA COLLECTION ■ METHODS TO THE IEP OBJECTIVES

Chapter 3 provides an example of an objective that includes both frequency and duration measures: When warming up with his PE class and when encouraged by peers, Lon will perform each different exercise for a minimum of three minutes before stopping, for 10 consecutive PE classes. To assess

Lon's progress in meeting this objective, the data sheet must be configured to capture both pieces of information—specifically, information related to how long (duration) he engaged in each exercise as well as the number (frequency) of exercises performed. There are many ways to collect this information. For example, actual duration data for each exercise may be collected: four minutes for Exercise 1; two minutes for Exercise 2; and three-and-a-half minutes for Exercise 3 (see Table 6.9). A basic template can be created with blank spaces and/or lines to write in information as it changes (e.g., different exercise, different durations). By noting the specific exercise performed, information is gathered on which exercises the student is more likely to complete for longer periods of time. Depending on the goal, the exercise regime might be modified based on this information (e.g., order of the exercises might be changed).

Table 6.9 Linking Data Collection Method With the IEP Objective—Example 1

Lon's PE Objective: Lon will perform each exercise for a minimum of three minutes per exercise for 10 consecutive PE classes.		
Instructions: Note type of exercise and time spent exercising (round to the nearest half minute) per exercise.		
3/23/09	Exercise 1: *Sit Ups* Duration: *2 minutes*	Exercise 2: *Arm rolls* Duration: *3 minutes*	Exercise 3: *Stretching* Duration: *3 1/2 minutes*
3/24/09	Exercise 1: *Toe touches* Duration: *3 minutes*	Exercise 2: *Walking* Duration: *1 minute*	Exercise 3: *Stretching* Duration: *3 minutes*
	Exercise 1: _____ Duration: _____	Exercise 2: _____ Duration: _____	Exercise 3: _____ Duration: _____

Another and simpler way to capture this information is through a yes-or-no system in which "yes" indicates the student engaged in a given exercise for three minutes or more and "no" means the student engaged in the exercise for less than three minutes (see Table 6.10). Again, a template can be created leaving space to write in the exercise with the "Yes or No" already on the data sheet, requiring the person to simply circle the correct response. This simpler version may not only save time but also could be adapted so the student himself collects the data. For example, pictures could be embedded into the data sheet and the student records "yes" or "no" by using a blotter (e.g., a bingo blotter) to highlight the correct response. This teaches additional skills (e.g., reading and writing) while also teaching the student to self-regulate and record his performance.

Both examples highlight the need to align the data sheet with the objective in order to ensure the information captured is relevant and informative.

Table 6.10	Linking Data Collection With the IEP Objective—Example 2

Lon's PE Objective: Lon will perform each exercise for a minimum of 3 minutes per exercise for ten consecutive PE classes.

Instructions: Monitor whether Lon exercises for required amount of time and if he correctly documents his performance. Provide feedback.

Key: Yes = Lon performed the exercise for 3 minutes or more
No = Lon performed the exercise for less than 3 minutes

3/9/09			
	Sit Ups	Arm Circles	Stretching
	Yes ⬭No⬭	⬭Yes⬭ No	⬭Yes⬭ No
3/10/09			
	Toe Touches	Walking	Stretching
	⬭Yes⬭ No	Yes ⬭No⬭	⬭Yes⬭ No

COLLECTING DATA WHILE TEACHING ■ IN GENERAL EDUCATION CLASSROOMS

Given the hectic pace of most classrooms and numerous expectations placed on those providing instruction, collecting data will probably only occur if it can be done quickly and easily. Those providing instruction must be able to teach, support positive and on-task behaviors, and manipulate adaptive materials. Methods of collecting data must not interfere with instruction, take up too much room, or be too time consuming.

Designing Data Sheets—Keep It Simple

Data sheets should be designed to be as straight-forward and easy to complete as possible while providing key information. All data sheets should include the student's name and the objective. If a key is included (see Tables 6.4, 6.6, 6.8, & 6.10), clearly describe the most relevant information so that the assessor can quickly capture the data needed. It is helpful to include simple instructions (see Tables 6.1–6.14) so the forms can be completed by anyone working with the student, including peers, paraprofessionals, related services staff, and substitute staff. Use of a template that includes most of the information is also helpful—this reduces the time needed to input information. For example, by including "yes or no" in the template, the person recording the data can simply circle the appropriate response. Similarly, by including a blank line followed by minutes (e.g., _____ minutes), the person simply writes in a number. An added benefit of using templates is that it makes it clearer to the person recording the data what specific information is needed. Creating data sheets on a computer makes it easier to quickly change, update, or modify the form as needed. Finally, the forms need to be readily available so time is not wasted looking for them. Making data collection as easy and efficient as possible is the goal.

How Often to Take Data

As discussed earlier, data collection does not need to occur at every opportunity. For example, when first teaching a new skill or concept, the student will need time to understand the expectations and to begin to demonstrate some understanding of the task. In this case, it may be wise to delay data collection for several weeks. Once the student begins to understand the task at hand, data collection might begin but be taken only once or twice a week to gauge the student's performance (also referred to as "probes"). Once the student is making fairly steady progress, the frequency of data collection should increase accordingly.

When to Stop Data Collection

Those individuals who are collecting data will need to keep referring back to the criterion for mastery that was stated in the IEP objective to determine when that level of mastery has been reached. Once the objective has been met, data collection is no longer required. At this point, the teacher may want to review all of the data in their totality (months of data) to look for patterns. For example, how long did it take the student to learn "Skill D," and how did that time period compare with the learning rate for "Skill A, B, and C"? Was there a pattern with regard to prompt level—for example, moving from a physical prompt to a verbal cue took more time than fading from a verbal to a gesture cue? Answers to these questions can help teachers to further refine instruction and teaching strategies.

Another approach is to take follow-up data to ensure that the student continues to display the newly acquired skill over time. This type of data is also referred to as "maintenance" data. Initially, the teacher may want to take follow-up data every couple of weeks. If these data show that the student continues to perform the skill then the schedule can be reduced to once a month or every couple of months.

EXAMPLES OF COLLECTING DATA ■ DURING INSTRUCTIONAL TIMES

Three examples will be presented across grade levels and content areas to demonstrate the various ways in which relevant and meaningful information on student performance can be gathered. In all of these examples, the individual providing instructional support is also assuming responsibility for collecting data.

Elementary School

Ms. Halen is teaching her fourth-grade class Roman numerals: what they mean, how they are written, and how they are used. She has previously discussed Roman history as part of a social studies lesson and reviews this topic during math. She asks the class questions about seeing Roman numerals in any books or other sources. She has them look at the beginning of one or two of their texts, and they talk about why Roman numerals are used. She demonstrates how to write some basic numbers, comparing them to Arabic numbers. She passes out a worksheet that students are to complete on their own. The standard addressed by this lesson relates to understanding and applying numbers, ways of representing numbers, the relationships among numbers, and different numerical systems.

Malikah is a fourth grader in this class who really likes coming to school and seeing her friends. Malikah uses eye gaze and some movements with her left arm and hand to indicate her messages using a variety of communication tools (e.g., objects, pictures, vocalizations, dedicated communication devices). She also uses a wheelchair and has several pieces of positioning equipment she uses throughout the day. In math, Malikah is learning to sequence numbers and recognize the larger of two numbers. During the class discussion, Malikah has access to pictures used in social studies and is working on identifying different vocabulary words. Ms. Halen will call on her to pick the larger of two numbers in front of her. When Malikah responds, the paraprofessional (or other support person) will convey her answer to Ms. Halen. If Malikah is incorrect, Ms. Halen will ask her if she's sure it's the largest number in a joking tone, and then she uses the number Malikah has given her to ask the class how it would look as a Roman numeral. When Ms. Halen is explaining how to write a specific number, the paraprofessional teaches Malikah why one number is bigger (using "Roman" coins, drawing stick Roman people, or using smiley faces, which Malikah likes). Using a simultaneous prompting strategy, she presents two numbers at least five inches apart and asks Malikah to find the larger number. She immediately says and shows her the correct number. Then she explains why it's larger, using a number line, counting the drawings or "coins," and so on. The paraprofessional does this several times with different numbers and keeps attuned to the class so that Malikah is listening when Ms. Halen asks her for the larger of the two numbers in front of her. Ms. Halen's questions to Malikah serve as probes prior to the instruction to see what Malikah is learning (new numbers that have not been taught are used).

The paraprofessional uses a simple data sheet (see Table 6.11) as she teaches. The objective is clearly stated, and she just needs to write in the two numbers presented. She only collects probe data (when Ms. Halen asks Malikah the question and Malikah is to respond with no prompting). The paraprofessional records the number in the left to right arrangement offered to Malikah and then circles her response and indicates whether it is correct or not. If correct, Malikah is praised and shown with the number line why she's correct. If incorrect, the paraprofessional will make drawings using the two numbers or show pictures, etc. to explain the error and help her see which number or amount is larger.

Table 6.11	Sample Data Collection Sheet for Identifying the Larger of Two Numbers

Malikah's objective: When presented with two different single or double digit numbers from 1–30, Malikah will indicate the larger of the two numbers with 80% accuracy for 10 opportunities.

Standard: AZ Math Standard in Number Sense: Understand and apply numbers, ways of representing numbers, the relationships among numbers, and different number systems.

Instructions: Record the numbers presented and their placement (right or left) and whether the response was correct (+) or incorrect (−).

Date	Numbers Presented and Their Placement		+ = Correct
	Left	Right	− = Incorrect
3/26/09	21	(13)	−
"	13	(23)	+
"	(10)	8	+
"	18	(10)	−
"	(11)	9	+
"	(20)	15	+
"	27	(23)	−
"	30	(29)	−
"	9	(14)	+
"	(12)	4	+
"		**Total Correct (Success/Opportunity)**	6/10

All students are learning about numbers, the relationships among numbers, and how to represent numbers. While Malikah may not learn Roman numerals, she does know most of her letters, which the Roman numerals support (e.g., she may not learn that C=100, but she can identify the C from the V, D, L, M, etc.).

The data sheet in Table 6.11 uses S/O data and includes the additional information of the number presented as well as where the number was placed (to the student's right or left). Analysis of these data suggest that Malikah appears to know which number is greater for numbers around 10 and under, but when she is less sure of her answer, she is more likely to respond to the number on her right. This additional information helps us to see that Malikah *will* scan the two options (she selected 10, 11, and 12, which were placed on her left) before making a selection. These data also tell us that additional instruction is needed in understanding numbers larger than 20.

Middle School

In Mr. Perino's seventh-grade science class, students are learning to distinguish different species, recognize similar characteristics, and rationalize placement of an organism in a certain species. The standards being addressed are the following: Developing an understanding of the structure and function in living systems, Developing an understanding of populations and ecological systems, and Developing an understanding of diversity and adaptations. Mr. Perino is using large group instruction and calling on individual students to answer questions and add to the discussion.

Bershawm has some speech, but it is often either echolalic or unintelligible. He works with a speech-language pathologist (SLP) who presents him with a picture of a specific mammal versus a bird, tortoise, and insect. When the class is talking about characteristics of mammals (for example) and what scientific methods support the development of a particular species, Bershawm is to identify the dog or cat, for example; state the number of legs; whether it has fur or not; and if warm or cold blooded. He is also to identify what letter the name of the animal, bird, or insect starts with. Mr. Perino will call on Bershawm throughout the discussion to hold up a bird or mammal, and Bershawm will select the correct picture (the SLP may cue him verbally to find a particular animal) and hold it up for the teacher to see. The teacher then asks all students why Bershawm's selection would fit within a certain category and species of animal life. Bershawm's IEP objectives are to identify individual letters, respond when called upon, and make differentiations with regard to shape, size, or color. He is also working on identifying similarities of common items (or in this case, living organisms).

The SLP attends to the information being presented by the teacher as well as responses from students. She presents Bershawm with pictorial options related to what the teacher is discussing. She also makes eye contact with the teacher throughout the lecture or discussion to determine when he is going to call on Bershawm. Then she cues Bershawm to listen to the teacher in case he should be called on. When Bershawm decides what to show the teacher (whether he is to select a mammal, bird, or insect or basic dwelling sites such as nests, caves, fields), the SLP records his unprompted responses on the data sheet (see Table 6.12). If he makes a mistake, the teacher will correct him, and the SLP will provide additional explanation regarding what he had chosen and why it is incorrect. The teacher continues on, eliciting more in-depth information from the other students while this corrective feedback from the SLP is occurring. Then more options are offered for different questions. Mr. Perino will continue to ask Bershawm simple questions during this part of the lesson to ensure his active participation and involvement.

Table 6.12	Sample Data Sheet for Bershawm's Responses in Seventh-Grade Life Science Class

Bershawm's Objective: Bershawm will identify the correct picture from a field of 4 to answer questions related to science content, correctly answering 80% of the questions asked per unit, for 6 units of study.

Instructions: Note the question asked, picture options presented, and note if the answer is correct or incorrect.

DATE: 3/26/09

Prompt by teacher	Picture Options Presented	Correct	Incorrect
Show me a mammal	bird spider bear (tree)		✓
Show me a small mammal	(kitten) crocodile elephant bird	✓	
Show the class a butterfly	butterfly (bird) dinosaur bug		✓
Show me something that doesn't fly	butterfly bird (dog) bee	✓	
Show me something that lives in a tree	(turtle) elephant bird pig		✓
Total		2	3

Note that the type of data gathered in this example (Table 6.12) is simply frequency data. However, as noted above, additional information is included in the data sheet—specifically, the questions asked and the order in which the picture options are presented. Again, we can use this information to better understand the student's performance. For example, is there a pattern with regard to positioning of the pictures? From the limited data provided, it appears that Bershawm tends to select the first picture; two times this was the correct response, and two times it wasn't. Additional data are needed to better understand Bershawm's performance.

High School

In Mr. Schumacher's 12th-grade world history class, students are studying Asia—the age of feudalism, growth of trade, conflicts, and contributions to the world. Mr. Schumacher uses a variety of approaches in his instruction, such as lecture, class discussion, and exploration on the Internet, videos, Chinese literature, and artifacts he has obtained from his travels abroad. Students pair up and work on projects and tutor each other for upcoming exams.

Carlien benefits from the varied visual media used in the class, and she has a classmate that she really likes working with. Carlien has autism with a moderate intellectual impairment. She has some verbal skills but often does not use them or repeats a specific word or phrase numerous times. She is learning to use two to three word phrases as well as pictorial and written symbols on different communication devices (high and low tech) to express herself. Large groups are difficult for Carlien, so she sits in the front row on the far side of the room so she can turn away from the other students as needed. She also uses an FM system at times to focus on Mr. Schumacher and headphones to block background noise when she expresses this need. She can become quite frustrated with tasks and with her difficulty with communicating her feelings and will yell and shake her body at these times. Sometimes Mr. Schumacher will ask her to step outside the classroom to calm down for a few minutes. A support person accompanies her and encourages her to take some deep breaths, gives her deep pressure hugs upon request, and helps her to return to class where the task will be changed somewhat (e.g., given different options).

In the lessons on Asia, Carlien is learning to recognize some simple words, make associations, categorize, and respond verbally to comprehension questions. A peer tutor helps Carlien on certain days, and on other days, she is supported by the special educator, speech-language pathologist, or paraprofessional. She is shown three categories (e.g., Asian people, products from Asia, and buildings) with pictorial representation and is then given one pictorial and labeled item for her to determine which category it belongs to. She will use these categories to complete a report on Asia. Other students are working on papers they are writing regarding a topic of their choice. Carlien's friend is working with her on the paper. Her friend is writing most of the paper on the computer, but Carlien contributes to it using her categorization of pictures with brief explanations. Their paper is on Asian products that have contributed to civilization.

As her friend does research and writes the paper, she will stop frequently and ask Carlien for her opinion, pointing to different pictures on the computer screen (e.g., what should I say now? Why?). Carlien is to respond with a short phrase or sentence (e.g., "There are more things there"), and her friend will incorporate her decision into the paper. While the one student is writing and researching on the Internet, the peer tutor supporting Carlien is having her sort various pictures into three categories and explain why. The peer tutor will show her the three categories (for example, people, products, and buildings) and then will model putting some pictures into each category with a simple rationale. She then presents Carlien with a picture and asks her where it would go. Carlien can usually do this skill if she is focused in on the correct stimulus and not irrelevant information (e.g., background of a picture). The peer tutor waits approximately two seconds and then points to the item pictured and asks if it is a person, a thing that can be sold, or a building. This is usually all the prompting that Carlien needs, although if necessary, another cue might be to draw her attention to the three possible categories and label each one. When Carlien places the picture onto one of the three piles, the peer tutor will ask her why she is putting it in that category. Carlien will usually respond with one or two words about the picture (e.g., "girl"). When she does this, the peer tutor will ask her to tell her more about the girl and why it goes in the people category. If she responds with a three to four-word phrase (e.g., "because she's people" or "she's like a woman"), Carlien will get credit for the sort. If she repeats the one or two-word utterance with no explanation or if she tries to put the picture into another category that is incorrect, the peer tutor will tell her the category and provide a correct model verbally for the rationale while ensuring that the picture gets placed in the correct pile.

Throughout the writing of the paper, Carlien's friend will ask her to give her another product to write about, and Carlien will have to make the right selection from the three groups in front of her and hand her peer one of the pictures in the product pile. If she does this correctly, her peer will ask her to explain why they should write about what's pictured. Carlien is again to provide a three to four-word rationale for including the pictured item in the paper (e.g., "I like tea" or" my mom drinks tea"), which her friend tries to incorporate into the paper. If Carlien hands her an incorrect picture, the peer will correct her and repeat her question for a product. If Carlien doesn't respond within two seconds, she'll point to the correct pile.

Table 6.13 Sample Data Sheet for Carlien's Activity of Categorization

Carlien's Objective: When presented with three categories using a picture or words of a given topic, Carlien will name a specific picture or labeled item, place it in the appropriate category, and explain why with a short phrase (e.g., China makes this) with 80% accuracy per topic of study (of at least five items) for 12 different topics of study.

Standard: World History—Students will demonstrate an understanding of the state of the world about 1000 CE.

Instructions: Note the topic and the three categories, the picture to be categorized, whether the response was correct or not, and Carlien's rationale of why she is placing the picture in a given category.

Date	Lesson or Topic/Categories	Item to be Categorized	Correct (+) or Incorrect (−)	Carlien's Explanation
4/2/09	Topic: Asia Categories: (1) people, (2) transportation, and (3) products	Man	+/+	"Man is a people"
"	"	Horse	−/−	put with products, "goes here"
"	"	Woman	+/+	"a woman is a people"
"	"	Silk	−/−	put with people, "she wears this"
"	"	Tea	+/+	"you drink this"
"	"	Temple	+/−	Correct category, "big"
Success/Opportunity			4/6 (67%)	3/6 (50%)

The peer tutor (or other person providing instruction at this time) keeps track of Carlien's progress by using the data sheet depicted in Table 6.13. This person records the subject being studied, writes down the three categories for the lesson, indicates whether or not Carlien was correct in her sorting of the labeled pictures, and writes down her verbal explanation for each picture sorted. She also records what is being sorted so that any particular difficulties that Carlien may be having with sorting can be quickly identified. Since the categories do not change during one lesson, the data recording time is minimal (e.g., just the item to be sorted, whether correct or incorrect, and her verbal rationale). Such data may show that while Carlien can sort the items correctly, she may not be providing the desired verbal explanation to accompany each picture.

TEST TAKING BY THE CLASS ■

Test-taking time in a general education class can become a challenging situation for students with severe disabilities. A tendency may exist to remove students during test-taking situations to ensure quiet for the rest of the students. However, tests can and should be adapted so that the target student has similar expectations as other students. Furthermore, testing the student at the same time as others can provide valuable progress data. Being removed from a class due to test taking identifies the student as a visitor to the class with lowered expectations.

Depending on the student and subject, the IEP goal and objective may address mastery as a percentage achieved on a certain number of unit tests or quizzes. For example, to demonstrate knowledge learned on core content in science, a student may be expected to meet 80% accuracy on the majority of adapted science unit tests during the year. When this is the case, testing the student on curricular material (albeit adapted) at the same time as others in the class makes perfect sense. The test with its adapted questions and the student's responses serve as valuable data toward meeting this objective. See Tables 6.13 and 6.14 for examples of IEP objectives written showing mastery on a certain number of tests as the criterion. Since the number of questions on any adapted test may vary, it is important to note both success (number of correct answers) and opportunities (number of total questions) to better understand performance over the long run. Also, finding out from the science teacher or classroom teacher responsible for science instruction how many tests will occur on science content for the school year will determine the number of tests on which the student must show some mastery.

Notice that the type of information gathered in Table 6.14 is frequency data in the form of S/O. In this case, success refers to the number of correct responses (5), while opportunities refer to total number of spelling words (10). Additional information noting the specific spelling word and the options presented to her was also gathered to better understand Jennifer's performance. For example, as we look at this data sheet, some patterns begin to emerge. Jennifer consistently identified the *c* sounds (*cattle* and *cowboy*). She identified the middle sounds in *rifle*, *ranch*, and *lasso*, and may have confused the *f* sound

Table 6.14 Sample Data Collection Sheet for Letter Identification

Jennifer's Objective: Given four letter options and when the word is said slowly to her, Jennifer will correctly identify the first letter of 8 of 10 spelling words per spelling test for 70% of all such tests.

Standard: AZ Grade 3: Identify and manipulate the sounds of speech.

Instructions: Record spelling word, placement of letter, which letter she selected, and if the response was correct (+) or incorrect (−).

Date: 4/24/09 Spelling words	Letter Options and Placement of Letters in Front of Student				Key + = correct − = incorrect
Jump	(T)	J	H	S	−
Cattle	S	R	D	(C)	+
Fences	C	S	F	(P)	−
Pumpkin	(P)	I	K	N	+
Lasso	O	L	(S)	A	−
Cowboy	B	(C)	E	O	+
Ranch	A	S	R	(N)	−
Grain	R	M	A	(G)	+
Barbecue	K	Q	(B)	R	+
Rifle	(I)	R	L	F	−
				Total Correct (S/O)	5/10 = 50%

with the *ph* sound. Clearly, additional data are needed before more definitive conclusions can be drawn, but it is apparent that this information can better help teachers in their day-to-day instruction with students.

■ TRAINING PARAPROFESSIONALS AND OTHERS TO TAKE DATA

Anyone can take data—teachers, paraprofessionals, related service staff, and peers. As a result, everyone will need to have some training with regard to creating appropriate data collection forms, learning how to objectively collect data, and learning how to analyze the data collected. Yell, Ryan, Rozalski, and Katsiyannis (2009) stress the importance of training everyone to collect and use data to design appropriate educational programs. The first step is to make the data sheet as simple and clear as possible. Several examples have been provided (see Tables 6.1–6.14). The consistent variables among these data sheets are (1) clear and succinct instructions, (2) a template with required information highlighted in some way, and (3) a simple key that explains symbols or abbreviations. The second step is to explain the data sheet; here, the focus should be on explaining why certain types of data are being collected. For example, in Tables 6.11, 6.12, and 6.14, data collection included noting the placement of the options presented to the student. This is being done to better understand the student's performance (e.g., Is the student more likely to select the first or last option?). If a pattern does emerge, this may mean that the student is not scanning all possible options before responding. Or it may mean that the student doesn't know the answer and therefore simply picks the first or last option presented. The point is, without this additional information, we may never come to understand the student's response. We cannot assume that others taking this data will understand this rationale—it is worth taking the time to explain the reasons why the data are being collected.

The third step is to practice taking the data in the actual situation in which performance data would normally be collected. It may be helpful for the teacher and the paraprofessional (or peer, related service staff, volunteer) to take data together for a short amount of time and then compare their results. This process will help to clarify any misunderstandings; for example, the student began to select Option A, hesitated, and then selected Option D instead. Option D was the correct answer and the student should receive credit for self-correcting (record response as correct). This process will be especially important in data collection that involves recording of prompt level. Noting prompt level can be complex in that it requires that the person taking the data has a clear understanding of the different types of prompts—specifically, what a partial physical prompt looks like (e.g., guiding the student's elbow and letting go) in comparison to a gesture cue in which the teacher points to the picture as a cue to select a given picture. Several training sessions may be needed to better understand the different types of prompts and how they may change as the teacher begins to fade them out.

THE NEED FOR ALTERNATE ASSESSMENT ■

NCLB of 2001 requires that all students be held accountable for acquiring specific skills as set forth in grade-level standards. For those unable to be assessed by standardized grade-level assessments, alternate assessment is available. The U.S. Department of Education (USDOE) allows for reduced depth, breadth, and complexity in alternate assessments to be used with the small percentage of students who need this option. The USDOE also allows for a variety of alternate assessment options to include portfolio, checklists, and one-to-one individualized format based on performance (USDOE, 2005). Therefore, each state can opt for a different alternate assessment to determine progress made by students with more significant disabilities.

To maintain high expectations for all students, states are to align alternate assessments with standardized assessments at each grade level. However, states continue to struggle with developing meaningful alignment (Browder et al., 2004, 2005; Lynch & Adams, 2008; Towles-Reeves, Kleinert, & Muhomba, 2009). Without meaningful alignment teachers may be teaching students skills that are not assessed on the alternate form of the mandated standardized assessment for this population. Concerns from teachers in the field highlight the lack of relevance to day to day instruction, the time taken away from meaningful instruction, and the increased demands on time (Crawford & Tindal, 2006; Flowers, Ahlgrim-Delzell, Browder, & Spooner, 2005; Perner, 2006; Towles-Reeves & Kleinert, 2006). This disconnect between what is being taught and what is being assessed is a challenge to the field.

Obviously, further growth and development in the areas of accountability and assessment are needed. Teachers need to feel that the assessments truly measure what students have learned and are worth the time and effort committed to them. In fact, experts recommend that students be assessed on what has been taught (Kampfer, Horvath, Kleinert, & Kearns, 2001; Parrish & Stodden, 2009). Therefore, students should be taught skills and knowledge that are aligned with grade-level standards, and their alternate assessment should also be linked to these same standards. Then, what teachers teach their students will be assessed on the alternate assessment. Such an alignment across both instruction and assessment would serve to lessen the current frustration that teachers have expressed for alternate assessments.

Students with moderate to severe disabilities are not likely to reach grade-level standards. However, this fact should not prevent these students from being educated in and benefiting from an inclusive educational program. When educated in general education classrooms, students have greater access to the core curriculum and benefit from higher expectations for academic progress (Roach & Elliott, 2006). Being unable to meet grade-level standards should not be a deterrent for including these students in typical classes. Not every student without disabilities will reach proficiency on every standard, yet they are allowed access the core curriculum in general education classrooms. Ensuring meaningful access to the core curriculum, making it as relevant as possible, providing systematic instruction, and supporting students to be successful should be the teaching goals for everyone responsible for a student's quality education.

■ SUMMARY

Chapter 6 has taken an in-depth look at the importance of meaningful data collection as well as the many different ways in which this can occur. No one right way exists for data collection to measure student progress, but rather, the data forms will change to address the topic being studied, the type of data collected, the need for additional information on student learning, and the manner in which the student indicates what he or she knows. Of critical importance is the need to actually collect the data so that student learning can be measured objectively and next steps determined more accurately. Making data collection simple, straightforward, and part of a routine may be the best way to ensure that this important aspect of instruction actually occurs.

Various individuals on the team will collaborate in the data collection process. Adults on the team as well as peers may be responsible for collecting data on different skills and activities across any school day. Therefore, training all those responsible for data collection on objective means of recording student progress (or lack of progress) is an important part of the teaming process. Data collected and analyzed will determine if students are making expected and desired progress or whether instructional plans and materials need to be altered. Therefore, everyone on the team must understand its importance and be diligent in carrying out this responsibility.

Although it is impossible to present every conceivable option for determining next steps for students when they have mastered present IEP goals and objectives, Chapter 7 will offer some suggestions for this process. Building on the student's accomplishments as determined via precise and objective data collection will be one consideration for future learning objectives. Other considerations may be more personal in nature and involve student interests (that may change), as well as familial needs and expectations, and changing life situations.

7

He's Getting It! Now What? Taking Learning to the Next Level

KEY CONCEPTS

- Next steps need to be individually determined and reflect student progress, unique situation, and needs.

- Individual's interests and goals, state standards, and task analyses of meaningful activities can all help in determining appropriate next steps.

- Learning does not stop upon graduation from public school.

Demonstrating progress on Individualized Education Plan (IEP) goals and objectives shows that the student is learning, and the instruction is appropriate. However, progress on discrete skills cannot overshadow the need to look at the bigger picture for the student. Strengths and needs change as the student progresses through the school years. Cognitive, physical, and sensory skills can improve or decline as the student ages. Different life circumstances (e.g., a major move, death of a family member, severe illness) can all impact future decisions. The need exists to understand both what the student is currently doing in the present context as well as what potential future environments may offer.

Careful assessment of student achievement (as discussed in Chapter 6) in both academic as well as nonacademic skills is needed to gain a comprehensive and accurate picture of the student's strengths. When skills have not been mastered, the educational team needs to carefully consider the importance of the skill(s) to the student and whether or not it should remain a targeted skill. Greater modifications may be in order as well as a different instructional procedure. The team may decide that ways exist to bypass the required skill or to work on ways for the individual to seek assistance as needed (a communication skill). For example, a student may never be able to independently obtain needed items to complete tasks due to a severe physical impairment and instead needs to learn to use a communication device to request help to perform this aspect of the task. For other students, learning all the essential steps in a task is quite feasible and will lead to greater independence in a number of areas. No two students are exactly alike, and therefore, next steps for students must be individually decided.

■ INVOLVING THE STUDENT IN PLANNING NEXT STEPS

In general, active involvement of the student in determining next steps is recommended (Carter, Lane, Pierson, & Stang, 2008; Wehmeyer, 2005; Wehmeyer, Garner, Yeager, Lawrence, & Davis, 2006). Even quite young children should be able to participate in identifying things they would like to do and skills they would like to learn. As stated in Chapter 1, assisting individuals at any age to achieve greater self-determination is a basic premise of this book. For individuals who do not use speech to express themselves, alternative modes of communication can be used (Beukelman & Mirenda, 2005; Downing, 2005; Iacono, 2003). Students can be asked simple questions and offered pictorial and/or object choices to express their preferences. The more experience the student has, the better able he or she will be to understand the questions and make an informed decision.

The degree of active involvement also will be tempered by the age of the student, with very young children typically having less involvement than older students. Family members will be the main determinants in how much they feel their child can and should participate. Some families will expect their child to play a major role in determining next steps, while others will feel it is more important for adults to decide. The culture, background, religious and spiritual beliefs, language, experiences, and beliefs of the family should always be respected during such planning meetings (King, Baxter, Rosenbaum, Zwaigenbaum, & Bates, 2009; Poston & Turnbull, 2004). Listening respectfully to the desires and beliefs of all parties and sharing information in a nonjudgmental manner are advised, especially when disagreements occur.

Person-Centered Planning

A recommended practice in the field designed to include the student in active decision making regarding the future is the practice of person-centered planning (PCP). PCP is a process of taking a highly individualized approach to planning someone's life (Holburn, Gordon, & Vietze, 2007; Holburn & Vietze, 2002). Typically, individuals who are very familiar with the student (e.g., family, friends, neighbors, teachers, and paraprofessionals) gather together to consider different options, express a vision for the future, identify potential barriers, determine needed supports, and design a plan to reach desired goals. Those at such a planning activity assume varying levels of responsibility for assisting the target individual to obtain individually determined goals. Once a plan has been decided on and implemented, this group will typically need to determine if the plan is being implemented as originally envisioned, whether it is meeting the individual's needs and desires, and arrange for modifications as needed. The plan is dynamic and designed to change with the needs, interests, abilities, and life situation of the individual. The ultimate goal of using PCP as a planning tool is to increase the individual's overall quality of life (Thompson et al., (2009). For specific examples of using PCP, especially in a pictorial format to help those who are nonreaders, see Holburn et al., (2007).

Developing a Plan

Potential next steps can be developed using information obtained from the PCP. This plan should be flexible so that changes can be readily made as needed. However, the plan should include next steps in skill development for the coming year as well as a larger picture of what the student's life could look like following school years. The plan should be systematically developed and contain the following steps: consider all options, determine priorities, undertake for a trial period, and reevaluate the plan. These steps will be described in the following paragraphs.

Consider All Options

When planning for future steps it is wise to brainstorm among team members to determine as many different options as possible (Holburn et al., 2007). Options could include continuing on a similar path as before with regard to learning skills, maintaining some aspects of the same general direction while changing others, or completely changing a student's program to better address individual needs. Obviously, aspects of the student and how that student learns (e.g., efficiency in mastering skills, student strengths and interests) will have an impact on the options determined. Desired goals that emerged during a PCP meeting would be part of the possible options for the student. While some options may appear somewhat fanciful, it may be better to err in the direction of having higher expectations than to be too restrictive.

Various options need to be discussed in terms of all academic areas as well as nonacademic areas (e.g., communication, social skills, vocational skills, self-help skills, physical development). For example, in discussing mobility issues for the student who uses a wheelchair, potential options involved learning how to push his own wheelchair, learning the use of an electric wheelchair, learning to request assistance from a peer to help him get places, learning to use a walker for short distances, learning to use an adapted tandem bike, and learning to use a public bus that is wheelchair accessible. Though there was some discussion that the student might not have the necessary foundational skills to learn to use an electric wheelchair, a tandem bike, or a public bus, these were still presented as possible options given the importance of independent and semi-independent mobility for this student. An effort should be made to avoid limiting expectations for the student but to strive to be creative in presenting various options. For another student, potential options for enhancing communication skills included continued work using objects and parts of objects, broadening use of vocalizations to address certain purposes, learning American Sign Language, and becoming proficient on a complex electronic device. While some discussion focused on the student's inability to effectively make use of an electronic device, not having access to a device prevents the student from demonstrating what she may be able to learn. This dilemma of whether or not to provide students with complex devices prior to them being able to demonstrate proficiency on the device places the student in a "catch-22" position. That is, the student can't demonstrate proficiency because he doesn't have the device and can never get the device until proficiency is demonstrated. Like many of us who are not capable of utilizing all the capabilities of our computers, not having a computer until proficiency was demonstrated would not help the situation. We become more efficient with our tools the more we have access to them and learn how to best use them. We need to be very careful not to inadvertently place the student in such an untenable situation. The focus should be on the types and amount of support the student will need to reach desired goals independently or semi-independently.

Determine Priorities for the Student

From the list of potential options, those most critical for the student's enhanced performance presently as well as in the near future should take precedent over other options that may become more critical later on. Priorities should emerge across the range of academic skills (reading, writing, math, social studies, science) as well as in nonacademic skills (e.g., communication, social skills, daily living skills, self-control). Priority skills should be those that increase the student's participation in valued school activities and will be most apt to enhance the student's future learning as well as social acceptance and belonging. In determining priority skills, the desires of the student as well as those of the family should be considered especially important. The family in particular may want a specific skill or activity learned to help their family engage in more activities together and enhance interactions. Of course, the student may have particular interests and even passions that should definitely be considered as priorities for next steps.

Provide a Trial Period

The next steps chosen for a student may not be the perfect solution, and therefore, a trial period is needed to determine whether or not they represent a good fit for the student. Students with severe disabilities may need considerable time to understand expectations and begin to demonstrate what they have learned. Therefore, sufficient time needs to be allowed before changes to the program occur. The individual members on the team will need to buy into the plan so that everyone can support its implementation. Such a buy-in will likely require compromise by several individuals on the team. All members will need to make sure that they are implementing the plan correctly, as it would be easy to undermine a plan when individual team members are unable to compromise. Therefore, agreeing to give a plan for a student serious consideration and effort is advised. After a month of consistent instruction using evidence-based practices, the student should begin to demonstrate some understanding of the task. Other students may demonstrate progress in much less time.

The trial period will likely differ per student given differences in age, cognitive ability, motivation, physical skills, and other variables. Progress, or lack of progress, on specific skills should be carefully monitored during the trial period to determine if the plan is appropriate (e.g., makes sense for the student). Bearing in mind that this is a trial period may help the team to consider some options that may initially have been thought to be unattainable or not practical. Sometimes a student's interests may lead the team to consider something that may be particularly difficult to teach and a trial period is needed to see what may result.

Review and Revise the Plan

Depending on results from the trial period, the team can determine if the plan is on the right track for the student or not. Although the IEP can be written for the duration of a year, needed changes can and should occur at any time during that time period. A student should not be expected to follow a course of action that is not helping the student learn important skills. While plans can and should be revised, sufficient time should be allowed for the trial period to determine if it is appropriate for the student or not.

Revising the plan could involve changing targeted skills, modifying the criterion to be reached, altering how the student will demonstrate the skill and/or what accommodations may be needed, or reducing or increasing the number of skills to be learned within a task. Revisions could also involve amending the teaching strategies used to teach the student if current strategies appear to be ineffective. For example, if a student is having difficulty using an electronic communication device to participate in class, options that support the use of the device, such as static overlays positioned directly in front of the student, as well as accepting natural gestures and vocalizations, may be used jointly with the device. Changing the ways that others respond to the student's use of various modes of communication may also support the student's progress.

WRITING IEP OBJECTIVES TO ■ REFLECT NEXT STEPS

Once students have mastered IEP objectives and goals, more challenging objectives and goals need to be written. At times, next steps may seem quite obvious, while at other times, multiple directions could emerge as possible options confounding the decision. For example, if a student has mastered the skill of completing prewritten sentences with words and/or pictures or by identifying the correct noun that is missing, a next step would be for the student to complete the sentence with a noun and a verb missing. The goal would be to increase the student's ability to write sentences (with picture or word cards)—a writing and communication skill. On the other hand, for a student who has mastered the communication skill of greeting peers and teachers, several next steps are possible. The student could learn to initiate an interaction by pointing to pictures or messages in her or his conversation book, or she or he could learn to respond to peers' questions or statements. The student could also learn to ask questions of peers or to maintain a conversation for a certain number of turns. If she or he has only learned to greet one or two peers, this could be expanded to greet more peers across different environments. When several different options exist, the team needs to decide which of the skills would most benefit the student— socially, academically, and communicatively. The student could work on two or three different skills that would all contribute to her or his communication progress.

■ USING STANDARDS AND PERFORMANCE INDICATORS TO DETERMINE NEXT STEPS

When the student is demonstrating clear progress toward achieving content standards as determined by performance indicators or objectives, using the sequence of skills described in the standards may be an appropriate approach. For example, a third-grade standard in language arts states that students will generate and answer literal, inferential, interpretive, and evaluative questions to demonstrate understanding of what is read. A student, Reva, has mastered her IEP objectives of responding consistently with 80% accuracy to factual questions of who, what, and where with stories read in language arts. She struggles with more interpretive and reasoning questions of why and how. Therefore, depending on other important variables in Reva's life, a next step for her could be to develop mastery of how and/or why questions (with pictorial accommodations as needed). The more this student can understand with regard to information read to her, the more she will gain access to more information and knowledge. Furthermore, understanding why events occur in fiction or nonfiction material may help her with her own life situations.

As another example, a student may have mastered the recognition of numbers 1 through 10 but no higher. The second-grade math standard on number sense states that students will read, write, and represent whole numbers to 1,000. Therefore, given no contra-indicators, a potential next step for this student may be to work on recognizing double-digit numbers and their relationships to each other. Recognition of larger numbers may be beneficial to the student in numerous future adult activities, such as banking, shopping, finding addresses, and so on. Continuing to learn number skills in a more typical developmental sequence may be just what this student needs.

A careful scrutiny of performance indicators for grade-level content standards can result in clearly important and feasible next steps for students. While all performance indicators may not be suitable or beneficial, some may be. For example, a seventh-grade Earth science standard states that the student will describe the composition and interactions between the structure of the earth and the atmosphere. One performance indicator for this standard states that the student will explain erosion, deposition, plate tectonics, and volcanism. For a student with very limited language skills and a very basic knowledge of Earth science, this indicator may not be attainable. However, another performance indicator at the same grade level states that students will classify rocks and minerals by their characteristics such as grain, color, texture, and hardness. Since this student is learning to sort, such a performance indicator may be quite appropriate as he can sort rocks by their weight, color, markings, and so on. Therefore, using the content-level standards in different subjects for a student may be an excellent starting point to determine next steps. See Table 7.1 for examples across grade level and subject matter in determining next steps from standards and performance indicators.

Table 7.1 Examples of Potential Next Steps According to Content Standards

Content Standard	Present Skill Level	Potential Next Steps
Kindergarten: Writing Write (print) first and last name.	Niko has learned to identify his first name from four options. He has also learned to identify the first letter of his name.	A logical next step for Niko would involve him learning to identify his last name from two or three options and/or to identify the other three letters in his first name.
Grade 3: Number Sense Describe and compare the attributes of plane and solid geometric shapes and use their understanding to show relationships and solve problems.	Although he does not name them, Tyron can sort up to four common shapes (e.g., circle, square, triangle, and rectangle) with approximately 85% accuracy.	Given his communication needs and understanding of the world, a next step for Tyron may be for him to identify common objects that have a particular shape (e.g., ball, clock, book, CD, piece of pizza, table). He can also work on counting the number of sides for those that are applicable.
Grade 6: Comprehending Literary Text Identify, analyze, and apply knowledge of the structures and elements of literature.	Zan really loves to have people read science fiction to him. He can recognize who the heroes are and what makes them heroic. However, he seems uninterested in other forms of literature.	To broaden his interests in reading, a next step for Zan may be to experience other genres of literature and be able to tell the difference between fantasy and nonfiction or between different forms of fiction (e.g., sci-fi, fantasy, mysteries)

(Continued)

Table 7.1 (Continued)

Content Standard	Present Skill Level	Potential Next Steps
Grade 8: Physical Science Students collect and organize data to identify relationships between physical objects, events, and processes. They use logical reasoning to question their own ideas as new information challenges their conceptions of the natural world. **Performance Objective:** Understand and explain that the benefits of the Earth's resources, such as fresh water, air, soil, and trees, are finite and can be reduced by using them wastefully or by deliberately or accidentally destroying them.	Polly has learned to respond verbally to who, what, and where questions. However, she struggles when questions involve explaining the how or why.	Polly can learn to respond to how and why questions involving the Earth's resources, such as why do we have fewer trees or how does a large fire get started? Learning to respond to such questions will help her not only in science, but in all other subjects as well.
Grade 12: Social Studies Economics Analyze the ways in which supply and demand, competition, prices, incentives, and profits influence what is produced and distributed in a competitive market system.	Bree has learned to read prices on items she would like to buy. She has also learned to pay for items using a one-dollar-more strategy or using a debit card or credit card.	Bree could benefit from learning that the same item could be more or less expensive depending on where it is purchased. She can learn to do some comparative shopping using ads in retail flyers or on the Internet to determine the lowest price to pay.

■ USING TASK ANALYSES TO DETERMINE NEXT STEPS

As presented in Chapters 2, 3, and 6, task analysis of activities is a recommended practice for teaching students with moderate to severe disabilities. Breaking down the task to delineate the necessary steps required for completion aids in mastering the activity as well as helps the teacher identify which steps are the most challenging. If an entire activity is deemed important for the student, then looking at the individual steps of the task to determine skill level would be helpful in writing subsequent IEP goals and objectives. For example, in the activity of reading a story or entire book, steps involved include getting the book, opening it to the correct page, finding the right place to begin reading, turning the pages, and comprehending what was read. A student may have mastered the steps of getting the book, opening it, and listening to the words being read (an adaptation) but has yet to master turning pages when cued or comprehending what is read. These skills should then be targeted as next steps, with accommodations as needed.

Some steps of an important activity may never be mastered by a student due to physical or cognitive limitations, and adaptations will be a permanent aspect of the activity. If the activity is an important one for the student to be involved in, then learning as many of the steps (or adapted steps) as possible should be the goal. The following example may clarify.

A fourth-grade student, Devon, has gained skills working in small group situations with peers. However, he still needs to make more progress to be a clearly contributing member. The following analysis of a typical small group lesson is depicted below.

Science Class—Small Group Work

1. Get materials
2. Get into groups
3. Perform experiment
4. Discuss results
5. Complete report
6. Clean up
7. Return to seats

While Devon has learned to get some materials, get into his group, participate in the experiment, help clean up, and return to his seat (Steps 1, 2, 3, 6, & 7), he struggles with the main intent of small group work (discussing findings and completing reports). When Step 4 (discuss results) is further analyzed to determine smaller skills Devon needs to learn to be an active member of his group, next steps can be identified.

Step 4. Discuss Results—Task Analysis for Devon

a. Make choice of pictorial options regarding experiment
b. Tap peer on arm to gain attention
c. Hand pictorial/written decision to peer
d. Repeat steps two to three times during group work

Devon needs to work on taking the initiative to gain a peer's attention and make a comment related to the experiment. He also needs to increase the number of turns taken to contribute to the discussion. So, although he is an active participant in the group work, a next step for Devon could involve targeting his part in the discussion step of the small group work. These skills are considered important for Devon because they appear in a number of different learning situations, and his team envisions them occurring in similar work or social settings in the future.

■ USING LIFE NEEDS TO DETERMINE NEXT STEPS

At times, traditionally prescribed next steps may not be the best option. Student characteristics and specific situations may take precedent over standard performance indicators. Personal situations may change that have an impact on goals for students. What had at one point seemed important to learn may no longer be considered essential. For example, writing by hand may have been targeted at one point for a student, but as the student aged and physical impairments prevented the ease of this approach, use of an adapted keyboard became much more of a priority. As King et al. (2009) revealed, parents of high school students with autism and Down syndrome expressed different goals than parents of similar students at the elementary level. King et al. (2009) interviewed 16 Canadian families to identify any impact of a disability on belief systems. The parents of high school students expressed a stronger desire for greater independence versus safety, placed greater emphasis on their son or daughter obtaining a job and contributing to society, and worried more about maintaining friendships for their child than did parents of younger children.

When remaining years in school are limited, next steps for learning may target skills that will be easiest to learn and most immediately beneficial to the student's daily life as an adult. For example, a student, Ian, is in the 10th grade and still struggles to recognize single-digit numbers. Given the few years remaining in school, it may be appropriate to consider certain number skills that may be most useful to him. For example, instead of teaching all numbers, it may make sense to teach numbers on common bills (ones, fives, tens, twenties). Recognizing numbers on common bills (a different task than recognizing clearly written numbers in black on a white background) would support daily purchases. These same numbers could also be used for pin numbers (to also support the activity of making purchases).

For the student in eighth grade who continues to struggle with basic writing skills, a different approach may be warranted. If he knows what he wants to say, can sound out several letters, but cannot remember how to produce these letters for his phonetically spelled words, teaching the use of a very small and portable computer and/or PDA may be a better use of school time. Such a skill fits well with our technologically oriented world, may relieve frustration, and supports the student to express himself in writing.

These examples highlight the importance of keeping future plans dynamic and flexible for students. While plans may change, the ultimate goal is to support the student to learn as many meaningful skills across a wide array of academic and nonacademic areas as possible to benefit the student's quality of life as an adult. Quality of life issues are serious ones for all individuals but particularly those individuals with moderate and severe disabilities. Research findings have failed to demonstrate that these individuals are attaining a high quality of life (Beadle-Brown, Murphy, & Wing, 2005; Keogh, Bernheimer, & Guthrie, 2004; Sheppard-Jones, Prout, & Kleinert, 2005). Educational teams need to keep quality of life issues for the unique individual clearly in mind when planning next steps as the student progresses through the school system.

POSTSECONDARY OPTIONS ■

When thinking of the future and making future plans with the student, all options available for typically developing students should be considered. Options to consider beyond the high school years include going to college, working, volunteering, living independently, and adult recreation. Academic goals considered important for the student may still be targeted after the student graduates from high school. An increasing number of students with moderate to severe intellectual disabilities are attending postsecondary institutions of learning to further their education (Hart, Mele-McCarthy, Pasternack, Zimbrich, & Parker, 2004). Different options exist to support this continuation of academic programs, including school district support, vocational aid programs, and legislation. In the United States, the Higher Education Opportunity Act (2008) was established to expand higher educational opportunities by increasing the number of Pell grants for students with intellectual disabilities. Like K–12 educational programs, these advanced programs at colleges and universities will need to be individualized with the necessary support for the student to be successful and meet stated outcomes.

While many postsecondary options for students with intellectual disabilities are on college campuses yet separate from the mainstream of student life (Hart, Zimbrich, & Parker, 2005), some college programs are being developed that are academic in nature and inclusive. Carroll, Blumberg, and Petroff (2008) describe the Liberal Arts undergraduate program at the College of New Jersey for students with intellectual disabilities. A specially designed four-year program entitled Career and Community Studies offers core coursework that are inclusive classes, with individualized supports for students and collaborative teaming. Students in this program take courses on human abilities, career exploration, consumer math, and others and participate in internships during their final three years.

As with education during the school years, postsecondary options also should be inclusive in nature. With the right kind of supports, the same benefits that students with and without disabilities experience from preschool through high school should also be apparent for college-age students (Carroll et al., 2008; Casale-Giannola & Kamens, 2006; Grigal, Neubert, & Moon, 2002). Learning together should continue to support interactions in other walks of life.

■ NEXT STEPS FOR NONACADEMIC SKILLS

While this text has intentionally targeted primarily academic skills for students with moderate to severe disabilities (to demonstrate how these skills could be taught within general education classrooms), nonacademic skills are equally important. All aspects of the student's life should be considered when planning next steps. The team needs to evaluate learning opportunities in academics, communication, social skills, vocational arenas, recreation, and daily living skills. For example, a student typically responds to others who ask questions, but he rarely if ever initiates interactions with others. This lack of initiation can be very limiting socially, making him dependent on others to approach him and ask the right questions. Therefore, teaching this student to initiate interactions with peers and adults alike could be a very important next step. Initiation could involve approaching a person and handing that person a picture or object with a written message on it.

Certain nonacademic skills can be very relevant as next steps for a particular student but should not be considered necessary for every student. For example, a student, Wes, has learned to pull on his pants and a T-shirt. The fine motor skills involved in buttoning and snapping are greater than what Wes can acquire given his severe physical disabilities. Therefore, most of his clothes can be pulled on. A next step for Wes may be to learn how to use a Velcro fastener (e.g., grasp, pull apart, and press together). Such skills can be learned when dressing for a PE class, during the use of a restroom, and putting on and removing a coat prior to entering or exiting a building. For a student with even more severe physical disabilities, the preceding example may be irrelevant and targeted skills could involve communicating with others to choose different clothes and ask for assistance to put them on. Next steps in nonacademic skills, as in academic skills, must be individually determined per student, as each student's situation is quite unique.

■ SUMMARY

This final chapter has provided some options to consider when determining next steps for a given student. Students need to be challenged to continue to learn new skills that are meaningful for their present and future life. Teachers can turn to grade-level standards, task analysis of activities, or familial and student interests to help in the determination of appropriate next steps for learning.

Learning does not stop when students reach the age when school services stop (usually at 22 years). Adults with moderate and severe disabilities have proven their ability to continue learning well after their K–12th-grade education ends. See studies by Stromer, Mackay, Howell, and McVay (1996), Brady and McLean (1996), and Pershey and Gilbert (2002) for examples of adults with moderate to severe intellectual disabilities acquiring new literacy skills long after leaving the school system. Therefore, those providing educational support for the student need to maintain realistic yet high expectations for learning that will follow the student into adulthood. Learning as many skills as possible during the school years will build a solid foundation for continued learning throughout the student's adult years.

Educational goals for a student may change as he or she progresses through the grades and toward graduation. Factors such as the student's learning rate, improved or diminishing physical and cognitive abilities, educational support at home, and interests may all impact decisions regarding next steps for a student. Using grade-level standards and typical, age-appropriate activities can help guide decision making. However, recognizing that these only serve as a potential guide and are not rigid requirements should allow some much needed flexibility in developing an individualized plan. A clear vision for the student that facilitates the student's attaining the highest quality of life with friends and meaningful activities is the ultimate goal of education.

References

Agran, M., Blanchard, C., Wehmeyer, M., & Hughes, C. (2002). Increasing the problem-solving skills of students with developmental disabilities participating in general education. *Remedial and Special Education, 23,* 279–288.

Agran, M., & Wehmeyer, M. L. (2003). Self-determination. In D. L. Ryndak & S. Alper (Eds.), *Curriculum and instruction for students with significant disabilities in inclusive settings* (pp. 259–276). Needham Heights, MA: Allyn and Bacon.

Alberto, P. A., Fredrick, L., Hughes, M., McIntosh, L., & Cihak, D. (2007). Components of visual literacy: Teaching logos. *Focus on Autism and Other Developmental Disabilities, 22,* 234–243.

Albin, R. W., & Horner, R. H. (1988). Generalization with precision. In R.H. Horner, G. Dunlap, & R. L. Koegel (Eds.), *Generalization and maintenance: Lifestyle changes in applied settings* (pp. 99–120). Baltimore: Paul H. Brookes.

Angell, M. E., Bailey, R. L., & Larson, L. (2008). Systematic instruction for social-pragmatic language skills in lunchroom settings. *Education and Training in Developmental Disabilities, 43,* 342–359.

Ault, M. J., Gast, D. L., & Wolery, M. (1988). Comparison of progressive and constant time-delay procedures in teaching community-sign word reading. *American Journal of Mental Retardation, 93,* 44–56.

Barnes, K. J. (2003). Service delivery practices and educational outcomes of the related service of occupational therapy. *Physical Disabilities: Education and Related Services, XX(2),* 31–48.

Barudin, S. I., & Hourcade, J. J. (1990). Relative effectiveness of three methods of reading instruction in developing specific recall and transfer skills in learners with moderate and severe mental retardation. *Education and Training in Mental Retardation, 25,* 286–291.

Beadle-Brown, J., Murphy, G., & Wing, L. (2005). Long-term outcome for people with severe intellectual disabilities. *American Journal on Mental Retardation, 110,* 1–12.

Beukelman, D. R., & Mirenda, P. (2005). *Augmentative and alternative communication: Management of severe communication disorders in children and adults* (2nd ed.). Baltimore: Paul H. Brookes.

Biederman, G. B., Fairhall, J. L., Raven, K. A., & Davey, K. A. (1998). Verbal prompting, hand-over-hand instruction, and passive observation in teaching children with developmental disabilities. *Exceptional Children, 64,* 503–512.

Billingsley, F. (1998). Behaving independently: Considerations in fading instructor assistance. In A. Hilton & R. Ringlaben (Eds.), *Best and promising practices in developmental disabilities* (pp. 157–167). Austin, TX: Pro-Ed.

Billingsley, F. (2003). Principles and practices for instructing students with significant needs in inclusive settings. In D.L. Ryndak & S. Alper (Eds.), *Curriculum and instruction for students with significant disabilities in inclusive settings* (2nd ed., pp. 362–381). Boston: Allyn and Bacon.

Billingsley, F. F., & Kelley, B. (1994). An examination of the acceptability of instructional practices for students with severe disabilities in general education settings. *Journal of the Association for Persons With Severe Handicaps, 19,* 75–83.

Blatt, B. (1981). *In and out of mental retardation: Essays on educability, disability, and human policy.* Baltimore: University Park Press.

Blue-Banning, M., Summers, J. A., Frankland, H. C., Nelson, L. L., & Beegle, G. (2004). Dimensions of family and professional partnerships: Constructive guidelines for collaboration. *Exceptional Children, 70*, 167–184.

Boe, E. E., & Cook, L. H. (2006). The chronic and increasing shortage of fully certified teachers in special and general education. *Exceptional Children, 72*, 443–460.

Bolton, J., & Mayer, M. D. (2008). Promoting the generalization of paraprofessional discrete trial teaching skills. *Focus on Autism and Other Developmental Disabilities, 23*, 103–111.

Bond, R. J., & Castagnera, E. (2003). Supporting one another: Peer tutoring in an inclusive San Diego high school. In D. Fisher & N. Frey (Eds.), *Inclusive urban schools* (pp. 119–142). Baltimore: Paul H. Brookes.

Bradford, S., Shippen, M., Alberto, P., Houchins, D., & Flores, M. (2006). Using systematic instruction to teach decoding skills to middle school students with moderate intellectual disabilities. *Education and Training in Developmental Disabilities, 41*, 333–343.

Brady, N. C., & McLean, I. K. (1996). Arbitrary symbol learning by adults with severe mental retardation: Comparison of lexigrams and printed words. *American Journal of Mental Retardation, 100*, 423–427.

Broer, S. M., Doyle, M. B., & Giangreco, M. F. (2005). Perspectives of students with intellectual disabilities about their experiences with paraprofessional support. *Exceptional Children, 71*, 415–430.

Brooks, A., Todd, A. W., Tofflemoyer, S., & Horner, R. H. (2003). Use of functional assessment and a self-management system to increase academic engagement and work completion. *Journal of Positive Behavioral Interventions, 5*, 144–152.

Browder, D. M., Ahlgrim-Delzell, L., Flowers, C., Karvonen, M., Spooner, F., & Algozzine, R. (2005). How states implement alternate assessments for students with disabilities. *Journal of Disability Policy Studies, 14*, 209–220.

Browder, D. M., Ahlgrim-Delzell, L., Spooner, F., Mims, P. J., & Baker, J. N. (2009). Using time delay to teach literacy to students with severe developmental disabilities. *Exceptional Children, 75*, 343–364.

Browder, D., Flowers, C., Ahlgrim-Delzell, L., Karvonen, M., Spooner, F., & Algozzine, R. (2004). The alignment of alternate assessment content with academic and functional curricula. *The Journal of Special Education, 37*, 211–223.

Browder, D. M., Mims, P. J., Spooner, F., Ahlgrim-Delzell, L., & Lee, A. (2008). Teaching elementary students with multiple disabilities to participate in shared stories. *Research and Practice for Persons With Severe Disabilities, 33*(1–2), 3–12.

Browder, D. M., & Spooner, F. (2003). Understanding the purpose and process of alternate assessment. In D.L. Ryndak & S. Alper (Eds.), *Curriculum and instruction for students with significant disabilities in inclusive settings* (2nd ed., pp.51–72). Boston: Allyn and Bacon.

Browder, D. M., & Spooner, F. (Eds.). (2006). *Teaching language arts, math, and science to students with significant cognitive disabilities*. Baltimore: Paul H. Brooke.

Browder, D. M., Spooner, F., Algozzine, R., Ahlgrim-Delzell, L., Flowers, C., & Karvonen, M. (2003). What we know and need to know about alternate assessment. *Exceptional Children, 70*, 45–61.

Browder, D. M., Spooner, F., Ahlgrim-Delzell, L., Flowers, C., Karvonen, M., & Algozzine, R. (2003). A content analysis of the curricular philosophies reflected in states' alternate assessments. *Research and Practice for Persons With Severe Disabilities, 28*, 165–181.

Browder, D. M., Spooner, F., Ahlgrim-Delzell, L., Harris, A. A., & Wakeman, S. (2008). A meta-analysis on teaching mathematics to students with significant cognitive disabilities. *Exceptional Children, 74*, 407–432.

Browder, D. M., Trela, K., & Jimenez, B. (2007). Training teachers to follow a task analysis to engage middle school students with moderate and severe developmental disabilities in grade-appropriate literature. *Focus on Autism and Other Developmental Disabilities, 22,* 206–219.

Browder, D. M., Wakeman, S. Y., Spooner, F., Ahlgrim-Delzell, L., & Algozzine, B. (2006). Research on reading instruction for individuals with significant cognitive disabilities. *Exceptional Children, 72,* 392–408.

Browder, D. M., & Xin, X. P. (1998). A meta-analysis and review of sight word research and its implications for teaching functional reading to individuals with moderate and severe disabilities. *Journal of Special Education, 32,* 130–154.

Brown, L., Branston, M. B., Hamre-Nietupski, S., Johnson, F., Wilcox, B., & Gruenewald, L. (1979). A rationale for comprehensive longitudinal interactions between severely handicapped students and nonhandicapped students and other citizens. *American Association for the Education of the Severely/Profoundly Handicapped, 4,* 3–14.

Brown, L., Branston, M. B., Hamre-Nietupski, S., Pumpian, I., Certo, N., & Gruenewald, L. (1979). A strategy for developing chronological age-appropriate and functional curricular content for severely handicapped adolescents and young adults. *Journal of Special Education, 13,* 81–90.

Brown, L., Ford, A., Nisbet, J., Sweet, M., Donnellan, A., & Gruenewald, L. (1983). Opportunities available when severely handicapped students attend chronological age appropriate regular schools. *The Journal of the Association for the Severely Handicapped, 8*(1), 16–24.

Brown, L., Nietupski, J., & Hamre-Nietupski, S. (1976). The criterion of ultimate functioning and public school services for severely handicapped students. In M. A. Thomas (Ed.), *Hey, don't forget about me: Education's investment in the severely, profoundly, and multiply handicapped* (pp. 58–82). Reston, VA: Council for Exceptional Children.

Brown, L., Nisbet, J., Ford, A., Sweet. M., Shiraza, B., York, J., & Loomis, R. (1983). The critical need for nonschool instruction in educational programs for severely handicapped students. *Journal of the Association for Persons With Severe Handicaps, 8,* 71–77.

Bui, Y. N., & Turnbull, A. (2003). East meets west: Analysis of person-centered planning in the context of Asian American values. *Education and Training in Developmental Disabilities, 38,* 18–31.

Campbell, D. J., Reilly, A., & Henley, J. (2008). Comparison of assessment results of children with low incidence disabilities. *Education and Training in Developmental Disabilities, 43,* 217–225.

Cannella, H. I., O'Reilly, M. F., & Lancioni, G. E. (2005). Choice and preference assessment research with people with severe to profound developmental disabilities: A review of the literature. *Research in Developmental Disabilities, 26,* 1–15.

Capizzi, A. M. (2008). From assessment to annual goal: Engaging a decision-making process in writing measureable IEPs. *TEACHING Exceptional Children, 41*(1), 18–25.

Carlson, E., & Billingsley, B. (2001). *Working conditions in special education: Current research and implications for the field.* Paper presented at OSEP Project Directors' conference, July 2001.

Carnahan, C. R., Williamson, P., Clarke, L., & Sorensen, R. (2009). A systematic approach for supporting paraeducators in educational settings: A guide for teachers. *TEACHING Exceptional Children, 41*(5), 34–43.

Carroll, S. Z., Blumberg, E. R., & Petroff, J. G. (2008). The promise of liberal learning: Creating a challenging postsecondary curriculum for youth with intellectual disabilities. *Focus on Exceptional Children, 40*(9), 1–12.

Carter, E. W., Clark, N., Cushing, L., & Kennedy, C. H. (2007). Moving from elementary to middle school: A smooth transition for students with severe disabilities. In K. Freiberg (Ed.), *Educating exceptional children* (18th ed., pp. 187–192). Dubuque, IA: McGraw-Hill.

Carter, E. W., Cushing, L. S., Clark, N. M., & Kennedy, C. H. (2005). The effects of peer support interventions on students' access to the general curriculum and social interactions. *Research and Practice for Persons With Severe Disabilities, 30,* 15–25.

Carter, E. W., Cushing, L.S., & Kennedy, C.H. (2009). *Peer support strategies for improving all students' social lives and learning.* Baltimore: Paul H. Brookes.

Carter, E. W., & Hughes, C. (2005). Increasing social interaction among adolescents with intellectual disabilities and their general education peers: Effective interventions. *Research and Practice for Persons With Severe Disabilities, 30,* 179–193.

Carter, E. W., & Hughes, C. (2006). Including high school students with severe disabilities in general education classes: Perspectives of general and special educators, paraprofessionals, and administrators. *Research and Practice for Persons With Severe Disabilities, 31,* 174–185.

Carter, E. W., Hughes, C., Copeland, S. R., & Breen, C. (2001). Differences between high school students who do and do not volunteer to participate in peer interaction programs. *Journal of the Association for Persons With Severe Handicaps, 26,* 229–239.

Carter, E. W., & Kennedy, C. H. (2006). Promoting access to the general curriculum using peer support strategies. *Research and Practice for Persons With Severe Disabilities, 31,* 284–292.

Carter, E. W., Lane, K. L., Pierson, M. R., & Stang, K. K. (2008). Promoting self-determination for transition-age youth: Views of high school general and special educators. *Exceptional Children, 75,* 55–70.

Carter, E. W., Sisco, L. G., Brown, L., Brickham, D., & Al-Khabbaz, Z. A. (2008). Peer interactions and academic engagement of youth with developmental disabilities in inclusive middle and high school classrooms. *American Journal on Mental Retardation, 113,* 479–494.

Carter, E. W., Sisco, L. G., Melekoglu, M. A., & Kurkowski, C. (2007). Peer supports as an alternative to individually assigned paraprofessionals in inclusive high school classrooms. *Research and Practice for Persons With Severe Disabilities, 32,* 213–227.

Casale-Giannola, D., & Kamens, M. (2006). Inclusion at a university: Experiences of a young woman with Down syndrome. *Mental Retardation, 44,* 344–352.

Causton-Theoharis, J. N., Giangreco, M. F., Doyle, M. B., & Vadasy, P. (2007). Paraprofessionals: The sous chefs of literacy instruction. TEACHING *Exceptional Children, 37*(6), 18–24.

Causton-Theoharis, J. N., & Malmgren, K. W. (2005). Increasing peer interactions for students with severe disabilities via paraprofessional training. *Exceptional Children, 71,* 431–444.

Chen, D., & Downing, J. E. (2006). *Tactile strategies for children who have visual impairments and multiple disabilities: Promoting communication and learning skills.* New York: American Foundation for the Blind Press.

Cihak, D., Alberto, P. A., Taber-Doughty, T., & Gama, R. I. (2006). A comparison of static picture prompting and video prompting stimulation strategies using group instructional procedures. *Focus on Autism and Other Developmental Disabilities, 21,* 89–99.

Clark, K. M., & Green, G. (2004). Comparison of two procedures for teaching dictated-word/symbol relations to learners with autism. *Journal of Applied Behavior Analysis, 37,* 503–507.

Clayton, J., Burdge, M., Denham, A., Kleinert, H. L., & Kearns, J. (2006). A four-step process for accessing the general curriculum for students with significant cognitive disabilities. *TEACHING Exceptional Children, 38*(5), 20–27.

Cloninger, C. J. (2004). Designing collaborative educational services. In F. P. Orelove, D. Sobsey, & R. K. Silberman (Eds.), *Educating children with multiple disabilities: A collaborative approach* (4th ed., pp. 1–30). Baltimore: Paul H. Brookes.

Cole, C. M., Waldron, N., & Majd, M. (2004). Academic progress of students across inclusive and traditional settings. *Mental Retardation, 42,* 136–144.

Colozzi, G. A., Ward, L. W., & Crotty, K. E. (2008). Comparison of simultaneous prompting procedure in 1:1 and small group instruction to teach play skills to preschool students with pervasive disabilities. *Education and Training in Developmental Disabilities, 43,* 226–248.

Conroy, M. A., Asmus, J. M., Ladwig, C. N., Sellers, J. A., & Valcante, G. (2004). The effects of proximity on the classroom behaviors of students with autism in general education settings. *Behavioral Disorders, 29,* 119–129.

Copeland, S. R., Hughes, C., Agran, M., Wehmeyer, M. L., & Fowler, S. E. (2002). An intervention package to support high school students with mental retardation in general education classrooms. *American Journal on Mental Retardation, 107,* 32–45.

Copeland, S. R., Hughes, C., Carter, E. W., Guth, C., Presley, J., Williams, C. R., & Fowler, S. E. (2004). Increasing access to general education: Perspectives of participants in a high school peer support program. *Remedial and Special Education, 26,* 342–352.

Copeland, S. R., McCall, J., Williams, C. R., Guth, C., Carter, E. W., Presley, J. A., et al. (2002). High school peer buddies: A win-win situation. *TEACHING Exceptional Children, 35*(1), 16–21.

Cramer, S. F. (2006). *The special educator's guide to collaboration.* Thousand Oaks, CA: Corwin.

Crawford, L., & Tindal, G. (2006). Police and practice: Knowledge and beliefs of education professionals related to the inclusion of students with disabilities in a state assessment. *Remedial and Special Education, 27,* 208–217.

Cross, A. F., Traub, E. K., Hutter-Pishgaki, L., & Shelton, G. (2004). Elements of successful inclusion for children with significant disabilities. *Topics in Early Childhood Special Education, 24,* 169–183.

Cummings, K., Atkins, T., Allison, R., & Cole, C. (2008). Response to intervention: Investigating the new role of special educators. *TEACHING Exceptional Children, 40*(4), 24–31.

Cushing, L. S., Clark, N. M., Carter, E. W., & Kennedy, C. H. (2005). Access to the general education curriculum for students with severe disabilities: What it means and how to accomplish it. *TEACHING Exceptional Children, 38*(2), 6–13.

Cushing, L. S., & Kennedy, C. H. (1997). Academic effects on students without disabilities who serve as peer supports for students with disabilities in general education classrooms. *Journal of Applied Behavior Analysis, 30,* 139–152.

Danzer, G. A., de Alva, J. J. K., Krieger, L. S., Wilson, L. E., & Woloch, N. (2007). *The Americans.* Geneva, IL: McDougal Littell.

Devlin, P. (2005). Effect of continuous improvement training on student interaction and engagement. *Research and Practice for Persons With Severe Disabilities, 30,* 47–59.

Dole, M. B. (2008). *The paraprofessional's guide to the inclusive classroom: Working as a team.* Baltimore: Paul H. Brookes.

Dore, R., Dion, A., Wagner, S., & Brunet, J. P. (2002). High school inclusion of adolescent with mental retardation: A multiple case study. *Education and Training in Mental Retardation and Developmental Disabilities, 37,* 253–261.

Downing, J. E. (2003). Accommodating motor and sensory impairments in inclusive settings. In D. L. Ryndak & S. Alper (Eds.), *Curriculum and instruction for students with significant disabilities in inclusive settings* (2nd ed., pp. 411–431). Boston: Allyn and Bacon.

Downing, J. E. (2005). *Teaching communication skills to students with severe disabilities* (2nd ed.). Baltimore: Paul H. Brookes.

Downing, J. E. (2006). On peer support, universal design, and access to the core curriculum for students with severe disabilities: A personnel preparation perspective. *Research and Practice for Persons With Severe Disabilities, 31,* 327–330.

Downing, J. E. (2008). *Including students with severe and multiple disabilities in typical classrooms: Practical strategies for teachers* (3rd ed.). Baltimore: Paul H. Brookes.

Downing, J. E., & Peckham-Hardin, K. D. (2007). Inclusive education: What makes a high quality education for students with moderate-severe disabilities? *Research and Practice for Persons With Severe Disabilities, 32,* 16–30.

Downing, J. E., Ryndak, D. L., & Clark, D. (2000). Paraeducators in inclusive classrooms: Their own perceptions. *Remedial and Special Education, 21,* 171–181.

Downing, J. E., Spencer, S., & Cavallaro, C. (2004). The development of an inclusive charter elementary school: Lessons learned. *Research and Practice for Persons With Severe Disabilities, 29,* 11–24.

Doyle, M. B. (2008). *The paraprofessional's guide to the inclusive classroom: Working as a team.* Baltimore: Paul H. Brookes.

Doyle, M. B., & Giangreco, M. F. (2009). Making presentation software accessible to high school students with intellectual disabilities. *TEACHING Exceptional Children, 41*(3), 24–31.

Duker, P., Didden, R., & Sigafoos, J. (2004). *One-to-one training: Instructional procedures for learners with developmental disabilities.* Austin, TX: Pro-Ed.

Dymond, S. K., Renzaglia, A., Gilson, C. L., & Slagor, M. T. (2007). Defining access to the general curriculum for high school students with significant cognitive disabilities. *Research and Practice for Persons With Severe Disabilities, 32,* 1–15.

Dymond, S. K., Renzaglia, A., Rosenstein, A., Chun, E. J., Banks, R. A., Niswander, V., et al. (2006). Using a participatory action research approach to create a universally designed inclusive high school science course: A case study. *Research and Practice for Persons With Severe Disabilities, 31,* 293–308.

Dymond, S. K., & Russell, D. L. (2004). Impact of grade and disability on the instructional context of inclusive classrooms. *Education and Training in Developmental Disabilities, 39,* 127–140.

Edeh, O. M. (2006). Cross-cultural investigation of interest-based training and social interpersonal problem solving in students with mental retardation. *Education and Training in Developmental Disabilities, 41,* 163–176.

Education Act for All Handicapped Children of 1975, 20 U.S.C. 1401 (1975).

Etscheidt, S. (2005). Paraprofessional services for students with disabilities: A legal analysis of issues. *Research and Practice for Persons With Severe Disabilities, 30,* 60–80.

Etscheidt, S. (2006). Progress monitoring: Legal issues and recommendations for IEP teams. *TEACHING Exceptional Children, 38*(3), 56–60.

Falkenstine, K. J., Collins, B. C., Schuster, J. W., & Kleinert, H. (2009). Presenting chained and discrete tasks as non-targeted information when teaching discrete academic skills through small group instruction. *Education and Training in Developmental Disabilities, 44*(1), 127–142.

Farmer, J. A., Gast, D. L., Wolery, M., & Winterling, V. (1991). Small group instruction for students with severe handicaps: A study of observational learning. *Education and Training in Mental Retardation, 26,* 190–201.

Ferguson, P. M. (2008). The doubting dance: Contributions to a history of parent/professional interactions in early 20th century America. *Research and Practice for Persons With Severe Disabilities, 33*(1–2), 48–58.

Finke, E. H., McNaughton, D. B., & Drager, K. D. R. (2009). All children can and should have the opportunity to learn: General education teachers' perspectives on including children with autism spectrum disorders who require AAC. *Augmentative and Alternative Communication, 25,* 110–122.

Fisher, M., & Meyer, L. (2002). Development and social competence after two years for students enrolled in inclusive and self-contained educational programs. *Research and Practice for Persons With Severe Disabilities, 27,* 165–174.

Flowers, C., Ahlgrim-Delzell, L., Browder, D., & Spooner, F. (2005). Teachers' perceptions of alternate assessments. *Research and Practice for Persons With Severe Disabilities, 30,* 81–92.

Flowers, C. P., Browder, D. M., Ahlgrim-Delzell, L., & Spooner, F. (2006). Promoting the alignment of curriculum, assessment, and instruction. In D. M. Browder, & F. Spooner (Eds.), *Teaching language arts, math, and science to students with significant cognitive disabilities* pp. 295–312. Baltimore: Paul H. Brookes.

Ford, A., & Davern, L. (1989). Moving forward with school integration: Strategies for involving students with severe handicaps in the life of the school. In R. Gaylord-Ross (Ed.), *Integration strategies for students with handicaps* (pp. 11–33). Baltimore: Paul H. Brookes.

Foreman, P., Arthur-Kelly, M., Pascoe, S., & Smyth-King, B. (2004). Evaluating the educational experiences of students with profound and multiple disabilities in inclusive and segregated classroom settings: An Australian perspective. *Research and Practice for Persons With Severe Disabilities, 29,* 183–193.

Fowler, C. H., Konrad, M., Walker, A. R., Test, D. W., & Wood, W. M. (2007). Self-determination interventions' effects on the academic performance of students with developmental disabilities. *Education and Training in Developmental Disabilities, 42,* 270–285.

Frank, D. V., Little, J. G., & Miller, S. (2009). *Science explorers: Chemical interaction.* Upper Saddle River, NJ: Prentice Hall.

Friend, M., & Cook, L. (2007). Interactions: Collaboration skills for school professionals (5th ed.). Boston: Pearson.

Fuchs, D., Mock, D., Morgan, P. L., & Young, C. L. (2003). Responsiveness-to-intervention: Definitions, evidence, and implications for the learning disabilities construct. *Learning Disabilities Research and Practice, 18,* 157–171.

Gast, D., Ault, M., Wolery, M., Doyle, P., & Belanger, S. (1988). Comparison of constant time delay and the system of least prompts in teaching sight word reading to students with moderate retardation. *Education and Training in Mental Retardation, 23,* 117–128.

Ghere, G., & York-Barr, J. (2007). Paraprofessional turnover and retention in inclusive programs: Hidden costs and promising practices. *Remedial and Special Education, 28,* 21–32.

Giangreco, M. F. (2006). Foundational concepts and practices for educating students with severe disabilities. In M. E. Snell & F. Brown (Eds.), *Instruction of students with severe disabilities* (6th ed., pp. 1–27). Upper Saddle River, NJ: Pearson.

Giangreco, M. F., Backus, L., Cichoskikelly, E., Sherman, P., & Mavropoulous, Y. (2003). Paraeducator training materials to facilitate inclusive education: Initial field-test data. *Rural Special Education Quarterly, 22*(1), 17–27.

Giangreco, M. F., & Broer, S. M. (2005). Questionable utilization of paraprofessionals in inclusive schools: Are we addressing the symptoms or causes? *Focus on Autism and Other Developmental Disabilities, 20,* 10–26.

Giangreco, M. F., & Doyle, M.B. (2007). Teacher assistants in inclusive schools. In L. Florian (Eds.), *The SAGE handbook of special education* (pp. 429–439). London: Sage.

Giangreco, M. F., Halvorsen, A., Doyle, M. B., & Broer, S. M. (2004). Alternatives to over-reliance on paraprofessional in inclusive schools. *Journal of Special Education Leadership, 17*(2), 82–90.

Giangreco, M. F., Yuan, S., McKenzie, B., Cameron, P., & Fialka, J. (2005). Be careful what you wish for . . .: Five reasons to be concerned about the assignment of individual paraprofessionals. *TEACHING Exceptional Children, 37*(5), 28–34.

Greenwood, C. R., Arreaga-Mayer, C., Utley, C. A., Gavin, K. M., & Terry, B. J. (2001). Classwide peer tutoring learning management system: Applications with elementary-level English language learners. *Remedial and Special Education, 22*, 34–47.

Greenwood, C. R., Horton, B. T., & Utley, C. A. (2002). Academic engagement time: Current perspectives on research and practice. *School Psychological Review, 31*,328–349.

Gresham, F. M., Reschly, D. J., Tilly, W. D., Fletcher, J., Burns, M., Prasse, D., et al. (2005). A response to intervention perspective. *The School Psychologist, 59*, 26–33.

Grigal, M., Neubert, D. A., & Moon, M. S. (2002). Postsecondary options for students with significant disabilities. *TEACHING Exceptional Children, 35*(2), 68–73.

Haberman, M. (1991). The pedagogy of poverty versus good teaching. *Phi Delta Kappan, 73*, 290–294.

Harcourt. (2007). *Social studies. The United States: Making a new nation.* Orlando, FL: Harcourt School Publishers.

Harrower, J., & Dunlap, G. (2001). Including children with autism in general education classrooms: A review of effective strategies. *Behavior Modification, 25*, 762–784.

Harry, B., & Klingner, J. (2006). *Why are so many minority students in special education?* New York: Teachers College Press.

Hart, D., Mele-McCarthy, J., Pasternack, R. H., Zimbrich, K., & Parker, D. R. (2004). Community college: A pathway to success for youth with learning, cognitive, and intellectual disabilities in secondary settings. *Education and Training in Developmental Disabilities, 39*, 54–66.

Hart, D., Zimbrich, K., & Parker, D. (2005). Dual enrollment as a postsecondary education option for students with intellectual disabilities. In E. E. Getzel, & P. Wehman (Eds.), *Going to college: Expanding opportunities for people with disabilities* (pp. 253–267). Baltimore: Paul H. Brookes.

Hedeen, D. L., & Ayres, B. J. (2002). "You want me to teach him to read?" Fulfilling the intent of IDEA. *Journal of Disability Policy Studies, 13*, 180–189.

Higher Education Opportunity Act. (2008). Public Law 110–315. 20 USC 1001.

Holburn, S., Gordon, A., & Vietze, P. M. (2007). *Person-centered planning made easy.* Baltimore: Paul H. Brookes.

Holburn, S., & Vietze, P. (Eds.). (2002). *Person-centered planning: Research, practice, and future directions.* Baltimore: Paul H. Brookes.

Horner, R. H., Albin, R. W., Sprague, J. R., & Todd, A. W. (2000). Positive behavior support. In M. E. Snell & F. Brown (Ed.), *Instruction of students with severe disabilities* (5th ed., pp. 207–243). Upper Saddle River, NJ: Merrill.

Horner, R. H., Albin, R. W., Todd, A. W., & Sprague, J. (2006). Positive behavior support for individuals with severe disabilities. In M. D. Snell & F. Brown (Eds.), *Instruction of students with severe disabilities* (6th ed., pp. 206–250). Upper Saddle River, NJ: Prentice.

Horner, R. H., Carr, E. G., Halle, J., McGee, G., Odom, S., & Wolery, M. (2005). The use of single-subject research to identify evidence-based practice in special education. *Exceptional Children, 71*, 165–180.

Horner, R. H., Sugai, G., Todd, A. W., & Lewis-Palmer, T. (2005). Schoolwide positive behavior support. In L.M. Bambara & L. Kern (Eds.), *Individualized supports for students with problem behaviors: Designing positive behavior plans* (pp. 359–390). New York: The Guilford Press.

Hughes, C., & Agran, M. (1993). Teaching persons with severe disabilities to use self-instruction in community settings: An analysis of applications. *Journal of the Association for Persons With Severe Handicaps, 18*, 261–274.

Hughes, C., Carter, E. W., Hughes, T., Bradford, E., & Copeland, S. R. (2002). Effects of instructional versus non-instructional roles on the social interactions of high school students. *Education and Training in Mental Retardation and Developmental Disabilities, 37*, 146–162.

Hughes, C., Copeland, S. R., Wehmeyer, M., Agran, M., Cai, X., & Hwang, B. (2002). Increasing social interaction between general education high school students and their peers with mental retardation. *Journal of Developmental and Physical Disabilities, 14*, 387–402.

Hughes, M. W., Schuster, J. W., & Nelson, C. M. (1993). The acquisition of independent dressing skills by students with multiple disabilities. *Journal of Developmental and Physical Disabilities, 5*, 233–252.

Hunt, P., Soto, G., Maier, J., Muller, E., & Goetz, L. (2002). Collaborative teaming to support students at risk and students with severe disabilities in general education classrooms. *Exceptional Children, 69*, 315–332.

Hunt, P., Staub, D., Alwell, M., & Goetz, L. (1994). Achievement by all students within the context of cooperative learning groups. *Journal of the Association for Persons With Severe Handicaps, 19*, 290–301.

Iacono, T. (2003). Pragmatic development in individuals with developmental disabilities who use AAC. In J. C. Light, D. R. Beukelman, & J. Reichle (Eds.), *Communicative competence for individuals who use AAC* (pp. 323–360). Baltimore: Paul H. Brookes.

Idol, L. (2002). *Creating collaborative and inclusive schools.* Austin, TX: Pro-Ed.

Idol, L. (2006). Toward inclusion of special education students in general education. *Remedial and Special Education, 27*, 77–94.

Individuals with Disabilities Education Act of 1990, 20 U.S.C. § 1400 *et seq.* (1990).

Individuals with Disabilities Education Act of 1997, PL 105–17, 20 U.S.C. § 1400 *et seq.* (1997).

Individuals with Disabilities Education Improvement Act of 2004, PL 108–466, 20 U.S.C. § *et seq.* (2004).

Jackson, L., Wehmeyer, M., & Ryndak, D. L. (in press). Scientifically based educational practice for ensuring access to general education and the general education curriculum: A case for inclusive education. *Research and Practice for Persons With Severe Disabilities.*

Jameson, J. M., McDonnell, J., Polychronis, S., & Riesen, T. (2008). Embedded, constant time delay instruction by peers without disabilities in general education classrooms. *Intellectual and Developmental Disabilities, 46*, 346–363.

Jameson, M., McDonnell, J., Johnson, J. W., Riesen, T., & Polychronis, S. C. (2007). A comparison of one-to-one embedded instruction in the general education classroom and one-to-one massed practice instruction in the special education classroom. *Education and Treatment of Children, 30*, 23–44.

Janney, R., & Snell, M. E. (2004). *Modifying schoolwork* (2nd ed.). Baltimore: Paul H. Brookes.

Janney, R., & Snell, M. E. (2006). *Teachers' guides to inclusive practices: Modifying schoolwork* (2nd ed.). Baltimore: Paul H. Brookes.

Johnson, D., & Johnson, R. (1987). *Learning together and alone: Cooperation, competition, and individualization.* Upper Saddle River, NJ: Prentice Hall.

Johnson, D. W., Johnson, R. T., & Holubec, E. J. (1993). *Circles of learning: Cooperation in the classroom* (4th ed.). Edina, MI: Interactive Book Company.

Johnson, E., & Arnold, W. (2004). Validating an alternate assessment. *Remedial and Special Education, 25*, 266–275.

Johnson, J. W., McDonnell, J., Holzwarth, V. N., & Hunter, K. (2004). The efficacy of embedded instruction for students with developmental disabilities enrolled in general classes. *Journal of Positive Behavior Interventions, 6*, 214–227.

Jorgensen, C. M. (2005). The least dangerous assumption: Presuming competence of students with a label of mental retardation. *Disability Solutions, 6*(3), 1, 5–9.

Jorgensen, C. M., McSheehan, M., & Sonnenmeier, R. M. (2007). Presumed competence in the educational programs of students with significant intellectual and developmental disabilities before and after the Beyond Access professional development intervention. *Journal of Intellectual and Developmental Disabilities, 32*, 248–262.

Kampfer, S., Horvath, L., Kleinert, H., & Kearns, J. (2001). Teachers' perceptions of one states' alternate assessment portfolio program: Implications for practice and preparation. *Exceptional Children, 67*, 361–374.

Kamps, D. M., Greenwood, C., Arreaga-Mayer, C., Veerkamp, M. B., Utley, C., Tapia, Y., et al. (2008). The efficacy of classwide peer tutoring in middle schools. *Education and Treatment of Children, 31*, 119–152.

Katsiyannis, A., Zhang, D., Woodruff, N., & Dixon, A. (2005). Transition supports to students with mental retardation: An examination of data from the National Longitudinal Transition Study 2. *Education and Training in Developmental Disabilities, 40*, 109–116.

Kearns, J., Burdge, M. D., Clayton, J., Denham, A. P., & Kleinert, H. L. (2006). How students demonstrate academic performance in portfolio assessment. In D. M. Browder & F. Spooner (Eds.), *Teaching language arts, math, and science to students with significant cognitive disabilities* (pp. 277–294). Baltimore: Paul H. Brookes.

Keefe, E. B., & Moore, V. (2004). The challenge of coteaching in inclusive classrooms at the high school level: What the teachers told us. *American Secondary Education, 32*(3), 77–88.

Keefe, E. B., Moore, V., & Duff, F. (2004). The four "knows" of collaborative teaching. *TEACHING Exceptional Children, 36*(5), 36–43.

Keogh, B. K., Bernheimer, L. P., & Guthrie, O. (2004). Children with developmental delays twenty years later: Where are they? How are they? *American Journal on Mental Retardation, 109*, 219–230.

Ketterer, A., Schuster, J. W., Morse, T. E., & Collins, B. C. (2007). The effects of response cards on active participation and social behavior of students with moderate and severe disabilities. *Journal of Developmental and Physical Disabilities, 19*, 187–199.

King, G., Baxter, D., Rosenbaum, P., Zwaigenbaum, L., & Bates, A. (2009). Belief systems of families of children with autism spectrum disorders or Down syndrome. *Focus on Autism and Other Developmental Disabilities, 24*(1), 50–64.

Kleinert, H., McGregor, V., Durbin, M., Blandford, T., Jones, K., Owens, J., Harrison, B., & Miracle, S. (2004). Service-learning opportunities that include students with moderate and severe disabilities. *TEACHING Exceptional Children, 37*(2), 28–35.

Kluth, P., & Schwarz, P. (2008). *"Just give him the whale!" Twenty ways to use fascinations, areas of expertise, and strengths to support students with autism.* Baltimore: Paul H. Brookes.

Knight, T. (2003). Academic access and the family. In P. Kluth, D. Straut, & D. Biklen (Eds.), *Access to academics for all students* (pp. 49–68). Mahwah, NJ: Lawrence Erlbaum.

Kohl, F. L., McLaughlin, M. J., & Nagle, K. (2006). Alternate achievement standards and assessments: A descriptive investigation of 16 states. *Exceptional Children, 73*, 107–123.

Leblanc, M., Ricciardi, J. M., & Luiselli, J. K. (2005). Improving discrete trial instruction by paraprofessional staff through an abbreviated performance feedback intervention. *Education and Treatment of Children, 28*, 76–82.

Li, A. (2009). Identification and intervention for students who are visually impaired and who have autism spectrum disorders. *TEACHING Exceptional Children, 41*(4), 22–32.

Light, J., & McNaughton, D. (2009). *Accessible literacy learning (All): Evidence-based reading instruction for learners with autism, cerebral palsy, Down syndrome and other disabilities.* Pittsburgh, PA: Mayer-Johnson LLC.

Light, J. C., & Binger, C. (1998). *Building communicative competence with individuals who use augmentative and alternative communication.* Baltimore: Paul H. Brookes.

Lipsky, D. K., & Gartner, A. (1992). Achieving full inclusion: Placing the student at the center of educational reform. In W. Stainback & S. Stainback (Eds.), *Controversial issues confronting special education* (pp. 3–12). Boston: Allyn and Bacon.

Logan, K., Jacobs, H. A., Gast, D. A., Murray, A. S., Daino, K., & Skala, C. (1998). The impact of typical peers on the perceived happiness of students with profound multiple disabilities. *Journal of the Association for Persons With Severe Handicaps, 23,* 309–318.

Lohrmann, S., & Bambara, L. M. (2006). Elementary education teachers' beliefs about essential supports needed to successfully include students with developmental disabilities who engage in challenging behaviors. *Research and Practice for Persons With Severe Disabilities, 31,* 157–173.

Losardo, A., & Notari-Syverson, A. (2001). *Alternative approaches to assessing young children.* Baltimore: Paul H. Brookes.

Lynch, E. W., & Hanson, M. J. (2004). *Developing cross-cultural competence: A guide for working with children and their families* (3rd ed.). Baltimore: Paul H. Brookes.

Lynch, S., & Adams, P. (2008). Developing standards-based individualized education program objectives for students with significant needs. *TEACHING Exceptional Children, 40*(4), 36–39.

Macy, M., & Hoyt-Gonzales, K. (2007). A linked system approach to early childhood special education eligibility assessment. *TEACHING Exceptional Children, 39*(3), 40–44.

Mainger, R. W., Deshler, D., Coleman, M. R., Kozleski, E., & Rodriquez-Walling, M. (2003). To ensure the learning of every child with a disability. *Focus on Exceptional Children, 35*(5), 1–12.

McCarthy, C. B. (2005). Effects of thematic-based, hands-on science teaching versus a textbook approach for students with disabilities. *Journal of Research in Science Teaching, 42,* 245–263.

McDonnell, J., Johnson, J. W., Polychronis, S., Riesen, T., Jameson, M., & Kercher, K. (2006). Comparison of one-to-one embedded instruction in general education classes with small group instruction in special education classes. *Education and Training in Developmental Disabilities, 41,* 125–138.

McDonnell, J., Mathot-Buckner, C., Thorson, N., & Fister, N. (2001). Supporting the inclusion of students with moderate and severe disabilities in junior high school general education classes: The effects of classwide peer tutoring, multi-element curriculum, and accommodations. *Education and Treatment of Children, 24,* 141–160.

McLeskey, J., & Billingsley, B. S. (2008). How does the quality and stability of the teaching force influence the research-to-practice gap? A perspective on the teacher shortage in special education. *Remedial and Special Education, 29,* 293–305.

McLeskey, J., & Henry, D. (1999). Inclusion: What progress is being made across states? *TEACHING Exceptional Children, 31*(5), 56–63.

Mechling, L. C. (2005). The effect of instructor-created video programs to teach students with disabilities: A literature review. *Journal of Special Education Technology, 20,* 25–36.

Mechling, L. C. (2008). Thirty-year review of safety skill instruction for persons with intellectual disabilities. *Education and Training in Developmental Disabilities, 43,* 311–323.

Mechling, L. C., & Gustafson, M. (2009). Comparison of the effects of static picture and video prompting on the completion of cooking related tasks by students with moderate intellectual disabilities. *Journal of Special Education, 42,* 179–190.

Meyer, L. H. (2001). The impact of inclusion on children's lives: Multiple outcomes, and friendship in particular. *International Journal of Disability, Development, and Education, 48,* 9–31.

Mills v. Board of Education, 348 F. Supp. 866 (D.D.C) (1982).

Minarovic, T. J., & Bambara, L. M. (2007). Teaching employees with intellectual disabilities to manage changing work routines using varied sight-word checklists. *Research and Practice for Persons With Severe Disabilities, 32,* 31–42.

Miracle, S. A., Collins, B. C., Schuster, J. W., & Grisham-Brown, J. (2001). Peer-versus teacher-directed instruction: Effects on acquisition and maintenance. *Education and Training in Mental Retardation and Developmental Disabilities, 36,* 373–385.

Morse, T. E., & Schuster, J. W. (2004). Simultaneous prompting: A review of the literature. *Education and Training in Developmental Disabilities, 39,* 153–168.

Naraian, S. (2008). "I didn't think I was going to like working with him, but now I really do!": Examining peer narratives of significant disability. *Intellectual and Developmental Disabilities, 46,* 106–119.

Nevin, A. I., Villa, R. A., & Thousand, J. A. (2008). *A guide to coteaching with paraeducators: Practical tips for K–12 educators.* Thousand Oaks, CA: Corwin.

No Child Left Behind Act of 2001, PL 107–110, 115 Stat. 1425, 20 U.S.C §§ 6301 *et seq.* (2001).

Norman, J. M., Collins, B. C., & Schuster, J. W. (2001). Using an instructional package including videotechnology to teach self-help skills to elementary students with mental disabilities. *Journal of Special Education Technology, 16,* 5–18.

Ohtake, Y. (2003). Increasing class membership of students with severe disabilities through contribution to classmates' learning. *Research and Practice for Persons With Severe Disabilities, 28,* 228–231.

Owens, J. S. (2006). Accessible information for people with complex communication needs. *Augmentative and Alternative Communication, 22,* 196–208.

Parrish, P. R., & Stodden, R. A. (2009). Aligning assessment and instruction with state standards for children with significant disabilities. *TEACHING Exceptional Children, 41*(4), 22–32, 46–57.

Peck, C. A., Staub, D., Gallucci, C., & Schwartz, I. (2004). Parent perception of the impacts of inclusion on their nondisabled child. *Research and Practice for Persons With Severe Disabilities, 29,* 135–143.

Pennsylvania Association for Retarded Children (PAEC) v. Commonwealth of Pennsylvania, 334 F. Supp. 1257 (E.D. Pa.); 343 F. Supp. 279 (E.D. Pa.) (1971, 1972).

Perner, D. E. (2007). No child left behind: Issues of assessing students with the most significant cognitive disabilities. *Education and Training in Developmental Disabilities, 42,* 243–251.

Pershey, M. G., & Gilbert, T. W. (2002). Christine: A case study of literacy acquisition by an adult with developmental disability. *Mental Retardation, 40,* 219–234.

Post, M., & Storey, K. (2002). Review of using auditory prompting systems with persons who have moderate to severe disabilities. *Education and Training in Mental Retardation and Developmental Disabilities, 37,* 317–327.

Poston, D., & Turnbull, A. P. (2004). Role of spirituality and religion in family quality of life for families of children with disabilities. *Education and Training in Developmental Disabilities, 39,* 95–108.

Realon, R. E., Favell, J. E., & Lowerre, A. (1990). The effects of making choices on engagement levels with persons who are profoundly multiply handicapped. *Education and Training in Mental Retardation, 25,* 299–305.

Reis, S. M., Schader, R., Milne, H., & Stephens, R. (2003). Music and minds: Using a talent development approach for young adults with Williams syndrome. *Exceptional Children, 69,* 293–314.

Renzaglia, A., Karvonen, M., Drasgow, E., & Stoxen, C. C. (2003). Promoting a lifetime of inclusion. *Focus on Autism and Other Developmental Disabilities, 18,* 140–149.

Reynolds, M. (1962). A framework for considering some issues in special education. *Exceptional Children, 28,* 367–370.

Riesen, T., McDonnell, J., Johnson, J. W., Polychronis, S., & Jameson, M. (2003). A comparison of constant time delay and simultaneous prompting within embedded instruction in general education classes with students with moderate to severe disabilities. *Journal of Behavioral Education, 12,* 241–259.

Riley, G. A. (1995). Guidelines for devising a hierarchy when fading response prompts. *Education and Training in Mental Retardation and Developmental Disabilities, 30,* 231–242.

Roach, A., & Elliott, S. (2006). The influences of access to the general education curriculum on alternate assessment performance of students with significant cognitive disabilities. *Educational Evaluation and Policy Analysis, 28,* 181–194.

Rogers-Atkinson, D. L., Ochoa, T. A., & Delgado, B. (2003). Developing cross-cultural competence: Serving families of children with significant developmental needs. *Focus on Autism and Other Developmental Disabilities, 18,* 4–8.

Rose, D., & Meyer, A. (2002). *Teaching every student in the digital age: Universal design for learning.* Alexandria, VA: Association for Supervision and Curriculum Development.

Rose, D., & Meyer, A. (Eds.). (2006). *A practical reader in universal design for learning.* Cambridge, MA: Harvard Education Press.

Rosenberg, M. S., Boyer, K. L., Sindelar, P. T., & Misra, S. K. (2007). Alternative route programs for certification in special education: Program infrastructure, instructional delivery, and participant characteristics. *Exceptional Children, 73,* 224–241.

Ryndak, D. L., & Alper, S. (2003). *Curriculum and instruction for students with significant disabilities in inclusive settings* (2nd ed.). Boston: Allyn and Bacon.

Ryndak, D. L., Jackson, L., & Billingsley, F. (2000). Defining school inclusion for students with moderate to severe disabilities: What do experts say? *Exceptionality, 8,* 101–116.

Ryndak, D. L., Moore, M., & Delano M. (in press). Access to the general curriculum: The mandate and the role of context in research-based practice. *Research and Practice for Persons With Severe Disabilities.*

Ryndak, D. L., Morrison, A. P., & Sommerstein, L. (1999). Literacy before and after inclusion in general education settings: A case study. *Journal of The Association for Persons With Severe Handicaps, 24,* 5–22.

Ryndak, D. L., & Pullen, P. C. (2003). Education teams and collaborative teamwork in inclusive settings. In D. L. Ryndak & S. Alper (Eds.), *Curriculum and instruction for students with significant disabilities in inclusive settings* (pp. 131–150). Boston: Allyn and Bacon.

Ryndak, D. L., & Ward, T. (2003). Adapting environments, materials, and instruction to facilitate inclusion. In D. L. Ryndak & S. Alper (Eds.), *Curriculum and instruction for students with significant disabilities in inclusive settings* (2nd ed., pp. 382–411). Boston: Pearson.

Salend, S. J. (2008). Determining appropriate testing accommodations: Complying with NCLB and IDEA. *TEACHING Exceptional Children, 40*(4), 4–22.

Salend, S. J. (2009). Technology-based classroom assessments: Alternatives to testing. *TEACHING Exceptional Children, 41*(6), 48–58.

Salisbury, C., Palombaro, M. M., & Hollowood, T. M. (1993). On the nature and change of an inclusive elementary school. *Journal of the Association for Persons With Severe Handicaps, 18,* 75–84.

Sarokoff, R., & Sturmey, P. (2004). The effects of behavioral skill training on staff implementation of discrete trail teaching. *Journal of Applied Behavior Analysis, 37,* 535–538.

Schnorr, R. F. (1990). "Peter? He comes and goes . . .": First graders' perspectives on a part-time mainstream student. *Journal of the Association for Persons With Severe Handicaps, 15,* 231–240.

Schuster, J. W., Griffen, A. K., & Wolery, M. (1992). Comparison of simultaneous prompting and constant time delay procedures in teaching sight words to elementary students with moderate mental retardation. *Journal of Behavioral Education, 2,* 305–326.

Schuster, J. W., Morse, T. E., Griffen, A. B., & Wolery, M. (1996). Teaching peer reinforcement and grocery words: An investigation of observational learning and instructive feedback. *Journal of Behavioral Education, 6,* 511–533.

Schwarz, P. (2006). *From disability to possibility: The power of inclusive classrooms.* Portsmouth, NH: Heinemann.

Science, Arizona Edition. (2006). Orlando, FL: Harcourt School Publishers.

Scruggs, T. E., Mastropieri, M. A., & McDuffie, K. A. (2007). Coteaching in inclusive classrooms: A metasynthesis of qualitative research. *Exceptional Children, 73,* 392–416.

Scruggs, T. E., Mastropieri, M. A., & Okolo, C. M. (2008). Science and social studies for students with disabilities. *Focus on Exceptional Children, 42*(2), 1–24.

Seo, S., Brownell, M. T., Bishop, A. G., & Dingle, M. (2008). Beginning special education teachers' classroom reading instruction: Practices that engage elementary students with learning disabilities. *Exceptional Children, 75,* 97–122.

Sheppard-Jones, K., Prout, H. T., & Kleinert, H. (2005). Quality of life dimensions for adults with developmental disabilities: A comparative study. *Mental Retardation, 43,* 281–291.

Shipley-Benamou, R., Lutzker, J. R., & Taubman, M. (2002). Teaching daily living skills to children with autism through instructional video modeling. *Journal of Positive Behavioral Intervention, 4,* 165–178.

Shukla, S., Kennedy, C. H., & Cushing, L. S. (1999). Intermediate school students with severe disabilities: Supporting their social participation in general education classrooms. *Journal of Positive Behavior Interventions, 1,* 130–140.

Shumaker, J. B., Deshler, D. D., Bulgren, J. A., Davis, B., Lenz, B. K., & Grossen, B. (2002). Access of adolescents with disabilities to general education curriculum: Myth or reality? *Focus on Exceptional Children, 35*(3), 1–16.

Siegel, E., & Allinder, R. M. (2005). Review of assessment procedures for students with moderate and severe disabilities. *Education and Training in Developmental Disabilities, 40,* 343–351.

Sigafoos, J., Arthur-Kelly, M., & Butterfield, N. (2006). *Enhancing everyday communication for children with disabilities.* Baltimore: Paul H. Brookes.

Simonsen, B., Sugai, G., & Negron, M. (2008). Schoolwide positive behavior supports: Primary systems and practices. *TEACHING Exceptional Children, 40*(6), 32–43.

Singer, G. H. S., & Irvin, L. K. (1991). Supporting families of persons with severe disabilities: Emerging findings, practices, and questions. In L.H. Meyer, C. A. Peck, & L. Brown (Eds.), *Critical issues in the lives of people with severe disabilities* (pp. 271–312). Baltimore: Paul H. Brookes.

Smith, V. M. (2003). "You have to learn who comes with the disability": Students' reflections on service learning experiences with peers labeled with disabilities. *Research and Practice for Persons With Severe Disabilities, 28,* 79–90.

Snell, M. E. (2002). Using dynamic assessment with learners who communicate nonsymbolically. *Augmentative and Alternative Communication, 18,* 163–176.

Snell, M. E., & Brown, F. (2006). Designing and implementing instructional programs. In M. E. Snell, & F. Brown, *Instruction of students with severe disabilities* (6th ed.). Upper Saddle River, NJ: Pearson Education.

Snell, M. E., & Janney, R. (2005). *Collaborative teaming* (2nd ed.). Baltimore: Paul H. Brookes.

Soukup, J. H., Wehmeyer, M. L., Bashinski, S. M., & Bovaird, J. (2007). Classroom variables and access to the general education curriculum of students with intellectual and developmental disabilities. *Exceptional Children, 74,* 101–120.

Spooner, F., Baker, J. N., Harris, A. A., Ahlgrim-Delzell, L., & Browder, D. M. (2007). Effects of training in universal design for learning on lesson plan development. *Remedial and Special Education, 28,* 108–116.

Spooner, F., DiBase, W., & Courtade-Little, G. (2006). Science standards and functional skill: Finding the links. In D. M. Browder & F. Spooner (Eds.), *Teaching language arts, math, and science to students with significant cognitive disabilities* (pp. 229–244). Baltimore: Paul H. Brookes.

Spriggs, A., Gast, D. L., & Ayres, K. M. (2007). Using picture activity schedule books to increase on-schedule and on-task behaviors. *Education and Training in Developmental Disabilities, 42,* 209–223.

Stecker, P. M., Lembke, E. S., & Folgen, A. (2008). Using progress-monitoring data to improve instructional decision making. *Preventing School Failure, 52*(2), 48–58.

Stromer, R., Mackay, H. A., Howell, S. R., & McVay, A. A. (1996). Teaching computer-assisted spelling to individuals with developmental and hearing disabilities: Transfer of stimulus control to writing task. *Journal of Applied Behavior Analysis, 29,* 25–42.

Sugai, G., Simonsen, B., & Horner, R. H. (2008). Schoolwide positive behavior supports: A continuum of positive behavior supports for all students. *TEACHING Exceptional Children, 40*(6), 5.

Szczepanski, M. (2004). Physical management in the classroom: Handling and positioning. In F. P. Orelove, D. Sobsey, & R. K. Silberman (Eds.), *Educating children with multiple disabilities: A collaborative approach* (4th ed., pp. 249–310). Baltimore: Paul H. Brookes.

Taylor, P., Collins, B. C., Schuster, J. W., & Kleinert, H. (2002). Teaching laundry skills to high school students with disabilities: Generalization of targeted skills and nontargeted information. *Education and Training in Mental Retardation and Developmental Disabilities, 37,* 172–183.

Taylor, S. J. (1982). From segregation to integration: Strategies for integrating severely handicapped students in normal school and community settings. *The Journal of the Association for the Severely Handicapped, 8*(3), 42–49.

Taylor, S. J. (1988). Caught in the continuum: A critical analysis of the principle of the least restrictive environment. *Journal of the Association for Persons With Severe Handicaps, 13,* 41–53.

Thompson, J. R., Bradley, V. J., Buntinx, W. H. E., Schalock, R. L., Shogren, K. A., Snell, M. E., et al. (2009). Conceptualizing supports and the support needs of people with intellectual disability. *Individuals With Developmental Disabilities, 47,* 135–146.

Thompson, J. R., Meadan, H., Fansier, K. W., Alber, S. B., & Balogh, P. A. (2007). Family assessment portfolios: A new way to jumpstart family/school collaboration. *TEACHING Exceptional Children, 39*(6), 19–25.

Thousand, J. S., Villa, R. A., & Nevin, A. I. (2002). *Creativity and collaborative learning: The practical guide to empowering students, teachers, and families* (2nd ed.). Baltimore: Paul H. Brookes.

Thousand, J. S., Villa, R. A., & Nevin, A. I. (2007). *Differentiating instruction: Collaborative planning and teaching for universally designed learning.* Thousand Oaks, CA: Corwin.

Tindal, G., McDonald, M., Tedesco, M., Glasgow, A., Almond, P., Crawford, L., & Hollenbeck, K. (2003). Alternate assessments in reading and math: Development and validation for students with significant disabilities. *Exceptional Children, 69,* 481–494.

Towles-Reeves, E., & Kleinert, H. (2006). The impact of one state's alternate assessment upon instruction and IEP development. *Rural Special Education Quarterly, 25*(3), 31–39.

Towles-Reeves, E., Kleinert, H., & Muhomba, M. (2009). Alternate assessment: Have we learned anything new? *Exceptional Children, 75,* 233–252.

Turnbull, A. P., & Turnbull, H. R. (2001). Self-determination for individuals with significant cognitive disabilities and their families. *Journal of the Association for Persons With Severe Handicaps, 26,* 56–62.

Turnbull, A. P., Turnbull, H. R., Erwin, E. J., & Soodak, L. C. (2006). *Families, professionals, and exceptionality: Positive outcomes through partnerships and trust* (5th ed.). Upper Saddle River, NJ: Merrill/Prentice Hall.

U.S. Department of Education. (2005). *Alternate achievement standards for students with the most significant cognitive disabilities: Nonregulatory guidance.* Washington, DC: Office of Elementary and Secondary Education.

Vacca, J. J. (2007). Incorporating interests and structure to improve participation of a child with autism in a standardized assessment: A case study analysis. *Focus on Autism and Other Developmental Disabilities, 22,* 51–59.

Villa, R. A., Thousand, J. S., & Nevin, A. I. (2008). *A guide to co-teaching: Practical tips for facilitating student learning* (2nd ed.). Thousand Oaks, CA: Corwin.

Wagner, M., Newman, L., Cameto, R., Levine, P., & Marder, C. (2003). *Going to school: Instructional contexts, programs, and participation of secondary school students with disabilities.* Menlo Park, CA: SRI International.

Wallace, T., Anderson, A. R., Bartholomay, T., & Hupp, S. (2002). An ecobehavioral examination of high school classrooms that include students with disabilities. *Exceptional Children, 68,* 345–359.

Wehmeyer, M. L. (2005). Self-determination and individuals with severe disabilities: Re-examining meanings and misinterpretations. *Research and Practice for Persons With Severe Disabilities, 30,* 113–120.

Wehmeyer, M. L. (2006). Beyond access: Ensuring progress in the general education curriculum for students with severe disabilities. *Research and Practice for Persons With Severe Disabilities, 31,* 322–326.

Wehmeyer, M. L., Field, S., Doren, B., Jones, B., & Mason, C. (2004). Self-determination and student involvement in standards-based reform. *Exceptional Children, 70,* 413–425.

Wehmeyer, M. L., Garner, N., Yeager, D., Lawrence, M., & Davis, A. K. (2006). Infusing self-determination into 18–21 services for students with intellectual or developmental disabilities: A multi-stage component. *Education and Training in Developmental Disabilities, 41,* 3–13

Wehmeyer, M. L., Lattin, D. L., Lapp-Rincker, G., & Agran, M. (2003). Access to the general curriculum of middle school students with mental retardation: An observational study. *Remedial and Special Education, 24,* 262–272.

Wehmeyer, M. L., & Palmer, S. B. (2003). Adult outcomes for students with cognitive disabilities three years after high school: The impact of self-determination. *Education and Training in Developmental Disabilities, 38,* 131–144.

West, E. A. (2008). Effects of verbal cues of pictorial cues on the transfer of stimulus control for children with autism. *Focus on Autism and Developmental Disabilities, 23,* 229–241.

West, E. A., & Billingsley, F. (2005). Improving the system of least prompts: A comparison of procedural variations. *Education and Training in Developmental Disabilities, 40,* 131–144.

Westling, D. L., & Fox, L. (2009). *Teaching students with severe disabilities* (4th ed.). Upper Saddle River, NJ: Merrill/Prentice Hall.

Wilson, L. L., Mott, D. W., & Batman, D. (2004). The asset-based context matrix: A tool for assessing children' learning opportunities and participation in natural environments. *Topics in Early Childhood Special Education, 24*, 110–120.

Winn, J., & Blanton, L. (2005). The call for collaboration in teacher education. *Focus on Exceptional Children, 38*(2), 1–12.

Wolery, M., Anthony, L., Snyder, E. D., Werts, M. B., & Katzenmeyer, J. (1997). Training elementary teachers to embed instruction during classroom activities. *Education and Treatment of Children, 20*, 40–58.

Yell, M. L. (2006). *The law and special education* (2nd ed.). Upper Saddle River, NJ: Pearson/Merrill.

Yell, M. L., Ryan, J. B., Rozalski, M. E., & Katsiyannis, A. (2009). The US Supreme Court and special education: 2005–2007. *TEACHING Exceptional Children, 41*(3), 68–75.

Zemelman, S., Daniels, H., & Hyde, A. (2005). *Best practice: Today's standards for teaching and learning in America's schools* (3rd ed.). Portsmouth, NH: Heinemann.

Zhang, J., Gast, D., Horvat, M., & Dattilo, J. (1995). The effectiveness of a constant time delay procedure on teaching lifetime sport skills to adolescents with severe to profound intellectual disabilities. *Education and Training in Mental Retardation, 30*, 51–64.

Index

The Corwin logo—a raven striding across an open book—represents the union of courage and learning. Corwin is committed to improving education for all learners by publishing books and other professional development resources for those serving the field of PreK–12 education. By providing practical, hands-on materials, Corwin continues to carry out the promise of its motto: **"Helping Educators Do Their Work Better."**